Advanc

The Atta

"Every reader will find this book about attachment enlightening—and above all, moving. The author takes a personal approach and shows how learning about the new science of attachment helps him understand himself and his life—in fact, the lives of all of us. An easy, absorbing read!"
—Dr. Sue Johnson, author of *Love Sense: The Revolutionary New Science of Romantic Relationships* and *Hold Me Tight: Seven Conversations for a Lifetime of Love*

"I've always thought that attachment principles play a crucial role not just in child-rearing and romantic relationships, but in other aspects of our lives. Then along comes this book, which illustrates how attachment affects pretty much everything! Written beautifully and, most important, accessibly, *The Attachment Effect* does a magnificent job of revealing how attachment manifests at the workplace, in friendships, in religion, and even in politics!"
—Amir Levine, MD, bestselling coauthor of *Attached*

"This remarkable book can be read in several ways. Each makes us more informed and better off: as an overview of a major body of research and social psychological theory, as a source for improved understanding of ourselves, and to better attach to others."
—Amitai Etzioni, author of *The New Golden Rule: Community and Morality in a Democratic Society* and professor at George Washington University

"This richly informative, deeply researched, touchingly personal, and always readable book about the meaning and uses of attachment theory explores the hows and whys of our complicated connections with each other. It offers valuable insights into what makes a relationship fail or succeed, and how a better understanding of our attachment style might help to rescue a floundering relationship."
—Judith Viorst, author of *Necessary Losses*

The Attachment Effect

Also by Peter Lovenheim

In the Neighborhood: The Search for Community on an American Street, One Sleepover at a Time

Portrait of a Burger as a Young Calf: The Story of One Man, Two Cows, and the Feeding of a Nation

Reading Between the Lines: New Stories from the Bible (with Rabbi David A. Katz)

Becoming a Mediator (with Emily Doskow)

How to Mediate Your Dispute

Mediate, Don't Litigate: Strategies for Successful Mediation

The
Attachment
Effect

**Exploring the Powerful Ways
Our Earliest Bond Shapes Our
Relationships and Lives**

Peter Lovenheim

A TarcherPerigee Book

tarcherperigee

An imprint of Penguin Random House LLC
375 Hudson Street
New York, New York 10014

TarcherPerigee with tp colophon is a registered trademark of
Penguin Random House LLC.

Most TarcherPerigee books are available at special quantity discounts for bulk purchase
for sales promotions, premiums, fund-raising, and educational needs. Special books or
book excerpts also can be created to fit specific needs. For details, write: SpecialMarkets@
penguinrandomhouse.com.

LIBRARY OF CONGRESS CATALOGING-IN-PUBLICATION DATA
Names: Lovenheim, Peter, author.
Title: The attachment effect : exploring the powerful ways our earliest bond
shapes our relationships and lives / Peter Lovenheim.
Description: New York : TarcherPerigee, 2018. | Includes bibliographical
references and index.
Identifiers: LCCN 2017051906 (print) | LCCN 2017055157 (ebook) |
ISBN 9780525504405 (ebook) | ISBN 9780143132424 (paperback)
Subjects: LCSH: Attachment behavior. | Interpersonal relations. |
Self-esteem. | BISAC: PSYCHOLOGY / Interpersonal Relations. | SELF-HELP /
Personal Growth / Self-Esteem. | PSYCHOLOGY / Personality.
Classification: LCC BF575.A86 (ebook) | LCC BF575.A86 L684 2018 (print) |
DDC 155.9/2—dc23
LC record available at https://lccn.loc.gov/2017051906

Printed in the United States of America
4th Printing

Book design by Alissa Rose Theodor

Contents

Part III: Attachment All Around Us

Foreword

By Professor Harry Reis

When Peter Lovenheim first approached me about sitting in on my relationships class at the University of Rochester, I said sure. I'm always open to having visitors, especially those who, with the benefit of age and experience, might add a bit of perspective for my college-age students. Peter seemed interested, and I expected that he'd attend two or three times and then, like others before him, gracefully move on. But Peter's appetite was not sated by this small sampling of what has by now become a large and lively area of research. Instead, he pursued the class wholeheartedly, attending almost every lecture and then asking follow-up questions as we sat and chatted at the Twelve Corners Starbucks. Peter's questions were uncomplicated at first, yet even from the beginning they probed deeply into the subject matter of my class, pairing an intrinsic curiosity about relationships with his analytical journalistic training. It's not surprising that a woman at the neighboring table wanted in on our conversation.

Understanding how relationships work—what makes them thrive or wither, what makes them the source of life's most rewarding yet also most painful moments—has fascinated people for millennia. As far back as the earliest recorded history, one can find "rules" and ideologies about relationships. Scientific research is relatively new to this endeavor—a fair estimate would locate the start of this field around the middle of the twentieth century—and there's little doubt in my mind that attachment theory represents the best insight into the subject we have to offer right now.

Theories come and go in the social sciences, typically engendering an early flurry of excitement and activity and then gradually losing prominence as their novel insights are exhausted, and new and better theories take center stage. Not so attachment theory. I first heard about John Bowlby's theory in 1982, when I was on sabbatical at the University of Denver, where Phillip Shaver and Cindy Hazan were beginning to apply to adult romantic relationships ideas that had until then been focused primarily on infants and their caregivers. When their pioneering studies hit the scientific literature, the field literally exploded, spawning hundreds and then thousands of studies. I've been waiting since then for research on attachment theory to slow down, like so many other theories before it, but that hasn't happened. Remarkably, the vigor and generative force of attachment theory research continues unabated.

What makes this theory so robust? As Peter explains, attachment theory always captivates students. When I lecture about attachment theory, even the most distracted student soon starts to pay attention. The theory's main propositions are compelling in a way that few theories are—how can one not be fascinated by a theory that begins with a simple behavior common to most mammals and then expands, with just a few additional considerations, to explain why our earliest experiences with caregivers shape our relationships from childhood to old age? Attachment theory's observations are at once wise, astute, and intensely personal—it's hard to listen to an account of attachment theory without thinking, "Yes, that's it!"

Among scientists and practitioners, attachment theory gets its extraordinary explanatory power by blending serious, coherent theorizing with relevance to many of life's most important and deeply human concerns. For you, the reader, I promise that attachment theory will offer a fresh perspective on your relationships, your emotional life, and more. This is not, however, a self-help manual, at least in the tired sense of offering "twelve steps to enduring love and romance." Rather, this book will deepen your understanding of the *why* and the *how* of human connection and detachment, and it will point out the path for using this knowledge to make the most of your relationships.

I came to look forward to our semi-regular visits to the Twelve Corners Starbucks. There I learned that Peter is a keen observer with a persistently inquiring mind. Naturally, his questions got tougher as his knowledge about attachment grew. But over time something more endearing was revealed to me. In the pages that follow, you will see, as I did, that he is a brave and strikingly candid soul willing to challenge his own life history and lay bare his thoughts and relationships (a sign of "earned security," perhaps, or maybe a reflection of his earlier anxious attachment style: read on and decide for yourself). These qualities come together in Peter's intimate approach to this book, which juxtaposes insights from research and therapeutic practice with his personal experiences—experiences that are simultaneously poignant and revealing of attachment theory's message. I suspect this is no coincidence: the ultimate beauty of attachment theory is its ability to make sense of our relationships and emotions, and Peter's talent as a writer is to bring out that sensibility. Make no mistake—personal narrative aside, this book has both feet firmly grounded in the science and evidence-based practice of attachment theory. It's the kind of book that would please John Bowlby.

Introduction

It began wonderfully, as romances do, but later devolved into a turbulent on-again, off-again affair. In plainest terms, she was looking for a commitment I couldn't make, and I was looking for emotional intimacy she couldn't give. More times than I can count, we broke up and made up—the breakups were all hers, the makeups mostly mine. Then the cycle would start anew.

This went on for years.

How sad for each of us to have invested so much in a relationship that came to nothing. Yet why we could never make it work remained, I think for both of us, a mystery.

But then, months after the final breakup, I chanced upon something eye-opening. While visiting my daughter at college and leafing through texts from her psychology class, I came across an article about something called attachment theory. In it, the author describes what often happens when people with two particular attachment styles try to become couples:

> The couples . . . tend to become *extremely polarized*. The partner with the anxious attachment style is usually *anxious and demanding of more intimacy* while the partner with the avoidant attachment style *shuts down and withdraws*. There may be *numerous breakups and makeups*. . . . These relationships can be

explosive. . . . The avoidant partner is usually the one who *de-cides to leave* the relationship.

I didn't understand then what "attachment styles" were and wasn't familiar with the "anxious" and "avoidant" labels, but sitting there in my daughter's dorm room I got the gist. My former girlfriend's reluc-tance to open up emotionally and her tendency to pull away in re-sponse to conflict fit the attachment style called avoidant. And my need for emotional intimacy and my tendency to cling to a relation-ship rather than risk being alone fit the style called anxious.

The textbook authors went on to say that this toxic pairing of at-tachment styles is common—indeed, some researchers call it the "anxious-avoidant trap"—and that unless a couple understands it and learns to work around it, it's often a relationship killer.

The revelation came too late to help my ill-fated romance, but it did leave me intensely curious to learn more about this mysterious thing called attachment.

———

Attachment theory was developed by British psychiatrist and psy-choanalyst John Bowlby (1907–90). After World War II, Bowlby worked in orphanages, where he saw children who were given good food, housing, and medical care yet did not thrive. Many, in fact, died. None of the common theories of child development explained the phenomenon.

Over the next decades, taking ideas from fields as diverse as evolu-tionary biology, ethology, and social psychology, Bowlby developed his theory of attachment. In a nutshell, it asserts that because human ba-bies are born helpless, they are hardwired (as we say today) to search for and attach to a competent, reliable caregiver. Usually this is the mother, but it can also be the father, grandparent, nanny, or another adult who's present and providing for their basic needs.

The infant's search for consistent care is met with either success, leading to a sense of emotional security, or failure, with insecurity as a result.

The success or failure of that search actually shapes the infant's developing brain, affecting core emotions and personality structure, and thus creating a set of beliefs and expectations about relationships in general. These, in turn, influence what we feel and how we behave in relationships for the rest of our lives—with romantic partners, certainly, but possibly with everything and everyone else too. Call it "the attachment effect." In short, those first attachments are central and formative—and the stakes could not be higher.

For most of us, this early attachment experience occurs before our earliest memories, usually before age two. And yet it has the power to affect relationships, in Bowlby's words, "from the cradle to the grave."

This is because the attachment system, like the reproductive system, is a fundamental part of what it means to be human. It's the way nature engineered our survival. At birth, we seek out attachment to others who can reliably protect us and respond to our survival needs. In adulthood, we connect with a special few others whom we love and on whom we rely for safety and security. We're born to connect, and as long as we live we never stop needing connection.

We're born to connect, and as long as we live we never stop needing connection.

Researchers around the world have devoted their careers to understanding and testing attachment theory and have largely confirmed Bowlby's work. Hundreds, if not thousands, of new studies are done each year.

In the first years of life, psychiatrist Thomas Lewis and colleagues have noted, we form patterns about how relationships work; we store impressions of what love *feels* like. So central and formative is this first attachment that it influences how we relate not only to romantic partners but to many others too.

Some of the newest studies confirm that the influences of our earliest attachments extend well beyond intimate relationships with family and romantic partners. In fact, they extend to all kinds of relationships. At work, they affect how we relate to coworkers and bosses. In sports, they affect how we relate to teammates and coaches. In politics, they affect our political leanings and whom we choose to vote for. Even in the realm of the spiritual, they affect what religion we practice or choose not to practice, and how we relate to God.

Yes, even to God.

People fortunate enough to grow up with a secure attachment tend to enjoy—both as children and as adults—more satisfying and stable relationships. They feel worthy of being loved and cared for, and so have greater self-esteem. They tend to be more giving and tolerant toward others, and they show more resilience in the face of challenges such as personal illness and the death of a loved one. As parents, one of the greatest gifts we can strive to give our children is attachment security.

Those with insecure attachments—two types are "avoidant" and "anxious"—will tend to have a tougher time navigating relationships and may struggle with issues of intimacy and trust. Even so, new research suggests that people with insecure attachments may also have unique strengths. In a clever study where test subjects were exposed to what appeared to be a threatening situation (a room gradually filling with smoke because of a supposedly malfunctioning computer), people high in attachment anxiety—who are especially sensitive to threats—were the first to detect the danger. And those high in attachment avoidance—who prize independence and self-reliance—were the first to find a way out to safety.

And while most people go through life with the same attachment style they developed in early childhood, it is possible to change. Through the luck of a healthy, long-term relationship with a secure person—a teacher, mentor, coach, or romantic partner—or through self-reflection, therapy, or even through parenting, some people who should have had attachment insecurity due to unreliable or unresponsive caregiving nevertheless achieve attachment security. Researchers call this "earned secure attachment."

(To make a quick assessment of your own attachment style, see the appendix for a brief attachment quiz.)

For me, learning about my own attachment style has been life changing. By recognizing when my attachment system is affecting my behavior, I find I can often change or delay my normal reactions—particularly in emotional situations—enough to achieve a more favorable result. For example, when I've been in a relationship and my partner has canceled plans at the last minute, I can sometimes catch myself distrusting her statements or overreacting to the change—both typical ways people with anxious attachment respond to a real or imagined threat to a relationship. Similarly, when sick with a physical ailment, I can catch myself "catastrophizing"—projecting the worst possible outcome—which is typical of how people with anxious attachment react to illness. Once I understand that part of my response is my insecure attachment kicking in, I can ask myself if the facts support my reaction—and often they don't.

I also now notice the effects of other people's attachment styles. I see it in the different ways friends react to their children leaving home for college, or to a job loss, or to the death of a loved one. I see it in young friends dating and trying to find a match that works. I see it in my own adult children pursuing careers, marrying, and raising children of their own. Knowing that people's reactions are due in part to their attachment style can make us more understanding, supportive, and forgiving of each other—and help us find better ways to get along.

I set out to write this book to discover as much as I could about attachment theory and to help make people aware of how attachment affects us all. My journey begins with my own story. I wanted to understand my own attachment style and the reasons for it. To do this, I met and spoke with many of the top experts around the world in the field of attachment research. I probed into my relationships with my parents and other early caregivers, and I explored how those experiences may have influenced my closest adult relationships. Some of this, obviously, is very personal.

But once I understood my own attachment, I wanted to understand the attachment styles of others. I spoke with a variety of people to hear stories about how attachment—once they became aware of the theory—impacted their lives: in dating, child-rearing, marriage, their career, aging and dealing with loss, at work, in sports, in politics, and spiritually.

I heard from people who had strengthened their relationships, their work, and their lives. They include:

- **a mother raising her son in a way designed to produce a secure attachment (chapter 6, "Raising a Human Being");**

- **a young couple who saved their marriage by working with a therapist trained in a counseling technique based on attachment theory (chapter 7, "Dancing Close");**

- **a coach who helps his athletes reach peak performance by understanding each player's attachment style (chapter 11, "Before the Buzzer").**

And we'll meet others whose personal and professional lives have benefited from an understanding of the way different people's attachment systems interact, including:

- **two young people who improved how they interact on first dates by using attachment theory (chapter 5, "A Date for Coffee");**

- **and the owner of a small business whose staff work together successfully in part because of their diverse attachment styles (chapter 10, "Securing a Position").**

Additionally, we'll look at how attachment styles influence our political leaders and their ability to govern. To do this, I administered the Adult Attachment Interview—the gold standard for measuring attachment in adults—to a former nominee for US president (chapter 12, "Following the Leaders").

(All the principal people I write about are identified, with their permission, by real names unless otherwise indicated. In some instances I've changed time sequences for narrative purposes.)

From this book, I hope you'll learn not only how attachment affects all our lives but also how attachment affects *your own* relationships and life. In the epilogue, I discuss the ten top lessons we can take from understanding attachment—practical and useful things you can do to improve your life and the life of your community. In the appendix you'll find an attachment quiz to measure your own attachment style. The resources section lists organizations, books, and websites from which you can learn more about dating, child development and parenting, attachment-based couples counseling, and individual therapy, among other topics.

———

Today John Bowlby's groundbreaking work is widely accepted as a foundational theory in child development and social psychology—indeed, in virtually all the behavioral and social sciences. Attachment theory is "one of the broadest, most profound, and most creative lines of research in 20th- and 21st-century psychology," declare noted national researchers Jude Cassidy of the University of Maryland and Phillip Shaver of the University of California, Davis. It is "one of the most successful theories in psychological science," asserts Lee A. Kirkpatrick of the College of William and Mary. The view of Canadian psychologist and author Sue Johnson is typical of the esteem in which many in the field hold Bowlby:

> As a psychologist and as a human being, if I had to give an award for the single best set of ideas anyone had ever had, I'd give it to John Bowlby hands down over Freud or anyone else in the business of understanding people.

A truly majestic accolade came in 2005 when the Harvard Mountaineering Club, climbing near the Kyrgyzstan-China border, named a nineteen-thousand-foot, snow-capped peak Mount John Bowlby.

What would happen if society in general became more aware of attachment theory and its implications? Our culture, I believe, gets it entirely wrong when it continually sends the message that the most evolved individuals are those who are independent and don't need anyone else. That attitude—a remnant of the myth of American pioneer cowboys as lone adventurers—flies in the face of our biology. Our attachment system tells us, instead, that for safety and security we always need connection to at least a few special others and that only through interdependence do we become our strongest and most authentic selves.

Only through interdependence do we become our strongest and most authentic selves.

And yet, by idealizing independence over connection we end up with far too many people existing largely on their own, living apart from family, disconnected from neighbors, socially isolated. Today, according to a CBS News report, one in four Americans says they do not have a single other person to confide in. "A good deal of modern American culture," psychiatrist Thomas Lewis and colleagues have observed, "is an extended experiment in the effects of depriving people of what they crave most."

Not long after I became aware of attachment theory, I met Harry Reis, a professor of psychology at the university in my hometown of Rochester, New York. He'd soon be teaching attachment theory, he told me, as part of an upcoming course. If I liked, he said, I was welcome to sit in on the class.

It was a generous offer that I eagerly accepted. And that's where my journey of discovery began.

I believe a deeper popular understanding of how attachment works, one that extends beyond researchers and other experts, has the power to change lives for the better, making all our relationships richer and more satisfying.

Part I

———

What Is Attachment?

CHAPTER 1

When the Tiger Comes: Origin of the Attachment System

Every time I attended Harry Reis's class on attachment theory, I was late. That was because the start of Harry's class at the University of Rochester conflicted with the end of a writing class I was teaching at a nearby college, and even if I made all the lights and quickly found a parking space, the soonest I could get there was ten minutes after class began. So I'd enter the amphitheater-style lecture hall quietly through a side door and take a seat in the back.

That turned out to be an advantage, though, because from the back of the room I could see all one hundred or so students, including who was paying attention and who wasn't. That first day, I noticed, in the seats nearby, a young man reading e-mail, a young woman on Facebook, and a young man checking stock quotes.

"This is a damn good theory," Harry was saying as I took my seat that first day. He stood six foot three, had a deep, resonant voice, and spoke with a slow, deliberate cadence. "We think it explains an unbelievable amount of human behavior: about our childhoods, about intimate adult relationships, about nearly all relationships throughout our lives."

When I'd first realized Harry was one of the country's leading relationship researchers *and* that he lived and taught about attachment theory in my hometown of Rochester, New York, I invited him for coffee. Halfway through our meeting, a middle-aged woman sitting at the next table suddenly turned around to us and nearly shouted, "Wow! I'd pay to be at your table! What you're sayin' is so true. Wished I'd known all that when I was younger—it would've saved me a heap of grief!"

Oddly, Harry hadn't seemed surprised by the interruption.

"People hear about this attachment stuff," he told me, "and say, 'Yeah, that's what I want to study. That's what I want to understand.'"

I wanted to understand my own attachment style and how it may have been affecting my relationships and behavior. I'd been through a divorce and then a long-term romance. If knowing more about attachment could help me find a satisfying, stable relationship, that's what I was after. Later, my interests would broaden to include understanding how attachment influences people throughout their lives and throughout society: their relationships with family and friends, how they raise their kids, get along at work, cope with loss, and much more. Could attachment theory be a key to unlocking a deeper understanding of our behavior and everyday lives?

———

Onto a large screen, Harry projected photos of parents—human and nonhuman—holding and protecting their babies: a mother carried her child on her back; a father held his son on his knee; a cat nursed two kittens; a polar bear sheltered her baby under her body.

"Let's look at this first slide," Harry said. "Notice that in all these different species, there is a physically close, protective bond between an adult caregiver and an infant."

The room was quiet except for the clicking of a hundred students typing on laptops. Taking notes in longhand, I was a visitor from another generation.

Harry's next slide showed a black-and-white photo of a middle-aged British man looking distinguished in a tweed sport coat over a wool sweater.

"In Britain during World War II," Harry began, "fathers were off at war, and during the bombing of London many mothers were killed, so there were a rather large number of children brought to orphanages. And working in the orphanages was a young British psychiatrist and psychoanalyst named John Bowlby."

The red dot of Harry's laser pointed at the image of the distinguished-looking Brit.

"Bowlby was struck by the behavior of these infants," he continued. "What he observed was that even though the orphans were housed in a clean, germ-free environment, were fed well and given good medical care, they didn't thrive. They were underweight. They became depressed. Some died."

The young woman in front of me who had been on Facebook looked up from her laptop.

"And Bowlby observed another thing," said Harry. "He was struck by the way these infants called for, cried for, and watched the door for their mothers, what he called 'searching behaviors.' And he took that to be the human equivalent of what animals do—you know, if you've ever seen a young kitten or a puppy and some scary person walks in the room, what do they do? They run immediately back to their mother for safety."

Monkeys

Harry didn't mention it that day, but at about the same time Bowlby was noting the effects of maternal deprivation on orphaned children, Harry Harlow, a psychologist at the University of Wisconsin, was observing a related phenomenon in monkeys. His work would later influence Bowlby.

In his most famous experiment, Harlow separated baby rhesus monkeys from their mothers at birth. He then provided them a choice of two surrogate "mothers": one made of wire and holding a bottle of milk, the other also of wire but covered with a soft cloth and without any milk. The result? Most of the time, the infant monkeys clung to the soft-cloth mother—and ran to her whenever they were frightened; they used the wire mothers only for milk.

"These findings are legendary in psychology," Lee Kirkpatrick has written, "as well they should be. They demonstrated convincingly that, at least in rhesus monkeys, infants' interest in their mothers was not reducible to the need or desire for food or breast; [instead,] they spontaneously sought physical contact and comfort."

Babies and Their Caregivers

There is no such thing as a baby—meaning that if you set out to describe a baby, you will find you are describing a baby and someone. A baby cannot exist alone but is essentially part of a relationship.

—PEDIATRICIAN AND PSYCHOANALYST DONALD WINNICOTT

Harry Reis took a couple of steps away from the lecturer's table and faced the class.

"You know," he said, "horses can run within a day or two of birth. That's one of their ways of surviving. But we can't do that. Human babies have the longest period of vulnerability of any species on earth. For seven or eight years of your life, if there isn't someone taking care of you, forget it—you're dead. If a tiger comes, you have no chance of survival."

Human babies have the longest period of vulnerability of any species on earth.

Harry paused, scanning the class.

"Okay, so you're an infant," he continued, "and there's a tiger coming. What's your way of surviving? If you can find a caregiver and keep that caregiver close—someone who'll provide you food and shelter, and when the tiger comes, take you away from danger—this would be your way of surviving.

"So how do you locate and then keep close to that caregiver?"

As he moved toward an answer, I felt the class's tension rise.

"How do you find and hold close to that caregiver?" he repeated.

"You cry!" he shouted. "You cry, meaning, 'Something's going on that's scaring me! I want somebody to protect me!'"

Babies use other "seeking behaviors" too, Harry explained, such as turning their heads, following with their eyes, and reaching with their hands. "Bowlby argued that these behaviors—crying, staying near the caregiver, etc.—were designed to maintain physical closeness because infants who did that were more likely to survive."

These behaviors of babies, in other words, are not random. They are biologically designed to help a human infant survive by locating and attaching to a competent, reliable caregiver.

Harry again pointed the laser at the photo of the man in the tweed jacket.

"And the profound idea Bowlby came up with," he continued, "and in retrospect this seems like such a simple idea, is that there is an evolutionary system called the attachment system.

"The attachment system was designed," he explained, "to do one very simple thing: to create and keep physical closeness between infant and caregiver. Infants who displayed these behaviors and caregivers who responded were the ones whose genes were more likely to survive to the next generation. Infants who didn't do it, who said, in effect, 'pretty tiger' and wanted to go talk to the tiger, or caregivers who were more concerned about themselves and didn't go to pick up the infant, their genes did not get passed on.

"So it's a very, very simple, straightforward evolutionary adaptation," he said. "And you all have it. You don't have to go to the store to buy the program called Attachment System. It's hardwired into you. You come with it already installed."

As Harry said this, a young man next to me, playing Tetris, looked up.

Attachment Figure: A Secure Base and Safe Haven, in Close Proximity

"When we say a child has an 'attachment figure,'" Professor Reis explained, "we mean a person—and it's usually the mother—who fulfills three essential functions of the attachment system. The first is called 'proximity maintenance,' which means the caregiver is someone the child keeps close for safety and comfort. The next two are 'secure base' and 'safe haven': children need a secure base from which to explore and a safe haven to come back to when life gets scary."

And true attachment figures, whether for a child or adult, meet two additional criteria: that the threat of separation from the attachment figure causes anxiety, often accompanied by protest (in the case of a child that would be crying), and that the loss of the attachment figure causes grief.

"Okay," Harry continued, "so infants have this attachment system, which acts like a sort of radar. When something threatening happens—tiger, hunger—the radar activates and the infant thinks, 'Is my attachment figure near? Is she attentive, able to interpret my signals of distress, and available to provide the help I need?'"

Typically, children have multiple attachment figures. These may include both parents, maybe a grandparent or two, an older sibling, and regular care providers. From the child's perspective, however, these people are not interchangeable. A hierarchy of attachment figures exists, with one special primary figure (usually the mother) at the top. "If the child were suddenly frightened," notes Lee Kirkpatrick, "and all of his or her attachment figures were lined up in a row, the primary attachment figure is the one to whom the child would run first."

Mental Models

> In the first years of life . . . a child extracts patterns from his relationships . . . [and] stores an impression of what love feels like.
>
> —PSYCHIATRIST THOMAS LEWIS AND COLLEAGUES

"Bowlby believed that as you grow up," Harry continued to the class, "you form beliefs about what you can expect from significant others—that is, you learn, 'This is how powerful, caregiving people are going to relate to me.' These beliefs stem from our earliest experiences with attachment figures, mostly in the first two years. And these beliefs, once formed, form a 'mental model' in the child—actually create patterns in the brain—that will influence what that individual expects of relationships and how he behaves in relationships, not just in childhood but over the whole of a lifetime, or as Bowlby put it, 'from the cradle to the grave.'"

And it's these mental models, Harry noted, that cause the experiences of the infant to later affect that individual's behavior as an adult. "This points up one place where Bowlby differed with Freud," Harry added. "Freud believed that an awful lot of stuff that went on was in the infant's mind—you know, the infant imagined this libidinal attachment to his or her mother. Bowlby didn't buy that. Instead, Bowlby felt that the *actual interactions* that occur between a mother and child are what's important, and that the mental models formed from those interactions are what transform the infant's early experience into personality traits that last a lifetime.

"These early beliefs are about the self in relation to others," Harry continued. "Am I lovable? Am I someone other people are going to value and care for? How comfortable am I being close, depending on another person, making myself vulnerable to another person? When I need others, will they be there for me?

When I need others, will they be there for me?

"If the answer is yes," he went on, "the infant experiences a sense of security." Harry took a loudly exaggerated deep breath, imitating a relieved infant whose mother had perhaps just picked them up and run into a cave to protect them from a tiger. "'Okay, no big deal. I'm fine,' which produces a sense of confidence that nothing dangerous is going to happen. The radar gets shut down and everything's okay."

This person, explained Harry, will come out of childhood trusting that others are generally available and responsive, and will think, "I can trust people. I can allow myself to be close to people. I'm not afraid of intimacy."

This is a secure attachment.

"But what if the radar system says no?" asked Harry. "What if the child does *not* feel protected by a competent and reliable attachment figure?"

In that case, there are two defensive responses.

"First," Harry said, "is when the infant cries and cries, and the caregiver just doesn't give a damn, doesn't respond, leaves the infant alone. No proximity, no safe haven, no secure base. This child may think"— and here he channeled the voice of a frightened infant—"'There is no caregiver available who can take care of me and who will deal with this threat for me. I'm an infant; I can't even crawl. I'll stick around this caregiver because what other choice do I have? But I'm not going to get too close and I'm not going to protest too much because I've already discovered these things don't work.'

"This individual," Harry continued, "whose caregiver is *pretty much always* unresponsive, learns to shut down and avoid intimacy."

This is an "insecure avoidant attachment."

"The other defensive response," he said, "occurs in infants when the caregiver is *inconsistent*—sometimes responding, sometimes not. The caregiver is sometimes there, sometimes not; sometimes provides a safe haven and secure base, but sometimes does not. This infant says, 'I can't figure out how I get my caregiver to come over and take care of me. I don't know what to do. I'm feeling abandoned, so I better just put all my energy into trying to get that person over here *right now.*'

"Instead of shutting down," Harry explained, "this infant protests and cries even more. He clings and does everything possible to signal that he is really, really distressed and, 'By God, you're my caregiver and you just gotta take care of me!'"

This is an "insecure anxious attachment."

Drawing from a large number of studies, among the US population about 55 percent of people tend to be relatively secure, 25 percent relatively avoidant, and 20 percent relatively anxious.

"These are pretty constant results," Harry said.

They are also pretty consistent universally. Studies show similar breakdowns among attachment styles across the globe, with only slight variations among Western and non-Western nations, developed and developing societies.

I found Harry's point about mental models neatly summarized by Dr. Kirkpatrick. "In essence," he writes, "mental models represent the child's answer to the question: 'Can I count on my attachment figure to be available and responsive when needed?' The three possible answers are yes (secure), no (avoidant), and maybe (anxious)."

———

John Bowlby himself had an emotionally difficult childhood. Raised in a typical upper-middle-class English home of the early twentieth century, he and his siblings had little contact with his parents. "Like most upper- and middle-class mothers in the Edwardian time," biographer Suzan van Dijken has written, "John's mother handed over the care of her children to a nanny and some nursemaids."

His mother was self-centered and his father a bully, observes psychologist and author Robert Karen. The parents had a "stiff-upper-lip approach to all things emotional" and set themselves utterly apart from their children, handing over care of John and his siblings to a head nanny, a "somewhat cold creature" but the only stable figure in the children's lives. There was also a series of "undernannies"—young girls, none of whom stayed very long. Sent to boarding school at age eight, John Bowlby later told his wife he "wouldn't send a dog to boarding school at that age."

All of this, in Bowlby's view, had a "lasting negative impact."

To me, Bowlby's early childhood has a familiar ring.

One of my earliest memories, from about age three, is of my father leaving for work in the morning. He and I eat breakfast together—my mother and older brother and sister are upstairs dressing—and then he has to leave. I run to the living room and climb onto a window seat facing the driveway and as he drives off to work I kick and pound against the window, screaming for him not to go.

From the outside, I must have looked like a bendable Gumby stuck with suction cups to the window.

Only when I became a parent myself did I begin to wonder: my mother didn't work outside the house and would have been home, so when Dad left in the morning, why did I have a tantrum?

————

Between class sessions, Harry Reis and I met for coffee. He wore jeans, a fleece jacket, and hiking boots. Up close, I felt the striking difference between his six-foot-three frame and mine of five eight. I'd wanted to ask him about early childhood memories and their possible connection to a person's attachment history—specifically, mine.

"I have memories of childhood," I confided to him, "that make me wonder about my own attachment style." I explained that I have few memories of my mother, that my dad sometimes cared for me but so did my sister, who was seven years older, and there had been various nannies—just like Bowlby—none of whom I could remember.

"I'm not even sure who my primary attachment figure was," I confessed.

About my father, my memories were mixed. I remembered that when I was little he'd carry me piggyback upstairs to bed. I'd hold on tight and lean in close, pressing my cheek against his and because it was the end of the day, feeling the comforting scratchiness of his beard. But he could also be bullying. He had a sharp tongue, paddled me, and once dragged me by the arm out of the house to nursery school.

"I just don't know if any of that added up to a safe haven or secure base, or what kind of attachment experience I had," I told Harry.

He cautioned that the way we remember our parents and families and even ourselves at the earliest ages can be faulty. Point well taken, I thought. Having by then raised three children, I wouldn't want my kids to characterize their whole childhoods based on a few random incidents.

Still, I found it puzzling that out of all the events that would have occurred in those early years, the ones I seemed to recall suggested a lack of attachment to my mother or any consistent caregiver. And yet I couldn't even be sure the memories were accurate.

Fortunately, I still had a slender thread of a chance to find out. My mother had died six years earlier, but my father was still living. He was ninety-five, and for his age doing very well. Though he moved slowly, with a cane or walker, he lived on his own, drove, and enjoyed meals out with friends. Several times recently he'd fallen but sustained no major injuries. And his mind remained sharp: in recent months he'd read, among other books, a six-hundred-page biography of Lyndon Johnson and a dense history of ancient Carthage. Long retired from the printing business that he and his brother founded during the Depression, Dad soldiered on without complaint, spending long stretches of time alone.

Harry encouraged me to use my remaining time with him wisely. "Given his early caregiving relationship with you," he said, "his eventual loss will be difficult. Make sure you handle this properly."

Properly?

"Be sure whatever you need from him in terms of information, family stories, or emotional connection, you get—or just come to terms with the fact that you're never going to get it."

Soon after, on one of my regular afternoon visits to his apartment, I found Dad in a typical setting: in the corner of his small den, in a white leather reclining chair, TV and reading lamp on, newspaper open on his chest—asleep.

The skin on the backs of his hands and forearms was paper thin and mottled with purple bruises—this due to blood thinners he took for a heart condition. He was bald except around the sides and back of his head where there was a delicate fringe of gray. His heavy eyebrows were white; in each ear he wore a hearing aid. On his chin and cheeks was that familiar five o'clock beard, though most of the stubble was now gray.

I woke him gently, and we chatted about the day.

"Dad," I then said, "I'd like to ask you about some memories I have from when I was little. Would you be okay with that?"

"With what?" he asked. His hearing wasn't so good, but his voice remained deep and strong.

"With me asking you some questions," I repeated.

"Sure. Shoot."

I asked him about the time when I stood on the window seat so upset when he left in the morning.

"I remember your tantrums," he said, his voice steady but without emotion. "You reacted to the fact that I was going to work."

He said "tantrums" so I guessed it happened more than once.

"But," I continued, "wasn't Mother home?"

"What?"

"Mother didn't work," I repeated, speaking louder. "She must have been home, right?"

"She was, and I tried to turn you over to her," he said.

I asked about how long the tantrums went on for, thinking he might say a few days or even weeks.

"I think it went on for a year," he said.

Oh.

"You have to remember, Mother wasn't well."

In her late twenties my mother contracted what was always described as a mild case of polio.

"I was the strong person in the family," he continued. "I doubled in duties. I put you to bed, got you up, and fed all of you. But I didn't have much time. I had to get you all to school and get myself to work. That's why we had various help in the house.

"I used to say to you kids: 'Someday when I die, they'll put on my gravestone, *He was not only a father, but a mother too.*'"

Dad and I sat silently for a while, and then he drifted off to sleep. I switched off the reading light and muted the TV. Before I left, I kissed him softly, pressing my cheek to his, feeling the scratchiness.

The "various help" Dad had referred to included two live-in nannies. First was Miss Kelly, who was nearly seventy when Dad hired her. He made a room in the attic for her, and she moved in right after I was born. But just after I turned a year old, she died suddenly of a heart attack. My parents replaced her with another live-in, Mrs. Hepburn.

I have no memory of Miss Kelly or Mrs. Hepburn, but what I do remember is going at age three with my mother to the office of a child psychologist. The reason for the visit was that I had developed a stutter. In the psychologist's office, I sat in a big chair and tried to answer his questions. Then he had me wait outside while he talked with my mother.

Years later, I asked my mother about that visit. She said the doctor advised her and my father to fire Mrs. Hepburn, which they did.

"Why'd he want you to fire her?" I asked.

"He said I should take care of you myself. He said, 'This child doesn't know who his mother is.'"

———

When I arrived at Harry's next lecture, a slide on the screen announced an upcoming exam. But he had lightened the mood by including on the slide a drawing of a ghost and the words, "Happy Halloween."

"Next week is one of my favorite holidays," he announced. "Anyone who comes to class suitably attired will be suitably rewarded." He looked down at his notes, paused, then looked back up. "And just saying you're dressed like a college student won't count."

Harry began by reviewing the concept of mental models, noting that once attachment styles are formed, as we get older "they affect our behavior not only in close relationships but in many, many other kinds of situations, as well."

For example, he said, the theory applies "perfectly well" to people's relationship to their pets and to God.

Pets and God?

"There are some people who have relationships to their pets or to God—and I'm not equating God with your pets; I'm just saying there is a process that can be similar. You can be securely attached to God, or you can be anxiously attached: 'I'm worried what God is going to think about me and I'm constantly worried about pleasing God.' Or you can have an avoidant attachment: 'God doesn't care about what happens to me.'"

Harry asked us to do a mental experiment.

"Close your eyes," he said, "and try to recall an episode when your mother or father, or a romantic partner, behaved in a way that increased the sense of trust you felt toward him or her, and another time that reduced the sense of trust."

I thought immediately of a time when I was about three. I was trying to dress myself but was unsure which sock went on which foot. My mother was in another room, talking on the phone. I called to her, asking about the socks. She called back, "It doesn't matter. They can go on either foot." But I didn't think she was telling the truth, so I didn't put on the socks.

Harry projected a slide with bar graphs showing how in a study, when people were timed to see how fast they came up with each scenario, people with secure attachments recalled positive memories faster than negative ones. But avoidant and anxious people were faster at coming up with negative memories.

"One thing these mental models do is make certain kinds of beliefs and expectations always accessible, always at the top of our minds and easily tapped into," he explained. "They're like a computer's operating system. They take over and don't let the computer do anything it doesn't like."

Next, Harry put up a slide entitled "Attachment Patterns in Adulthood." The slide showed two axes, one for "avoidance" and the other for "anxiety."

"We really don't speak in terms of strict categories anymore," he said, but of people falling somewhere on these axes, relatively higher in avoidance and lower in anxiety, or low in avoidance but high in anxiety, and those who are low in each we call secure. Some individuals, Harry added, can actually be high in both avoidance and anxiety, in a quadrant labeled "disorganized." These are often children who have been neglected or maltreated. "This, of course, is the worst place to be," he said.

Harry, knowing well his college audience, said he would next summarize how attachment styles influence adults in romantic relationships.

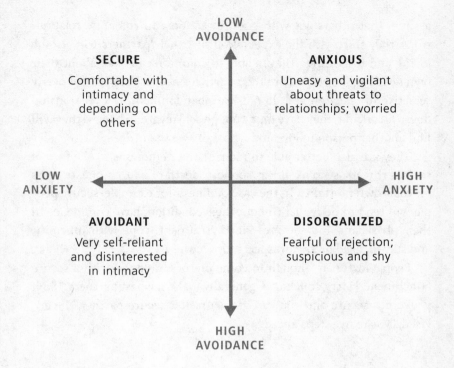

Three Attachment Styles

There is a thread connecting life in your mother's arms and life in your lover's arms.

—PSYCHOLOGIST THEODORE WATERS

Secure

People who in early childhood had reliable and competent caregivers—and hence a secure attachment—generally feel comfortable with intimacy, Harry explained. They're willing to trust and allow themselves to be vulnerable. They believe other people are basically good and assume that others act with good intentions. In romantic relationships, they start with the expectation that their partners will also be loving and responsive. They're able to communicate well about their own needs and to respond to their partners' needs. They are not overly sensitive to rejection and do not fear abandonment. If a relationship doesn't work out, they have high enough self-regard to believe they will find another person to love and who will love them.

They are also better able to manage their emotions in the face of serious threats, such as illness, job loss, death of a loved one, or fears for their own mortality. In the case of illness, for example, secure people will tend to be realistic about their condition, have confidence in their physicians and the prescribed treatment, cope with infirmity, and stay focused on the prospects for recovery.

People fortunate enough to come out of childhood with a secure attachment, Harry concluded, generally make the best partners. "So if you're not secure and you can get yourself a secure partner," he advised, "you're five steps ahead."

Avoidant

The experience of caregivers not responding to an infant and basically saying, "Take care of yourself," Harry said, produces adults who say things like "I'm uncomfortable being close to others. I find it difficult to trust or open up to others and difficult to allow myself to depend on others. Often partners want me to be more intimate than I feel comfortable being."

"Avoidant people," he continued, "are less invested in relationships; they just care about them less. They say things like, 'This intimacy stuff is a bunch of BS.' They believe strongly in self-reliance, that you should be able to solve all your problems yourself. They also don't like to self-disclose, and disapprove of people who do. In social situations, they can be charming but this is usually in a nonwarm manner, like being good at entertaining. When avoidant people are in a relationship, they are relatively poor at giving support when their partner needs it, and when conflict occurs, they tend to distance themselves.

In terms of emotion regulation, avoidant people tend to deny their feelings about a threatening situation—be it illness, job loss, or grief—and rather than rely on others to help, they will be inclined to try to fix it themselves.

Anxious

The individual who received inconsistent care as an infant likely craves intimacy as an adult. At the same time, though, he is vigilant about threats to the relationship and worries about what's going to happen. "Anxious people," Harry explained, "say things like, 'I worry my partner won't want to stay with me. I find others are reluctant to get as close as I would like. I want to merge completely with another person, and this desire sometimes scares people away.'"

He went on, "Much of this stems from the realization, 'When I wanted my mother to comfort me, she didn't, or at least I couldn't count on it, so I must not be very lovable, and so I have to keep tabs on other people.' Anxious people also have a 'come here, go away' thing—a push-pull quality in their desire for closeness, reflecting an intense need to be in relationship but at the same time resentment for feeling so insecure without one. They tend to be hypercritical toward partners, feeling let down or rejected when their partners show the slightest lack of attention. They also tend to think about this stuff more; they're often preoccupied with it.

"It's experiencing these big ups and downs—'This is it! No it's not!'—plus feeling that intense need for connection but at the same time resenting the insecurity, that produces in anxious people what is so characteristic of this attachment style: a general sense of ambivalence."

When faced with existential threats, anxious people tend to have difficulty regulating their emotions. When faced with the death of a loved one, for example, they will tend to grieve longer and more deeply than others. When ill, they will desperately want someone to "make it better," while at the same time catastrophizing—that is, imagining the worst possible outcome and finding it difficult to trust their own doctors.

Genetics

The genetic lottery may determine the cards in your deck, but experience deals the hand you can play.
                    —THOMAS LEWIS AND COLLEAGUES

As Harry continued lecturing, he posed a question: "Okay, but isn't it also possible that this stuff is genetic?"

I was sure that was on a lot of minds.

"It's a fair question," he said, "but we think that genetics, while a factor in attachment style, are not controlling."

He spoke of "cross-fostering" experiments. "You can take a mouse of a genetic strain that is prone to anxiety," he went on, "and say, 'Hey, what if this mouse is raised by a secure mother? Does the mouse come out secure like the mother or does the mouse come out anxious like its genes?'"

The "anxious gene," he explained, is one of the *5HTT* receptors, a gene implicated in anxiety and depression because it regulates uptake of the neurotransmitter serotonin.

"What we find," he continued, "is that it's the *combination* of high caregiver anxiety and the anxious gene that produces the most anxious offspring.

"There's something about the caregiver's behavior that seems to bring out the anxiety in the child, making the child more anxious," Harry said. "Look, at birth our brain circuits are plastic—flexible—they're ready to be wired in whatever way experience wires them, but not so much later on. So there's stuff that goes on with our caregivers that can either enhance or discourage development of these anxious circuits."

In fact, despite great effort, no definitive connection between genes and attachment has been found. In one study looking at the genomes of more than 2.5 million people, researchers found no significant relation between genes and attachment style.

Insecurity Has Its Advantages

While secure attachment may best enable an individual to find a mate and maintain a long-term, stable relationship, Harry noted, insecure attachment need not be seen as a disorder or as a sentence to a lifetime of relationship hell. If more than half the population is predisposed to insecure attachment, after all, we'd expect it to confer some advantage in evolutionary terms. In fact, during infancy, insecurity is adaptive: for children in a poor relationship environment, it can be protective— for the anxious child, it can help get Mom or another caregiver to pay attention, and for the avoidant child, it can help one avoid being hurt by rejection. In those situations, both options are more effective than just continuing to behave like a secure child.

Moreover, for adults, emerging research suggests that both avoidant and anxious attachments carry benefits that are valuable to both the individual and the community.

Israeli researcher Tsachi Ein-Dor and others, for example, have suggested that in early human settlements, tribal members with anxious attachments—ever vigilant to early signs of a threat—would have functioned as "sentinels," alerting others to danger. And tribal members with avoidant attachments—inclined to be self-reliant and act independently—would have functioned as "rapid responders," taking decisive yet dangerous action to protect the community.

On a personal level, insecure attachment also confers some benefits. Avoidant individuals—self-reliant and able to function without close proximity to significant others—do especially well at jobs that require solo travel or long hours working independently. And, as noted, it is often anxious individuals—ever sensitive to threats—who act as early warning systems of danger, the so-called "sentinel" function.

Incidentally, anxious people also tend to be highly sensitive to the emotional environment and therefore are likely to be overrepresented among writers, musicians, and others who express the human condition through art. Consider, for example, the opening lyric of John Lennon's song "Mother": "You had me / But I never had you." Still, contrast that lyric with the tribute to a mother's steadfastness in Paul Simon's "Loves Me Like a Rock": My mama loves, she loves me she gets down on her knees and hugs me."

Harry was beginning to wrap up.

"So, once you've got insecurity are you stuck with it forever?"

The answer, he said, is yes and no.

Yes, because, as Bowlby himself argued, mental models of attachment "tend to remain stable." The best current estimate of the stability of attachment styles over the life span is 70–75 percent. "This means," Harry explained, "that if we put people in an attachment category, 70 to 75 percent of them will live their lives in that category without changing."

Earned Secure Attachment

But as far as people being stuck with insecurity, Harry wanted the class to understand a concept called "earned security."

A quick glance around showed every student paying attention.

"People are 'earned secure,'" explained Harry, "if everything in your background suggests you should be insecure yet you are not."

Earned security comes from one of two things: first, a strong, meaningful relationship with another person—not a caregiver—who somehow substitutes for the caregiver. In childhood or adolescence, that could be an aunt or uncle, a foster parent, schoolteacher, mentor, or

coach. In adulthood, it could be a romantic partner or spouse in a successful, stable marriage or a therapist—"some incredibly influential
experience with another person that has a profound impact on you,"
Harry explained. Second, earned security can also come from deep
reflection and meaningful insight into one's own experience—often
with the aid of a therapist—that convinces oneself, "You know, my
early experiences really suck but maybe I can do better."

Harry said that most often earned security results from the combination of a strong, meaningful relationship plus personal insight.
"People with earned security are those who by all rights should be a
mess but who, through life experiences, have been able to achieve secure attachments. At some level," he added, "you're still anxious or
avoidant, but you know how to deal with it."

Class time was up.

"But a better question to ask than, 'Can I change?'" Harry said, getting in one last point, "is, 'Are there ways to live a life given my attachment style that can work around some of the bad things?' And the
answer is yes. You can learn to subvert the process. Even if you can't
change your attachment style, by being aware of its influence, you may
be able to change the outcomes, and if you can change the outcomes,
then who cares what your attachment style actually is?"

———

I looked over the students—most of them barely out of their teens—as
they pulled on sweatshirts and coats. Along with laptops and back-
packs, I now realized each carried an attachment style, the result of
experiences in early childhood over which they had no control and
about which they had little memory. I thought of all the choices and
relationships that would be affected by their attachment history:
friendships that would endure while others would not, passion and
heartbreak, marriage and perhaps divorce, even their choice of careers. I hoped some of what they had learned in Harry's class might
help smooth their way.

For myself, I realized that I likely carried out of Harry's classroom—and probably had carried for nearly sixty years—an anxious attachment style. Harry said, though, that these categories are a matter of degree. So how anxious was I? And could I take advantage of its good parts while, as Harry suggested, finding ways to work around the bad? While my attachment style had been established decades earlier, my investigation of this central and fascinating aspect of our personalities and lives had only just begun.

CHAPTER 2

Five Adjectives: Measuring Adult Attachment

Some months after I'd visited Harry Reis's class, I arranged to meet Mauricio Cortina, a psychiatrist, for coffee, in Washington, DC. In the preceding weeks, we'd exchanged e-mails and spoken once by phone, but this was the first time we'd met in person. As we talked, I found myself wondering if he could tell my attachment style just by our conversation—and then realized that wondering that was itself probably evidence of an anxious attachment style.

Dr. Cortina, sixty-seven, was of medium build, with a round face, thinning hair, and a soft voice. It was Tuesday—a day he normally didn't see patients—so he was dressed casually: polo shirt, khaki pants, and sneakers. He'd agreed to spend part of the day giving me the Adult Attachment Interview (AAI), considered the gold standard for measuring adult attachment. Unlike the "strange situation" procedure, which assesses a person's attachment as a child, the AAI aims to measure the current, adult state of attachment.

Soon after beginning his clinical practice in psychiatry in the 1970s, Dr. Cortina began reading John Bowlby.

"I said to myself, 'My God, this is good stuff!'" he told me. "It's a theory about vulnerable relationships, trust relationships. It's not everything—there are things that influence personality that are not attachment—but what it does capture is essential," he said.

He became, in his own words, an "early adopter" of attachment theory, eventually founding the Attachment and Human Development Center at the Washington School of Psychiatry. He was also trained to administer the Adult Attachment Interview.

Developed in the mid-1980s by psychologist Mary Main and colleagues at the University of California, Berkeley, the AAI is a structured interview designed to assess a person's attachment style. In the interview, people are asked open-ended questions about their childhood relationships with their parents, as well as experiences when they felt ill, threatened, or rejected, and how all these may have affected their adult personality. The goal is not to determine what the person's childhood experiences actually were—memory is considered too unreliable for that—but instead to discover the person's "mental model" of how he sees himself in relation to others. A 2009 report by Dutch researchers assessed more than 10,500 Adult Attachment Interviews conducted in the previous twenty-five years and found the coding system to be "remarkably robust across countries and cultures."

"Attachment theory is so much in my bones now," Dr. Cortina told me, "I sometimes use its questions in psychotherapy. And when I discuss attachment theory with patients who are parents, they say, 'Of course,' because they know in *their* bones that the relationship with their infant children is crucial in development."

"Is it helpful for people to know their own attachment style?" I asked.

"Yes, of course," he said. "Look, the expectations we have of others in terms of emotional availability form an important part of everyone's psychology and therefore of relationships. Can I lean on you? Can you lean on me? That's not the whole of psychology, but, my God, it's one of the most important elements of psychology."

Later Dr. Cortina and I talked about attachment style as just one aspect of an individual's overall outlook and behavior, and how just because someone may be securely attached doesn't mean that person won't face, for example, relationship stresses, heartache, or even depression. Obviously, there are always other factors besides attachment at play.

In terms of formative influences, Dr. Cortina mentioned genetics and how the cultural environment (family, economics, nurturing) determines which genetic components get expressed and which don't.

He mentioned siblings and peers, as well as broader cultural factors including institutions and schools. All these factors, and others, help form an individual's personality. And there are also ways to describe personality other than in attachment terms. For example, psychologists speak of the Big Five personality traits: extroversion, agreeableness, openness, conscientiousness, and neuroticism.

Still, said Dr. Cortina, "Attachment theory has given clinicians many more tools with which to understand human personality and behavior."

Hoping I wasn't being too intrusive, I asked Dr. Cortina, "Do you know your own attachment style?"

A colleague had once given him the test, he said, and although he never had it officially scored, he guessed it would come out secure "with elements of avoidance."

(Technically, the AAI classifies people as "secure," "dismissing," or "preoccupied." These terms parallel the more common terms I've been using in this book—"secure," "avoidant," and "anxious"—so for simplicity I'm going to continue using the same terms.)

Explaining the roots of his attachment style, Dr. Cortina said, "There was very little evidence that my mother was emotionally attuned, even though she was there for me. My mother and father loved me, and with my father I developed a very positive relationship. I grew up expecting very little of people—something I was completely unaware of until I discovered it in therapy."

His mother, who lived to be one hundred, had died only the previous winter.

Had he ever talked with his mother about these things?

"No," he said. "She was so oblivious about it, it would hurt her. She genuinely loved us, but she was so blind about it that it would have served no useful purpose. I would have hurt my mother very deeply if I'd gone into it."

Our conversation about his attachment style seemed to open a door, and Dr. Cortina began to tell me much more about his personal life: about his divorce and remarriage, how he believed he had "lucked out" with his second wife but nevertheless how early in the new marriage they had gone through a rough patch during which he had had panic attacks; about how during that time being a parent had anchored him; about his adult children—one of whom was considering becoming a therapist; about his grandchildren; and about how after his mother's death he was named executor of her estate and tried to mediate conflicts among his six siblings over the will.

I was surprised a psychiatrist was confiding so much personal information and was silently congratulating myself for being such a good interviewer when Dr. Cortina looked me in the eye and said, "I wanted to have this conversation with you, Peter, because later I'm going to be asking you very personal questions—some that might elicit painful memories for you—so I wanted to first tell you a little about myself, just to make it fair."

Oh.

Then we drove to his home office in Silver Spring, Maryland, where he would give me the Adult Attachment Interview.

———

"Okay," said Mauricio, placing a small tape recorder on his desk. "I'm ready when you are."

Somewhere between the café and his home, I'd begun to feel comfortable enough with Dr. Cortina to refer to him by his first name.

"I'm ready, Mauricio," I said, and put down my notebook.

We were seated in a large, book-lined room on one end of his modest, two-story home. He sat at his desk in a swivel chair, which was turned to face me; I sat on a futon sofa close by.

The AAI lasts about an hour and consists of twenty questions asked in a set order, along with specific follow-ups. The protocol requires it be recorded and transcribed so later it can be scored by an independent third party. Taking the AAI is "not as easy as it might appear," cautions one of its developers, Erik Hesse, of the University of California, Berkeley. The person must answer complex questions about their life history, many of which "he or she will never have been asked before." It moves along at a "rapid pace" and has among its aims to "surprise the unconscious." Overall, warns Hesse, "the process often appears to be a far more powerful experience than anticipated." Later, what the scorer will be looking for is not so much what was said but, instead, whether the narrative was coherent or filled with "contradictions and inconsistencies."

I'm going to recount here in detail much of what I said during the Adult Attachment Interview because I want you to see what the interview looks like and to simulate the intense experience.

(If you want to have your own attachment style professionally assessed, you may be able to locate professionals who, like Dr. Cortina, are accredited to administer the AAI. See attachment-training.com or write to Naomi Gribneau Bahm, coordinator of the AAI Trainers Consortium, at ngbreliability@gmail.com. Note that some researchers dissuade individuals from taking the AAI because errors by the interviewer or by the scorer may lead to inaccurate results. They prefer the AAI be given by a person's own therapist—if certified to administer it—who can interpret results based on a broad knowledge of the patient. Other attachment experts, however, see the self-knowledge that may come from taking the AAI as outweighing the risks. "The AAI would give anyone useful information about themselves," says Dr. Cortina. Bottom line: remember that any test is subject to human error, so if you do take the AAI, weigh the results accordingly. Another option is to take the Experiences in Close Relationships quiz, also called the attachment quiz, reprinted in the appendix. This quiz measures different factors from the AAI but also gives a general measure of attachment style.)

"Well, so let's start with the very first question," said Mauricio, pushing RECORD.

His gentle voice had taken on a slightly more formal tone. I guessed he was slipping into psychiatrist mode.

"Okay, so just to help me get into your family," he said, "if you could tell me where you live, where you were born, if you moved around much, what your dad and family did for a living—just a general orientation."

The room was silent except for the slight whirring of a microcassette as it spun inside the recorder.

"I was born in Rochester, New York," I began, "and have two older siblings, a brother ten years older, and a sister seven years older. My dad was in business with his two brothers. They founded and ran a commercial printing company."

"Did you move around much?" Mauricio asked. I'd failed to respond to that part of the question.

I told him my family moved from the city to the suburbs, where they had built a new home in 1957 when I was four years old. We were part of that large, late-fifties migration from city to suburbs.

"Any other adults living in the household?" he asked.

"Yes," I said, my parents had some live-in help. "The story is that my mom had contracted a mild case of polio when my older sister was born, so when I was born they hired an older woman to live in the house to help take care of me."

"Any memories of her?" he asked.

"No," I said, "but there were actually two women. One who died and the other who was let go."

"So, who would you say raised you?"

In less than two minutes, Mauricio, following the script for the AAI, had managed to get to the central question of my early childhood.

"That's the $64,000 question," I said, with a loud, nervous laugh. "I actually don't know who raised me. I don't think it was my mother."

"Okay," said Mauricio, betraying no emotion.

"I mean, how expansive do you want me to be in this answer?" I asked. "I can talk for a long time about it."

"I'm interested in your sense of who raised you," he said.

Mauricio, no doubt, had honed his interviewing skills over more than thirty years as a practicing psychotherapist, and though that morning he was following a prepared script, I was on the receiving end of his intensely focused attention. His whispery voice, which in the coffee shop had sometimes frustrated me because it was hard to hear, in the quiet of his office was soothing, even lulling. I felt at ease, and eager to answer his questions as fully and honestly as I could.

"I think it was probably my dad who raised me," I said. "I have very, very few memories of my mother and . . . no memories of these other women—the nannies. I've been told that when I was about one year old the first nanny died suddenly of a heart attack and was replaced by the second. I've seen pictures of the second one but I don't have any conscious memory of her. And then she was let go at the suggestion of a psychiatrist who my mother took me to see because when I started speaking I had a stutter, and they were concerned about that. Years later, when I asked my mother about this, she said the psychiatrist told her, 'This child doesn't know who his mother is. You have to get rid of the nanny and be the mother.'"

Mauricio asked me when all that had happened, and I said it must have been when I was about three.

Despite Mauricio's attention and soothing tone, it felt strange to be sharing these personal stories—all of them private and emotional and some of them embarrassing—and not have the person I was speaking to make any comment but instead just move on to the next question. Later, in reading about how the Adult Attachment Interview is structured, I came to see that the rapid pace of questioning was part of the protocol designed to elicit honest and unedited responses, but at the time it felt odd to be sharing these things and not even get back a shrink-like "I can imagine that was difficult."

"So, let's go on," said Mauricio. "I'd like you to choose five adjectives that describe your relationship with each of your parents. Take your time on this—it's not easy to come up with these five adjectives. And then I'm going to ask you why you chose them. You choose who you want to start with."

This seemed an odd request, but I was willing to go along.

"Okay," I said, "so my mother, five adjectives that describe her?"

"That describe your relationship with her."

"Oh, my relationship. Okay, but at what point in time?"

"Go as far back as you can," he said, "and then go forward."

The "five adjectives," I later learned, are a key part of the AAI. Erik Hesse explains that the "adjectival constellation" the person is asked to provide on the spot is a synopsis of the "general nature of the child-hood relationship." Once the adjectives have been given, the person has in effect "taken a stance" as to the kind of relationship he or she had with that parent. Then the person will be "systematically prodded" for specific memories to support the selection of each word.

The first two adjectives I gave were "distant" and "untrusting."

"But then after we moved, starting when I was five," I said, "it was 'warm' and 'loving' and 'reliable.'"

Then he asked me to think of specific memories that illustrated each adjective.

"Let's start with 'distant,'" said Mauricio.

"Well, I say 'distant' because I just don't have any memory of her— any physical contact with her. I can't remember a single instance of her holding me or comforting me or feeling like she was there," I answered.

"What about 'untrusting'?" he asked.

I told Mauricio the story about asking my mom which sock goes on which foot and not thinking she was telling the truth when she said it didn't matter. I also told him about having tantrums when my father left for work in the morning, even though she was home.

"Okay, then we go to the next adjective: 'warm.'"

"Well, we moved to the new house, new neighborhood, new school," I said, "and suddenly in my memory my mother is always present. She puts me to bed at night and comes to school events and is just like a regular mom."

Mauricio pressed: "Do you have an actual memory of her being always present?"

I didn't. But I could think of someone else who was always there.

"I have to introduce another character here," I began.

"Go ahead," said Mauricio.

"In the new house, we had a housekeeper. Her name was Irene. She was a black woman who had recently moved with her family from the South—part of what's now called the Great Migration. I became very close to her. And, in fact, she was the one who was always present when I got home from school. And I would—I don't know—in my memory my mother often isn't home when I get home but Irene is. And I think she would often be done with her work for the day and would make a snack for me. Sometimes we'd play cards. She'd—unlike my mother, she was a strong woman: physically strong, large, and I think emotionally strong. I was very much attracted to that."

From there, we went to "loving" and "reliable." Moving further along in age, now covering the period of elementary and middle school—all in the new house and new neighborhood—I didn't have any trouble telling Mauricio specific memories of both a loving and reliable relationship with my mom.

"Okay, now the same exercise with your father," said Mauricio. "Five adjectives, starting with the earliest memories."

Without much delay, I gave him "nurturing," "bullying," "distant," "loving," and "unavailable."

"Okay, let's start with 'nurturing,'" he said.

I told him about the very clear memory of my father carrying me piggyback up to bed. "And the part I always remember," I told Mauricio, "is leaning forward so my cheek is against his because it's the end of the day and I can feel the roughness of his beard. A five o'clock shadow, I guess. I remember how safe I felt with him carrying me and how close I felt holding on around his neck."

"This memory is before you moved, right?" Mauricio asked. "Around age four?"

"Probably three," I said.

Just then, the tape recorder clicked.

"You want to change the tape?" I asked.

While Mauricio tended to the recorder, I looked around the room. On a shelf near his desk was a framed photograph of an attractive, older woman in a broad-brimmed summer hat. Later Mauricio confirmed my guess that the picture was of his mother. She looked nice enough to me, not at all "oblivious," as Mauricio had described her, but then I wasn't her son and she hadn't raised me.

"Okay," said Mauricio, pushing RECORD, "I just want to repeat that the first adjective about your father was 'nurturing'—this very kinesthetic memory you have of him. Could you repeat that?"

"Kinesthetic?" I asked.

"Tactile," he said. "Describe it just one more time."

"Oh, him carrying me piggyback up to bed," I said again, "and my leaning my cheek against the roughness of his beard."

"So," he continued, "the second adjective you mentioned about your father was 'bullying.'"

"Yeah, well, that was the flip side of all the nurturing. He could be rough. I remember one day—still when I was around three or four—not wanting to go to nursery school, so I hid behind a big lounge chair in our den, but my father ordered me to come out, and then when I didn't he reached behind the chair and grabbed my arm and yanked me out and physically pulled me out of the house."

If Mauricio had asked, I could have showed him where on my arm my father had grabbed me. There was no mark; he hadn't physically hurt me. It was just that, fifty-six years later, I was pretty sure I still remembered the spot.

The third adjective you mentioned was "distant," said Mauricio.

I told him that's because, as I got a little older, the relationship with my father seemed "kind of forced or awkward." I remember once when I was in Cub Scouts there was a father-son dinner and it was almost embarrassing to want him to take me to that. "We went but it was awkward," I explained. Same thing happened when I asked him once to take me to a circus that I'd seen advertised on TV. He seemed to me much more comfortable and involved with my brother and sister and their homework and school activities than he was with me.

"On the other hand," I added, "while running for student council in sixth grade I had to give a speech to the whole school, and he actually came and stood in the back of the auditorium to listen. That meant a lot."

"Okay, shall we move to the number four adjective, 'loving'?"

"Did I say that?" I asked, laughing. "Well, I did feel that he loved me."

"Can you remember incidents that illustrate that?" asked Mauricio.

"Well, he was loving when he took me up to bed." I paused. "I sure wish I had more to say about that."

Another pause.

"My dad was a successful businessman," I said, "and provided well for us, and I think that's how he expressed his love for us. He'd be home nearly every night for dinner. And starting in maybe fourth grade, he'd help me with my homework."

"Well, let's move on to the last adjective," said Mauricio.

"What did I say?" I asked, laughing as I realized I couldn't recall the fifth adjective I'd stated only minutes before.

"'Unavailable,'" he said.

"Well, he was around but my interaction was more with my mother," I said, and left it at that.

As Mauricio consulted his script for the next question, I found myself wondering how I'd feel someday if one of my own children, whom I love so much, was giving five adjectives to describe their relationship with me.

"As a child," asked Mauricio, "when you were emotionally upset, what would you do?"

"Cry, have tantrums, go to my sister," I said. "My sister was the more consistently nurturing one. She was comforting and supportive. There was no physical place I would go. I don't remember feeling there was any safe place.

"My mother appeared kind of weak as a person," I continued, "and her comforting and nurturing didn't count, in a way. She seemed dependent on my dad. And I think that's what attracted me to Irene, the housekeeper who took two buses from where she lived in the city, got dropped off a mile from our house, and walked from the bus to our house in all kinds of weather, including snowstorms. She'd work at our house from nine till three or four in the afternoon, walk to the bus, take two buses back to where she lived, and then take care of her own family. As I saw it, she was always there, was patient and physically strong, had time to take care of me and play with me. If I got home from school and it was raining hard, she'd meet me at the bus and walk me home. I never had a problem getting her attention. So I'd come home from school and I'd sort of come home to her."

After that long soliloquy about the housekeeper, I felt dazed. "I'm sure we were talking about something else," I said with a laugh, "but I've forgotten what!"

"Well," said Mauricio, "we were talking about where you would go when you were emotionally upset, so right on topic."

He continued: "I know we've gone over this, but this is an important question. I'm just wondering, when you were upset or hurt do you remember being held or comforted by either of your parents?"

I said I was sure my mother held me if I was hurt, but I couldn't think of any particular time.

Mauricio then asked when was the first time I remember being separated from my parents.

"Separated?" I asked.

"Like going to camp," he said.

"I went to camp when I was nine," I said. "They sent me for the whole summer, which in retrospect seems a little weird, but I'll tell you an incident before that. This is a great illustration of how my family operated.

"So I'm seven and it's a Sunday and I'm out riding my bike in front of our house, and my father comes out to the sidewalk and says"—and here I affected what to my seven-year-old ears was my father's deep, gruff voice—"'Put your bike away. We're going to the hospital. You're going to get your tonsils out.' Oh, okay, I thought. That was the first I'd heard of getting my tonsils out."

I laughed in retelling the story.

"In those days," I continued, "it was common for kids to get their tonsils taken out, although I don't know how common it was that no one would tell you about it until it was time to go to the hospital. Anyway, so I put my bike away, got in the car, and they drove me to the hospital, and an hour later somehow I'm in pajamas in a bed and my parents are saying, 'You'll be fine, and we'll see you tomorrow when you wake up,' or something, and 'They're going to give you ice cream.'

"I remember that evening going into a common room with other kids who were there for some kind of operation," I continued, laughing, "and I remember thinking, 'This is pretty weird. How'd I get here?'

"They came the next day and later they took me home and I recovered," I told Mauricio. "It wasn't until I was much older that I looked back on that and saw how bizarre it was, but I'm also not sure how unusual it was. Parents were advised to do that in those days. I've joked about it with my family."

"With these first separations," asked Mauricio, "how did your parents respond?"

"Well, my father was probably"—here, I again affected a low, gruff voice—"'stiff upper lip.' My mother was very indulgent"—here, I used a high, quavering voice—"'Oh, you don't have to go. You can change your mind. We'll come and get you,' which, in retrospect, was also not a healthy approach. But those were the typical approaches: my father denying any emotional experience and my mother indulging the worst fears and anxieties. It's a great combination." Laughing, I added, "I don't recommend it!"

Turning to the next page of his script, Mauricio asked, "Okay, so did you ever feel rejected as a young child?"

"By whom?"

"By your parents."

"How young?"

"Any age."

"What does rejection mean?"

"Well, whether you felt that they rejected your bids for comfort or attention, or of needing them?"

"Yes, in the old house before age four," I said. "Particularly at night in bed. I felt very much alone and abandoned. In contrast to that, though, when we moved to the new house and new neighborhood, I gradually came to feel pretty much the center of the show, especially when my brother and sister went off to college. I also was academically more successful than my brother and sister. I did well in school, was active in student government, and those were new experiences for my parents, and they enjoyed all that, I think."

"Any feelings of being pushed away or ignored at the new house?" he asked.

"No," I said. "But you'd have to wonder how reliable my memory is, because how radically could my parents' behavior change just because of a change in venue?"

"Why do you think your parents acted that way toward you when you were little?" he asked.

"I don't think it was out of malice," I answered. "I think it was just what they thought about parenting. And they also had a seven- and ten-year-old who required a lot of attention. My brother had a lot of emotional difficulties and was probably a handful. My father was just not given to emotional expression—still isn't. My mother did have some physical weakness from polio, but I think her major problem was fearfulness and anxiety. The feeling I had was that this family was fully formed when I came along and I never quite fit into it. I still feel that way, actually. But I don't think it was out of malice at all."

"Were your parents ever threatening with you in any way?"

"My father would occasionally threaten me—spank me. He'd use a table-tennis paddle to spank me. That's about it, though."

"Any physical abuse?"

"No."

"Silent treatment or shaming?"

"No, just ridicule," I said. "I would often be ridiculed for being too sensitive about things. Also, I was still stuttering up until the fifth or sixth grade. That was humiliating within the family, partly because it was never discussed. But again, I think that was generational. Sometimes my father would make a comment at the dinner table if I was trying to say something and couldn't. He'd just say, 'Slow down!' But there was an edge to it; it wasn't like a sympathetic understanding. It was like, 'You're embarrassing me,' or 'You don't have to do that!'"

"Was that shaming for you?"

"Yeah, that was shaming. But I don't think it was intentional."

"He didn't intend to shame you?"

"No."

"But you felt shamed?"

"Yeah."

"What about people outside your family, Peter, who were ever threatening or punishing or shaming, or anything influential like that?"

"Influential?" I asked. "Well, I had a sixth grade male teacher who later was also my basketball coach. He was—I don't even know how to describe it—tremendously supportive and was the first male I encountered who seemingly got who I was and believed in me and just gave me more and more confidence, and he became a significant person in my life who I still keep in touch with."

"So he was a very important figure."

"Yeah, and I think it was significant that he was male."

"What about this housekeeper who you told me about? Did you keep in touch with her?"

"I did. I visited Irene as an adult, and I visited her in a nursing home in hospice care the day before she died."

"So that speaks to the significance she had for you, too."

"Yeah, the two of them were like an alternate set of parents," I said, laughing. "I didn't see it that way at the time, but just looking back . . ."

I didn't think to mention it during the interview, but our housekeeper—after she left our employment when I was about twelve—became a fixture in the local black community. She ran the kitchen at a large nursing home, put her children through college, and became a mentor to many young people, including several generations of black seminary students. When she retired, Rochester's mayor proclaimed it Irene Saunders Day. A testimonial dinner was held in her honor; my parents and I attended.

"Okay," said Mauricio, "let's move on to the next question. How do you think your overall experience with your parents affected your adult personality?"

I laughed again.

"Well, I'm here in your office, aren't I? Really, I think it had a profound effect on who I chose to marry and how we raised our children, and that being a father became the most important thing I did as an adult, and still is. And I think it—I mean, the biggest charge I always used to hear as a kid from my family was, 'You're too sensitive.' It was only recently I told that to a friend who is a rabbi and she said, 'You know, when your family accuses you of being too sensitive, the correct response is, "Thank you."' And I got what she meant, because I think all that experience did make me sensitive, and it's from that sensitivity, in part, that my wife and I were successful in raising children and nurturing them, and I think that sensitivity has also allowed me to become a writer and explore subjects that are important, so that stuff's been good."

Mauricio asked, "And what about the negative side? Do you think there were aspects that held you back in your development?"

"Yes, of course," I said. "I've had to battle against a profound sense of not being as competent as I would like to feel. Not trusting my own judgment about things. My marriage was ideal for raising children in a healthy way, but in other respects the woman I married was not an ideal choice as an adult partner—nor I for her—and ultimately this led to our divorce, which I deeply regret. I see the roots of a lot of who I am as an adult, good and bad, in those early experiences. I still struggle with it. But the good stuff's been good."

"So why do you think your parents behaved the way they did during your childhood?"

"Didn't we already cover that?"

"Yes, but some of these questions look at the same issues from different angles."

"A lot of it was generational," I began. "It was just how people parented in those days. And each of my parents had parents themselves. My father was raised by first-generation immigrants from Austria and Hungary, a Germanic culture. They spoke German at home. They grew up in the Depression. My father slept three to a bed with his brothers, was the youngest in his family, was very much aware of their poverty, and worked from the time he was nine years old. Though he was bright, he had no chance of going to college because there was no money for it. Instead, he had to work to support his family. And from what I've heard, his father was largely absent and his mother was very strong but could also be cutting, even caustic, so he probably grew up the best he could under those circumstances and brought all that to the table as a parent himself. I get that.

"My mother was also the youngest of three girls, and while she had a much more middle-class upbringing, I think she had some emotional issues as a child that were probably never addressed, and I don't think as a woman she ever fully matured. She was part of that generation of American suburban women who were not expected to really do much.

"And I don't think their parenting was probably very different from what was going on in many suburban homes around us."

Mauricio looked at his sheet but didn't immediately ask another question.

"I'm going to use this pause to be sure we don't miss anything," he said. "I'm going to check the tape."

He said we just had a few questions left.

"I feel like we're getting to know each other," I said, during the pause.

"I told you this was going to be an intense—"

"You were right!" I agreed, laughing.

"Okay," he said, "recording now. Peter, you've mentioned that your father is still living. Is your mother still alive, too?"

"No, my mom died at eighty-eight, about six years ago."

"So, can you tell me more about that, how you responded, what it was like for you?"

I laughed.

"You really want to know that?" I laughed again. "Well, she had a good death. She and my dad had been living in an apartment on their own. Mentally she was fine, but she got progressively weaker until one day she needed to be hospitalized for pneumonia, and then she died the next day.

"I didn't feel much," I continued, "and I still don't. There was this incident for me, though: a couple of days before she went to the hospital my father called and said my mom had fallen and he couldn't get her up. I went over, and she was lying on the floor and looking very helpless, and of course I went to help her up. But the thing was, when I reached down to pick her up I had this surge of anger that seemed to come out of nowhere and thought, 'Where were you when I needed to be held?!' I didn't say it out loud, of course, but that's what I thought. And then I helped her up.

"This coincided," I continued, "with a difficult period I was in. I'd been in a relationship that had just broken up, and I felt abandoned and lonely. I had come to understand enough of my history through therapy at that point to grasp that some of the difficulty I was having in my romantic relationships might be attributed to some of these early childhood issues. So I was very angry in general right then, at being alone, and so to come over and pick up my mother, in effect to nurture her—I just felt resentful."

I paused.

"I forgot the question!" I said, laughing.

"The next question," said Mauricio, "is about changes in your relationships with your parents after childhood, moving into adulthood."

This subject was safer ground.

"In middle school and high school," I began, "I had good relationships with them. After school, trying to find a career, I felt some tension because I was gradually coming to understand that my father did not actually know who I was, and it took me a long time to work my way toward doing what I ultimately ended up doing, which is writing and teaching, rather than being in business or law, which my father would have preferred or at least understood.

"Also, I was married for seventeen years, but as the marriage began to come apart I began to explore my own childhood, now with the benefit of having raised children, and I began to feel a mix of love and animosity, or resentment, toward my parents. Usually, I wouldn't talk about it, but once or twice when I was feeling so desperate because of the breakup of my marriage or subsequent relationship I told my parents—at the urging of a therapist—what I thought about these early things, and that didn't go over so well. Frankly, when you told me that you chose not to have a conversation like that with your own mother, I was thinking, 'Maybe I should not have had that conversation either,' because I know it was hurtful to my father, and I don't think he understands me any better for my having said it, and I'm not sure I got any benefit out of saying it, so I kind of admire your choice."

"Thank you," said Mauricio.

"What about your relationship with your father now?" he asked. "What would you say about it?"

"I've liked this time, most of it, to be closer to him," I said. "At the same time, the relationship is mixed. He's still hurting about the things I told him—those feelings about my childhood—and I still don't feel he knows who I am or that he appreciates my achievements. I call him every day, though, and see him several days a week and have dinner with him and along with my sister oversee his care, so it's a mixed bag.

"But I also anticipate his death and am concerned about how that will affect me, because I do think he was my primary attachment figure, and I'm sure I won't react to his death the way I did to my mother's, which was basically not having much reaction."

Again, no comment.

"I'd like to move to another sort of relationship," said Mauricio, "the current one with your children. How do you respond now that you're separated from your children? Do you ever have concerns or worries about being separated from them?"

"Well, this is the good part of the interview," I began. "My kids are twenty-eight, twenty-five, and eighteen years old. Both my former wife and I have very good relationships with the kids. We actually have a good relationship with each other, are very amicable, and managed to continue parenting together even after the divorce. The kids are all doing great. I'm staying with my daughter and her fiancé here in DC. I'm close with my other daughter in New York City, and my son just had a good first year of college. I don't have anything negative or troubling to say about it."

Mauricio—breaking character, perhaps—said he was glad to hear that.

"Anything you've learned from your childhood experiences?" he asked. "Anything you've gained from having the kind of childhood you had?"

This sounded like a summing-up question; we must have been nearing the end.

"It taught me a lot about being a parent," I said. "My former wife and I came out of childhood with our own wounds, and as a result we took parenting seriously. We found our way toward creating a family that was nurturing and safe, and also tried to know our kids for who they really are, and to encourage them to be who they are—even if they're different from each other or from us. I think that's the most important thing I've learned."

I hoped I didn't sound too mawkish.

"Looking to the future," said Mauricio, "I want to end by asking one more question: what do you hope your children have gained from your parenting?"

"I hope they came out of their childhoods feeling loved and protected, and known for who they really are, and accepted," I said. "And also encouraged to be themselves and to explore and try things. My wife and I were on the same page raising kids and enjoyed learning about child-rearing and learning how to do it as a family. I loved being a parent and deeply regret the divorce, because it was not good for the kids, but even with that I think overall we did pretty well, and I consider that my greatest achievement."

"Well, Peter," said Mauricio, as he reached toward the tape recorder, "maybe we should leave it there." And with that, he pushed STOP.

"Well, I feel pretty exposed!" I said, laughing.

"Yes, it is very exposing," he said. "And do you still want to have the interview scored?"

I definitely did want it scored, I said, because I wanted to know my attachment style.

"Well," he said, "I can also give you my personal opinion of how you'd score."

"You can?" I asked.

I wasn't expecting that.

"You're a classic earned secure."

Earned secure was what Harry Reis had talked about in class—the goal that all of us with less-than-perfect childhoods could aspire to. Although 75 percent of people live their whole lives within one attachment category, some do change.

"Really?" I asked. "That's a surprise to me."

"Because you see, this is the beauty of the Adult Attachment Interview," Mauricio explained. "It's not so much the experience; it's how you can tell the experience. It's the coherence of the narrative. Your case is a classic example: a childhood that was far from ideal in some aspects, in terms of what you have said about your mother and your father, but the point is that you can talk about it and you can describe it to me. That's what an earned secure does. Earned secures might have had a very difficult childhood, but even with the mixed adjectives about your dad, there's not—if I may use some psychological jargon— there's not a lot of defensive idealization or denigration. There's more a kind of 'this is the way it was.'"

"I would have thought I was classic insecure anxious," I told Mauricio.

"If you weren't reflective—and this is the beauty of the interview— yes, you would be. I mean, if you couldn't give me a more balanced view of the positives and negatives I'd be inclined to move you to more insecure."

"But how come I don't feel more secure," I said, "especially in regard to relationships?"

"Perhaps you don't feel as sure-footed as you'd like to in relationships," he said. "It's not that all those childhood issues are erased. Earned secure doesn't mean that everything's fine or that you don't struggle. It means you have enough understanding and enough distance that you can describe things with a certain objectivity. That's what being secure in general means."

"Maybe all these years of therapy were useful!" I said.

"I'm sure they were," agreed Mauricio, "and your own parenting and your reflecting on it. Your parenting was enormously useful. It's your life experience. You've thought a lot about this, and that's why I'm almost sure you're going to end up being scored earned secure."

I pointed out that in my research about earned security, I'd read that it can be achieved through therapy or self-reflection, through finding a mentor or a secure life partner, but that I'd never heard of achieving it through parenting.

"Well, parenting forces you to reflect, to think deeply about these important issues," Mauricio said. "As far as changing a person's attachment style, I don't think there's any research on it. This is just my own thinking."

I was skeptical but really wanted Mauricio to be proved right. I hoped that when the transcript of our interview was scored, he would be.

CHAPTER 3

When Mother Returns:
Attachment Styles in Children

Early on in the development of attachment theory, no one—not even John Bowlby—knew how to assess a young child's attachment style. But eventually a student of Bowlby's named Mary Ainsworth figured it out.

Ainsworth was living with her husband in London when she answered a classified ad placed by Bowlby for a research assistant. She took the job and became immersed in the questions Bowlby was studying about mother-child relations. Later, she went to Uganda to observe mothers and babies in their villages and then to Johns Hopkins University, in Baltimore, to study mothers and babies in their homes. It was there that she hit on the idea of a laboratory procedure—she called it the "strange situation"—to measure attachment style in young children.

The strange situation is composed of eight episodes of separations and reunions between a mother, her child, and a stranger. The episodes become gradually more stressful for the child—the emotional equivalent of a cardiac stress test—activate the attachment system, and reveal the child's attachment style. They uncover, in effect, the "mental model" of relationships that has already been created in the child's mind. The test culminates with an episode based on Ainsworth's brilliant insight that if you want to see the quality of a young child's attachment to his or her mother, watch what the child does, not when Mother leaves, but when she returns.

The strange situation has become the accepted measure for assessing attachment in early childhood—from about one to two years.

Indeed, in recognition of this, those Harvard climbers who named a mountain after John Bowlby named another after Mary Ainsworth; fittingly for a theory about keeping special people close, the mountain named after her is next to the one named after him.

The strange situation test is filmed and later evaluated—coded—by a specially trained person who was not present at the session. One of the leading American coders is Susan Paris of South Portland, Maine.

"We send most of our tapes to Susan—she's the best," a lab director in Maryland told me. "She probably codes for everyone in the country, and internationally too."

I visited Susan Paris at her home, where she showed me how she codes children with different attachment styles as they go through the strange situation.

"I'd like to look with you, first, at a very secure baby," said Susan, inserting into her computer a video of a boy of fifteen months.

We were seated in a cozy study in her modest ranch house in a quiet suburb. In her midfifties and of medium build, Susan had short graying hair, blue eyes, and a ready smile. By day, she taught special ed at a public school, but she'd been coding strange situation tapes for nearly thirty years.

As the tape began, we watched as a woman in her early thirties, with long dark hair, held her fifteen-month-old son. The blond little boy wore a gray T-shirt with a picture of a dinosaur on it. Visible under the waistband of his shorts was a diaper.

The strange situation test we were about to see, Susan explained, was part of research done at an American university. She had no idea what the research was about—and she didn't at the time she originally coded it either. "I don't like to know," she explained. "As in anything with human beings, we can bring our biases into the work, so I want to know as little as possible about the subjects or the aim of the study."

(A researcher had given Susan permission to view some strange situation tapes with me as long as no identifying information about the studies or participants was disclosed.)

On the tape, the mother sat the boy on the floor and walked toward a nearby chair, but as soon as she moved away the boy reacted by toddling toward her, so she got down on the floor with him, and they played with a ball and other toys.

"This looks nice," said Susan. "Nice reciprocal interaction."

Susan noted that as the boy becomes more comfortable in the strange place, he begins to move away from his mother to inspect the toys.

"Hi, I'm Mary," says a young woman as she enters the room. The woman playing the stranger was probably a graduate student in whatever psych department was running the experiment.

"Hi, Mary," says the mother.

"Okay," said Susan, "see what he's doing with his hands? He's pulling at his clothes."

I hadn't noticed it, but the boy was sort of pawing with both hands at his T-shirt.

"It's an indication of uncertainty," explained Susan. "Is this person safe? Is she a threat? And then the boy's like, 'Well, Mom doesn't seem to think so, so I guess I can relax.'"

While the boy plays, his mother goes back to the chair and chats with the stranger.

"Remember how attachment is about having a secure base from which to explore?" asked Susan. "You can see that very nicely in this little boy. He's interested in what the stranger is doing and wants to explore—so that pulls him over toward the stranger, but then he's like, 'Oh, I'm a little too far away from Mom,' and so he moves a bit back toward her. That's the balance."

When the mother leaves the boy with the stranger, he cries a bit but overall holds it together. When his mother comes back—the first of two reunion episodes—he reacts joyfully.

"So there she is, ta-da!" said Susan, speaking as if in the boy's voice. "And that's exactly what you want to see: immediate approach. As soon as she's there, he immediately turns to her. 'It's all I can think about!' He reaches and runs right into her arms. That is a hallmark of security," said Susan.

"I love you!" the mother in the video says, and the boy quiets. She puts him down but, as Susan observed, it is too soon. He gets fussy and she picks him up again. A few moments later, Susan pointed out the boy is now feeling safe in his mother's presence—his secure base is back. Mother puts him down, and he goes back to exploring the toys.

So much of this seems to be the mother's timing, I said—whether the boy gets what he needs at the moment.

"Exactly," agreed Susan. "Sometimes you'll see moms and dads with the best intentions but for whatever reason they're not attuned."

In attachment terms, "attunement" refers to a parent perceiving and responding to a child's needs. "No one gets it right 100 percent of the time," Susan later told me, "but the more a mother correctly interprets a child's signals and acts on them, the more attuned we say she is." In simplest terms, attunement means reading and following a child's cues. For a baby, that might include timing of feeding, minimizing intrusive touch, moving with and gazing at the baby in predictable patterns, and acting in harmony with the baby's mood rather than interrupting it.

We continued to watch the screen. On cue, the mother stands and leaves the room. Immediately, the boy screams. In Susan's narrative voice: "My worst fear! She's gone again!"

"He held it together last time," observed Susan, "but this time it's too much." The boy is alone in the room, the stranger having quietly left.

"Okay, here comes the stranger back," said Susan. By design, the stranger returns first so we can see how the boy responds and then compare it to how he responds in the final episode when his mother returns.

For some kids, explained Susan, this is the most stressful moment. "Their expectation was that it would be Mom coming through the door, so when it's not, you'll see some kids who have barely held on throughout the procedure and then they hear the door and they're all happy, but then they see the stranger and they completely lose it."

But, in fact, the boy is calmed by the stranger, at least a little. Gradually, his cries are shorter, and in between he tries to catch his breath.

"He does have some ability to regulate his own affect," said Susan, pointing out that the boy does occasionally look around the floor nearby, seemingly maintaining some interest in the toys.

"Hang on, she's coming right back," says the stranger.

The boy's shoulders rise and fall.

"He's trying, really trying," said Susan.

"Okay," Susan exclaimed as the final episode begins and the mother returns to the room. "Here she is!" The boy runs right to her. "And there he goes!"

His mother picks him up, and the boy holds on to her with both arms as she wipes his tears.

"He's holding on and clearly relaxed," said Susan. "He doesn't put his head down though. Doesn't quite mold."

"Mold?" I asked.

"A complete relaxation," she said, and made a gesture with her hands—an open hand over a fist—to suggest two things fitting perfectly together. "In coding, we use the term 'mold' to mean the child's body is molded to the caregiver and there's as much contact as possible. It's always chest to chest—frontal—heart to heart."

The mother puts the boy down and returns to her chair. For a moment, he stands still, looks around, and then begins playing quietly with the toys.

"That's good, but he's still a little gaspy," noted Susan. "Clearly, he's working to comfort himself and recover from the bout of crying."

The boy looks intently at his mother.

"He needs a little something more, a little more interaction," observed Susan, "so he looks at her and smiles—then resumes playing. And this is really important: he shares pleasure with her in his success—as he plays he looks at her with a smile. It's a sign of connection, and there's no avoidance or ambivalence about this contact: he says, in effect, 'I did this cool thing and I want you to know about it.'"

The strange situation was over.

"This boy really seemed to be working hard at managing his own affect, at self-regulation," said Susan, "such as when the stranger came back he could use that other person to bring his distress down. And at the end when he resumed playing and shared it with Mom, that clinched it, the shared positive affect. He has a nice, solid secure attachment."

If she'd actually been coding this tape as part of a study, explained Susan, there'd be a second coder—called a "reliability coder"—to independently assess at least 20 percent of a study's tapes. When she and the reliability coder compare results, Susan says, "We're usually 90 percent in agreement, and even when we miss, it'll be a close miss. It's a real vote of confidence in the protocol."

Susan said the next tape we'd see was of a year-old baby girl with an anxious attachment. I didn't tell Susan, but I felt nervous about watching this one. Even if Dr. Cortina, in his assessment of my Adult Attachment Interview, had "upgraded" me to earned secure, my underlying attachment style remained anxious, as I'm sure it was when I was little. I was uneasy about what it might look like.

The tape showed a blond, heavyset mother and a pale, skinny little girl with blond hair pulled severely back into two short pigtails that sat atop her head. The girl wore a white T-shirt with a big zero on it, which struck me as a bad sign.

In an early episode, the mother tried to play with her daughter by running a toy car up and down her arms. "Mothers of anxious babies," said Susan, "are apt to be intrusive like that, to roughhouse or to tickle. I think it's partly that they know they're not going to be able to comfort the child just with contact, and so they try all these other things."

The stranger hadn't even entered yet, and already the baby was crying.

Anxious babies, explained Susan, are not good at using their mothers as a secure base. "That's the essence of the anxious attachment style," she said, "to seek comfort but not to be able to be comforted because it hasn't been consistent and can't be trusted. They want their mother but they can't use the contact, and so they get angry." Or as one researcher put it, "The hallmark of this classification is seeking contact and then resisting contact angrily once it is achieved."

When the stranger entered, the baby got distracted for a moment but soon cried again. Still being held, she turned her body away from her mother. Certainly no "mold" there.

The mother put her down, and the baby wailed.

This child, Susan noted, had much less ability to self-regulate or self-soothe than the secure child we saw.

When the mother left the room, the baby screamed even more. When the mother returned, the baby went to her, and the mother picked her up, but immediately the baby, looking angry, turned her body away.

Watching that anxious little girl get angry when her mother returns reminded me of when I was about three and my parents were about to return home from a trip. To spot them the minute they came in, I'd positioned myself halfway up the stairs with a view of the front door. But at the first glimpse of them, I felt a rush of anger and ran up to my room. I remember at the time both being surprised by that reaction and not understanding it.

On the tape, the girl is still in her mother's arms but faces away and continues wailing. "And now what does Mother do?" asked Susan. "Does she say, 'Oh, honey, it's okay'? No, she shows her a magazine!" From a table near her chair, the mother takes a news magazine and waves it intrusively in her baby's face.

The baby leans back farther, screaming. Her mother says, "It's all right. She's all gone. She's all gone." Susan said, "Mother's thinking it's the stranger that has upset her baby when it's really Mom herself." The mother tries pulling her baby in close, but the baby backs away. Then the baby leans into her mother with her chin. "Look how awkward that is," observed Susan, sounding frustrated. "You don't snuggle into someone with your chin."

On the tape, the girl wails even louder.

"That's okay. That's okay," says her mother, but it isn't helping.

Susan concluded, "This is a classic, prototypical, extremely anxious child."

What might the future look like for that little girl? I asked Susan, as she removed the tape.

"My prediction is she'll be the kid who goes to preschool and cries inconsolably when the parent leaves and isn't able to calm down. And she'll be the kid who has a very difficult time handling all the little annoying things throughout the day: somebody will grab a toy from her and she'll fly off the handle."

Can she ever get back her emotional stability?

"Maybe, but I don't think you can ever get it back as good as if you'd gotten it in the first place," said Susan. "Those first years are critical for mental health, and if you don't experience safety and security then, it's exceedingly difficult to get it back later."

————

The next tape was of a girl of eighteen months whose attachment style was avoidant. These were children, I remembered from Harry Reis's class, who had consistently failed to receive care and as a result had largely given up seeking it.

The contrast with the secure child in the first tape and with the anxious girl in the second was startling. For example, when the girl's mother leaves, the girl has no visible reaction—none. She sits quietly among the toys, seemingly not missing her mother at all. Later the girl continues to play quietly when she is left alone. When the stranger returns, she stands up, looks at the stranger, says something, and goes over to her. "This is how we'd want to see the girl respond with the mother, not the stranger," observed Susan. But in the final episode, when the mother does return, the child just glances at her and then looks away. Her focus remains on the toys; she keeps her head turned away from her mother.

In the attachment literature, I'd read descriptions of how such children might behave—ignoring or looking away from their mother—but seeing it done by an actual child was disturbing.

"Those last two tapes were hard to watch," I said to Susan.

"They are, for sure," she agreed. "Of course, if I had a disorganized kid to show, that would be even tougher to watch."

"Disorganized?" I asked.

Susan then reminded me about a fourth category of attachment, "disorganized." Harry Reis had touched on it in his lecture. Some individuals, he'd said, can actually be high in both avoidance and anxiety. "This, of course, is the worst place to be," he said.

In the general population, only about 5 percent of children are categorized as disorganized, but among those who are maltreated, or where economic and family stresses strain the mother-infant relationship, that figure often rises steeply—some studies put it as high as 60 percent. Among children with negligent or abusive parents, it rises to nearly 80 percent. High percentages of disorganized attachment are also found among children raised in orphanages or other institutionalized care. This phenomenon is often seen, for example, among children adopted from orphanages in Eastern Europe. In a promising study, however, signs of disorganized attachment among Romanian institutionalized children decreased after placement in foster homes, especially if the children were placed before age two with highly sensitive foster parents who themselves had secure attachments.

That day, Susan didn't have any tapes to show me of children with disorganized attachment. But I wanted to see what it looked like, so I arranged to visit a facility where kids, some of whom may have disorganized attachment styles, reunite with their mothers.

———

A metal detector and series of locked doors protected the entrance to the Monroe County Pediatrics and Visitation Center. A sign taped to the outside door listed prohibited items, among them knives, switchblades, razor blades, box cutters, Mace, hammers, screwdrivers, wrenches, cutlery (spoons, forks, butter knives), Tasers, and metal hair picks.

I was curious about the ban on butter knives until a staff worker told me about a little girl with a scar on her neck where her father had burned her with a heated butter knife.

Inside, teddy bears hung from the branches of a Christmas tree in the waiting area. Next to the tree, clutching a purple bear, stood a two-year-old boy I'll call Isaiah. He'd arrived in a van along with three other toddlers and two babies in car seats—all picked up at day care or private homes and brought to the visitation center. This is the place in my hometown of Rochester, New York, where children in foster care come for court-ordered weekly visits with their birth parents.

(To protect confidentially, I've changed names and identifying information of children, parents, and some visitation center staff.)

"Hi, handsome boy!" a staff social worker named Marla said, greeting Isaiah. "You're all nice and bundled up." Marla pulled off Isaiah's camouflage ski cap, revealing a haze of curly, dark hair, and helped him off with his black snow jacket and boots. When he turned around, I could see the top of a diaper poking above the waistband of his jeans.

"I hope Mom comes today to see you," said Marla. An hour-long visit with his mother was scheduled to begin in ten minutes, but Isaiah's mother was known to often miss visits.

Marla was twenty-nine and before working at the visitation center had taught elementary school. Of average build, she nevertheless struck me as physically strong: I could equally imagine her comforting a toddler having a tantrum or restraining an aggressive teen.

"We give parents thirty minutes," she told me quietly, "and then if the parent doesn't show, we cancel the visit." If that happened, another van would take Isaiah back to day care.

Just then a phone rang.

"Oh, great!" Marla said. "Buzz her in. We'll be in 132."

"Mommy's here, little guy!"

Marla pressed her security badge against an electronic lock to buzz open the interior door, took Isaiah's hand, and together they started down a wide corridor toward the visitation rooms.

———

When researchers began using the strange situation to assess children's attachment styles, they found a small number who showed odd behaviors that didn't fit into any of the regular categories. In the last episode, when Mother returns, these children would begin to approach their mother but then freeze, or approach her walking backward, or hold up a hand in front of their face, or sink to the floor. Investigation into the backgrounds of these children showed that many had experienced abuse, neglect, or some other form of parental maltreatment.

Researchers placed these children into a fourth category of attachment called "disorganized." As explained by researcher Bert Powell and colleagues, "The underlying commonality is that these children seem to be seeking and fearing their caregiver at the same time." Unlike secure children, they note, who reach out to their caregivers when frightened, or avoidants who turn away defensively and focus on distractions, or anxious children who redouble their efforts to attach to the caregiver, children with a disorganized attachment show they are in a conundrum: "Their fear is insolvable because the source of their security is also the source of their fear." Powell and colleagues write:

> Children have a four-million-year-old instinct to run away
> from what frightens them and a four-million-year-old instinct
> to run toward their caregiver when they are frightened. When

what is frightening them is the caregiver, they are stuck, caught in a bind of wanting to go toward and go away at the same time.

It's not just overt abuse, such as hitting, that can cause this degree of fright in a child but also—with infants—other types of frightening and startling behaviors.

At the University of Maryland, for example, psychology professor Jude Cassidy shows her grad students a video of a mother who unintentionally produces in her five-month-old son a disorganized attachment. In the video, the mother harshly jangles toys in the baby's face, forcibly turns his head, laughs at his distress, and then growls and lunges at him like a tiger. "What baby's learning here," explains Dr. Cassidy, is that Mother "is not someone I can turn to for comfort when I'm upset. She's the person who's causing me to get upset." She continues: "I think this mom loves her baby, and I don't think she has any idea what she's doing, but that's what the baby's learning. That's toxically powerful. And it's really sad." Parents who themselves were abused as children and have disorganized attachment—as the mother in that video does—are more likely than others to abuse their children, yet it's also true that most parents who were abused do *not* go on to abuse their own children.

At the visitation center, I was curious what it would look like when Isaiah and his mother met. Would he exhibit some of the behaviors I'd read about when disorganized kids have reunions with their mothers: freezing, walking backward, turning in a circle? I was still running through the possibilities when a security door opened at the opposite end of the corridor and Isaiah's mother—a slim, attractive young woman with long black hair—came toward us. Marla let go of Isaiah's hand, and his mother quickly scooped him up, kissed him, and said over and over, "I love you, baby."

It was possible Isaiah did not have a disorganized attachment at all. The visitation room resembled a home environment—like a den or family room. There was a sofa, bookshelves, cupboards with toys and games, a small dining table and chairs, and in the middle an area rug soft enough to sit and play on.

While Marla and Isaiah's mother caught up on some matters of her parole, Isaiah found a music box in a cupboard and then sat on his mother's lap as he played.

The center offers two types of visits: supervised and monitored. During a supervised visit, the worker stays in the room with the family; during monitored visits—allowed when it's clear the parent can handle the situation without staff—the worker checks in every fifteen minutes. Isaiah's visits were supervised.

Isaiah's mother had brought lunch. They sat together at the table and with a plastic spoon (metal utensils being prohibited) she fed him what looked like a rice dish from a plastic tub. Twice Isaiah took the spoon and tried to feed her. "No, it's for you, baby," she said.

Children with disorganized attachment may try to control the interaction with their parent, sometimes by trying to entertain or reassure them. As one staff worker put it, "Some kids get all parental and try to control the visit so it goes well." Whether in trying to feed his mother and bring her toys that was what Isaiah was doing, I didn't know. Earlier I had seen another child, a girl of about three, try to feed her father lunch.

After lunch, Isaiah, all smiles and happy noises, went back to the cupboard and brought his mother more toys.

Children typically come to the center for months, Marla later explained, but occasionally for years. Most cases are for neglect, not abuse, although they have had cases involving sexual abuse, burns with cigarettes, broken bones, whipping with cords and belts, and shaken babies with brain damage, detached retinas, hearing loss, and spiral limb fractures. And there was the little girl with the butter knife.

Neglect is a broad concept that includes failure to provide adequate food, clothing, shelter, and medical treatment; lack of supervision or education; and failure to provide psychological safety, through ridicule, hostility, exposure to marital violence, or abandonment.

Isaiah, I later learned, was placed in foster care because his mother, who was just twenty when he was born, was unable to provide for him. "If you have food in the house one day and then not again for three or four days, that's a form of neglect and grounds for removal," Marla explained. Also, she had served jail time and was unable to arrange shelter and care for Isaiah in her absence. "She's been in jail for much of her son's life," Marla said.

I asked Marla if kids sometimes become attached to staff workers.

"Some kids are more attached to us than to their parents," she said.

I found that last point difficult to grasp until Marla pointed out that since the staff worker is present at every supervised visit, many children in foster care spend the same amount of time with their staff worker as they do with their birth parent, and often the staff worker— by training—is more attuned to the child's needs.

Isaiah was still on the floor, playing quietly with the toys.

"Maybe Isaiah would enjoy going to the playroom," Marla suggested.

The center's indoor playroom has a large climbing toy with a red, wavy slide and dozens of toys and games—most donated from the community. Two other children shared the playroom: a girl about a year old, with pigtails and pink hair clips, and a boy of about Isaiah's age, dressed all in black—I thought of him as a little Johnny Cash, especially when he picked up a toy guitar and starting strumming. Both were with a parent: the girl with her mom and the boy with his dad.

Isaiah made a beeline for the climbing toy. He smiled at everyone and played happily on his own. Later he pushed trucks along the linoleum floor, eventually finding himself in front of a wavy, fun-house mirror—the kind that distorts your image, making you taller, shorter, wider, or thinner depending on how far away you stand.

"What do you see in there, young man?" asked Marla.

And I guess that was the key question: what did Isaiah see?

He didn't answer Marla's question.

I didn't know and really could not know if Isaiah had a disorganized attachment—determining that would require that he and his mother be given the strange situation test—but it was a good bet that some of the kids who peered into that mirror did have disorganized attachment, and so Marla's question, "What do you see?" was apt. The essence of a disorganized attachment is the radical distortion of what should be the normal relationship between a parent and child, and the result is the distortion of a child's sense of security, well-being, and how he sees himself in relation to the world.

That distortion can be seen in the connection between disorganized attachment in early childhood and a type of adult psychopathology called "dissociative disorders." These include conditions such as split personality, memory loss, and symptoms similar to post-traumatic stress disorder. Self-hitting, cutting, and burning have also been linked to disorganized attachment, particularly in combination with childhood maltreatment.

When Isaiah went back to playing on the slide, his mother went over to a stack of toys and picked up an electronic alphabet board—it's a game where you push a letter and an electronic voice says the letter's name. She took the game to Isaiah—he was standing atop the slide—and pushed A and then B, trying to get Isaiah to repeat the letter names. But Isaiah just smiled, made his happy sounds, and slid down.

"He's got a speech problem," she said to me. It was only then I realized that I'd not heard Isaiah speak. He smiled a lot and made his pleasant sounds, but I had not heard him say any words. "Children entering foster care typically show evidence of developmental delays," one treatise on child development notes, "including . . . speech and language development." But not all "normal" two-year-olds speak yet either. So was this a symptom of maltreatment or possibly disorganized attachment? Just as with Isaiah's "parental" behavior in the visitation room, I had no way to know.

As Isaiah played on the slide, my eye caught an object I had not previously noticed: a child-sized gray-blue plastic chair. I knew that chair well; when our kids were little, we had an identical set at home. For hours and hours, our girls—when they were about the same age as Isaiah—would sit in them, at a matching table, happily drawing, coloring, and playing games. Seeing that chair made the gulf between what my kids started with and Isaiah's situation seem even starker.

If he did have a disorganized attachment, Isaiah's life would likely be harder, even on top of the economic and social disadvantages he faced. Studies show that kids with disorganized attachment and the dissociative disorders they spawn often lack the social skills and behavioral self-control to succeed in school, from Head Start and pre-K right up through high school. A 2010 meta-analysis of some sixty studies involving more than six thousand children found that those rated disorganized showed in later childhood markedly higher levels of oppositional behavior, hostility, and aggression. The risk was greater for boys, but girls were also at risk. And in a study of prison inmates, 36 percent were rated as disorganized, as were 82 percent of psychiatric patients. A forensic psychologist suggests that disorganized attachment may be a direct risk factor for later delinquency and violent criminality.

The troubling prevalence of disorganized attachment among at-risk kids comes at enormous cost, not only to these children and their families but also to the larger community. Fortunately, researchers are developing methods of intervention that actually can turn disorganized and other insecure attachments into secure ones.

In one such program, Child-Parent Psychotherapy, therapists meet weekly for a year with mothers and infants in the mother's home. They observe mother and infant together, challenge any distorted perceptions of herself and her child the mother may have as a legacy of her own upbringing, and help the mother respond sensitively to her child's needs. In a recent study of 137 maltreated thirteen-month-olds, 89.8 percent showed disorganized attachment (as measured by the strange situation) before going through the program, compared to just 32 percent after the program. A control group of maltreated children from the same demographic group who did not go through the program showed no similar drop in disorganized attachment.

In another program, called Circle of Security, groups of parents meet with workshop leaders to learn about attachment theory and good parenting skills. This intervention also has shown promising results in reducing rates of insecure attachment.

These programs are expensive, particularly the ones that involve home visitations, but the cost is tiny when compared to the costs to society of dealing with school dropouts, delinquency, and violent criminality.

———

"Ten minutes," Marla said to Isaiah's mother, indicating the visit was nearly over.

Isaiah's mother started packing up the lunch containers. Now, suddenly, Isaiah looked frightened; the perpetual smile was gone. His face remained frozen as his mother helped him put on his black winter coat and boots. When she put on her own coat, Isaiah lost it: he cried, and then he wailed.

Another staff worker appeared in the doorway. "Everything okay in here?" she asked.

"Isaiah," Marla gently coaxed, "give Mom a hug."

But Isaiah didn't go to his mother; he ran instead to Marla, hugging her legs to his bulky black snow jacket. She knelt to comfort him, but then, still wailing, he ran to the staff worker at the door and hugged her. She gently pried him loose and also pointed him back toward his mother.

"Go to Mom," she urged.

Isaiah spun in a circle, screaming, but then through his tears found his way back to his mom. She scooped him up, hugging and trying to comfort him. "I'll see you next week, baby. I love you, I love you," she said. Then she passed him to Marla.

"The problem is," the other staff worker said in a quiet voice so as not to be overheard, "he doesn't know who his mother is."

> *"He doesn't know who his mother is."*

That cut deep. It was the same thing a child psychologist had said to my mother about me when I was three years old and having problems learning to speak. Suddenly, I looked at Isaiah as he held tightly to his mother and, despite the half-century difference in our ages and the socioeconomic gulf that separated us, I felt a bond to this frightened and tearful little boy.

———————

Watching these young children—the secure and insecure ones in the strange situation tapes and, of course, Isaiah at the visitation center—powerfully demonstrated to me the importance of early attachment. Harry Reis, in his university lecture, had said that from these early experiences we form beliefs or "mental models" about what to expect in relationships and how to behave in relationships, and that these stay with us throughout our lives. These mental models persist, Harry explained, because they create "patterns in the brain" and channel our behavior.

I wondered: Can we actually see these patterns in the brain? Does modern technology allow us to do that? If so, could I see the patterns in my own brain? The strange situation might be ready for a high-tech update.

CHAPTER 4

In the Scanner:
Attachment and the Brain

"Let's just have you roll down your sock," she said, "and I'll put these electrodes right above your ankle."

Sarah, the young woman rolling down my sock, was the lab coordinator for James Coan, professor of clinical psychology at the University of Virginia. It was a lovely spring day—all birdsong and blooming magnolias—but we were in the basement control room of an off-campus building that houses a massive Siemens MRI machine. It was one of the machines Dr. Coan used in his lab to study the neuroscience of emotions and relationships.

I'd come to Coan's lab to learn about the biological underpinnings of attachment theory. Could our mental models of how relationships should work, formed by our early attachment experiences—"patterns in the brain" as Harry Reis had called them—actually be seen?

My other question was personal: was my own attachment style really "earned secure," as Mauricio Cortina had suggested after giving me the Adult Attachment Interview?

At Dr. Cortina's suggestion, I'd arranged for Shoshana Ringel, a Baltimore psychotherapist trained to code the Adult Attachment Interview, to review a transcript of my interview. After going through it line by line, coding each of my responses, she concluded that my primary attachment category is secure. Among other factors, she noted: "Ease with the topic, coherence of mind, forgiveness of parents and acceptance of parents' limits, and ease with imperfections in the self."

But she also saw evidence of some remaining attachment anxiety. She noted "some manifestations of preoccupation with attachment figures or past trauma, specifically mild preoccupation with unfortunate parenting experiences, or with potentially traumatic experiences."

All in all, however, Dr. Ringel's assessment was as Dr. Cortina had predicted: earned secure. But Jim Coan and other researchers, using functional magnetic resonance imaging (fMRI), had in recent years started to investigate, in Coan's words, "individual differences in attachment styles using measures of neural activity." Could anything visible in the brain confirm an attachment style?

While Sarah rubbed conductive gel above my ankle, a technician came in. Seeing Dr. Coan, who was seated next to me, the technician asked, "Hey, summer 'do?"

He was asking about Coan's haircut. The previous night, I'd watched a TEDx Talk Coan had given a few months before, and in it his auburn hair was pulled straight back into a ponytail—not the short, wispy ponytail middle-aged men sometimes wear but a full, bushy one more like the actual tail of a pony.

"Oh yeah," Coan answered, laughing. "You haven't seen me with short hair! Whaddya think?"

"It's a good look!" said the technician.

I had to agree. Coan has a slender, medium build and, at least to my eye, looked, without the mane—though still with a mustache and goatee—younger and fitter than his forty-four years.

In his TEDx Talk, titled "Why We Hold Hands," Coan told a story about how, as a young VA hospital clinician, he'd met a World War II veteran with post-traumatic stress disorder. This aged patient, Coan discovered, would only open up and talk about his war experiences if his wife of many years was holding his hand.

Curious as to why—in a neurological sense—hand-holding was so vital to his patient, Coan devised an MRI brain-imaging study. In it, subjects were put under threat of electric shock: if they were shown a blue circle, they knew they were safe, but if they were shown a red X, they knew there was a 20 percent chance that after a period of time they'd get an electric shock on their ankle. "We were making them very anxious!" he said. The subjects did this under three conditions:

while holding the hand of a stranger, while alone, and while holding the hand of their romantic partner.

"And here's what we found," he said. "If you're alone and in a tube and it's very loud and you're under threat of electric shock, your brain lights up like a Christmas tree." The brain has a lot to do, he explained: hating the experience, wanting to escape, but also self-regulating so you don't actually bolt from the machine.

If you're holding a stranger's hand, he said, parts of the brain associated with physical arousal, including heart rate and mobilizing the body to take action, are somewhat less active.

But if you're holding your partner's hand, he said, "We see massive decreases in the way the brain responds." People felt less threatened and didn't exercise regions of the brain for self-regulation and release of stress hormones. Instead, the hand-holding—if the relationship was good—seemed to take care of that.

That study won a lot of attention for Coan and for the lab he directs, the Virginia Affective Neuroscience Laboratory. Coan's work has been featured in the *New York Times*, the *Washington Post*, and other media, both national and international.

Back in the lab, Sarah stuck a plastic electrode—about the size of a half dollar—over the conductive gel on the left side of my ankle.

––––––

Earlier that day, Jim Coan had picked me up at my hotel, and we went for coffee. Seated on the outdoor patio of a café near campus, I asked if you put two kids in the MRI, one with secure attachment (I imagined the secure, fifteen-month-old boy in a dinosaur T-shirt I'd seen in the strange situation videos) and one with insecure attachment (I was thinking of Isaiah, the two-year-old I'd seen at the foster care visitation center), could you tell the difference by looking at their brain scans?

"Absolutely, 100 percent," he said. He cautioned, though, that no single part of the brain controls attachment behaviors. "What you'd see are differences distributed across all kinds of systems in the brain dedicated to all kinds of different tasks. There's no single module for organizing how we think about relationships."

As Coan noted, no one part of the brain lights up and says "secure" or "insecure" attachment, but there are regions of the brain known to be associated with emotions that are often experienced differently by people with different attachment styles. These include how we react to social cues, such as facial expressions; how we process feelings like pleasure, fear, and sadness; how we react to threats and to rewards; and how we respond to social approaches or rejection.

In one study, thirty new mothers whose attachment style had been measured with the Adult Attachment Interview were put in an MRI scanner and shown photos of their babies' faces. Researchers reported a "striking difference" in brain activation: mothers who were secure showed significantly more activity in regions associated with "reward processing" than mothers who were avoidant.

In another study, participants in the MRI scanner were asked to count dots on a screen and then shown faces—some smiling and some angry—of people they were told were evaluating their performance. In response, people with avoidant attachment showed "reduced activation" in regions of their brains associated with receiving social information while anxious individuals showed increased activation in regions associated with negative social signals. These results were consistent, researchers noted, with findings that avoidant individuals tend not to seek social support, while people with anxious attachments may show "enhanced vigilance" toward threats to the self.

And in an especially clever study of how attachment influences brain responses to social rejection, participants were told they'd be playing a virtual ball-tossing game in the scanner via the Internet with two other participants in other scanners. In reality, participants played with a preset computer program; the other two players didn't really exist. Halfway through the test, the other two "players" started tossing the ball back and forth only to each other, excluding the real participant who, for the remainder of the game, had to watch the other two play the game on their own. The findings? Participants with anxious attachment showed "heightened activation" in brain regions associated with social rejection, but those with avoidant attachments showed "dampened neural activation" in those same regions. "Thus, reactions to social rejection," concluded the researchers, "depended in part on individual differences in anxious and avoidant attachment."

"So if you put me in your MRI machine," I asked Jim Coan, "is there an experiment that might confirm the result I got in the Adult Attachment Interview?"

He said yes, maybe.

"I could probably find markers," he said, and offered to put me in the MRI and do the hand-holding experiment.

"The anticipatory anxiety you'll experience should produce some markers that reveal attachment type," he said, but warned he couldn't guarantee any result. "We may not be able to tell anything about attachment from just one sample with a single subject," he said. "There may not be enough data, plus we don't have a baseline on you. But we'll give it a try."

In fact, we'd have to do a modified version of the test, so there'd be even less data than usual. The protocol calls for three rounds of threatened electric shock: with a stranger, alone, and with a romantic partner. But since I'd come to Charlottesville alone—and at that point didn't actually have a romantic partner—we'd need to skip that last part.

"Let's go have lunch," said Jim, "and then I'm gonna put you in the scanner."

———

Jim Coan's undergraduate major, according to his vita, was psychology. Over lunch, I asked what had drawn him to study psych right out of high school. He replied that, in fact, he didn't even go to college right away. "Kind of wild" is how he described his eighteen-year-old self, and "not academically inclined." Instead, he "smoked grass" and worked in Spokane, Washington, in his stepfather's roofing and siding business. Only when he was twenty-one did he enroll at a community college. Later, at the University of Washington, he worked with prominent marriage psychologist John Gottman and, eventually, at age twenty-eight, began graduate studies in brain research.

Just then, Jim got a call from his wife, Cat, a photographer. Could he pick the kids up later? Jim and Cat have two daughters, then ages one and three.

It can get hectic, he admitted, being a husband, father, teacher, and active researcher—particularly since his work has gained such wide attention.

"It's been a mixed blessing that the work has gotten really popular— no, I mean, it's been a blessing—but I still haven't quite figured out how to say no, which means I always seem to be saying 'I'm sorry' and 'maybe' to a thousand people."

In fact, it had taken me months to connect with Jim—people kept telling me how busy he was.

"Yeah," said Jim, laughing. "Sorry about that."

In thinking over some of what I'd learned about Jim—nonconformist, bit of a maverick, and self-made—I was curious whether he accepted any orthodoxies, even those of attachment theory.

"So, Jim," I asked, "do you buy the whole attachment theory thing? Do you buy Bowlby?"

"Absolutely," he said, "but I think of it as psychology's Newtonian physics: it works for so many things—we can use it to send the equivalent of rockets to the moon—but yet it's not quite right."

In what way not "right"?

"It puts too much emphasis on attachment figures," he said. "It doesn't honor the degree to which humans are disposed to sociability."

How so?

"Humans are so fundamentally sociable that attachment figures are insufficient," he said, "especially for kids. So it leads to some bad recommendations, like some researchers get all up in arms about how we shouldn't send our kids to day care before two years old. This is absurd. Human babies are designed to have multiple caregivers almost immediately, and human mothers are not designed to feed and care for their young exclusively. That's where it's gotten us astray. It's bad for people; it's particularly bad for women."

But doesn't the notion of the mother-baby bond go to the heart of attachment theory?

"Yeah, well, that's where it's wrong," he said. "All that stuff with the strange situation and secure base and safe haven—it works really well with attachment figures but also with larger social networks."

We also place too much emphasis on attaching to just one person in adult relationships, he said.

"Kurt Vonnegut was sort of on to this," he said. "He said whenever he sees a couple fighting he wants to instruct them to shout at each other, 'You're not enough people!' and that's right on target."

I checked out the quote, and Jim had it just about right. It's from Vonnegut's novel *Timequake*, where he writes: "Fifty percent or more of American marriages go bust because most of us no longer have extended families. When you marry somebody now, all you get is one person. I say that when couples fight, it isn't about money or sex or power. What they're really saying is, 'You're not enough people!'"

But getting back to kids, was Jim saying that an infant could be raised by a larger number of caregivers?

"Not could be, should be," he said.

And there's research to support this?

"Mostly anthropological, but yeah," he said. "Bowlby drew a lot on studies of chimps and other apes for developing his attachment theory, trying to put an evolutionary spin on it. And it's true, apes keep their babies attached to their bodies until weaned, and nobody is allowed to touch them or get near them. But in terms of child-rearing, humans are not like other apes. All around the world, human mothers permit other people to handle their babies almost immediately, and their babies are clearly not suffering as a result."

"So if instead of being raised just by his or her mother," I asked, "a kid were raised by six people, men and women in the village—"

"Then the kid would see all those men and woman as attachment figures," said Jim, "just as they do the mom in the strange situation."

It's interesting to note, however, that on early Israeli kibbutzim—collective farms—where infants were made to sleep communally, away from their families, studies later showed an unusually large number of children with anxious attachment. Yet on modern kibbutzim, where family sleeping arrangements are standard, studies show normal distribution of attachment styles.

"The strange situation isn't wrong necessarily," Jim continued. "It's just that what we take from it is limited. We've omitted a large part of the story. What I fear is that what generates an insecure attachment, whether avoidant or anxious, is an overreliance on a single attachment figure who can't do it all—'cause she can't."

I mentioned the child-rearing movement called "attachment parenting." Advocates encourage a close and frequent physical bond between mother and baby.

"Well, they're wrong," he said. "And their advice is dangerous to children. I don't want to overstate it, but kids are resilient, and outside of real neglect and abuse, most of the outcomes they realize have little or nothing to do with parenting styles. This whole 'don't put your kid in day care' thing is bullshit; it's pointless. And socially regressive."

I wondered if Jim's point of view came partly from being a new parent himself.

"I don't think so," he said, "but maybe. Hadn't thought about it."

His older daughter—the three-year-old—is in day care?

"Yeah, and it's working out fine," he said.

And the younger one too?

"Since six months," he said.

Jim continued: "You know what makes good day care? That the caregivers are consistent, meaning it's always the same people. Bad day care is if the people caring for your kid keep changing. Familiarity and consistency of persons is what matters. People are designed to have multiple caregivers, but they're not designed to have multiple caregivers on a revolving door of unfamiliarity."

Jim continued, "My daughter has had the same day-care team for two and a half years. She kisses them and says 'I love you' when she leaves at the end of the day. That's what matters most."

After all I'd read about attachment theory, I knew Jim's point of view ran counter to most of the experts, but it was interesting and refreshing to hear. His notion of couples "not being enough people" for each other rang true; I could remember times in my marriage when I felt that way. And whether as a species we were meant to have one primary caregiver or many intrigued me too. So did the question of day care. Bowlby initially opposed day care but later in life came around to accept it as long as the care was of high quality and consistent— pretty much Jim's position. These were all questions I wanted to explore further.

———————

Now, back to where we started—the imaging lab, where Sarah was finishing sticking electrodes on my ankle.

Jim had described the MRI scanner as "a dangerous environment. You're in the bore of a large magnet that has about thirty times the gravity of Earth. Anything that's metal will hurtle in at tremendous force, and if your body's in the way, it will go through you. So you have to be sure you have no metal on you. Even a paper clip could be dangerous."

I was told to remove any metal on my body—watch, pens, tape recorder—and to empty my pockets.

"And how do the magnets not affect your brain?" I asked.

"They're not really acting on your brain," said Jim. "They're acting on hydrogen atoms in your brain."

I didn't find that particularly comforting, but Jim assured me he'd been in the scanner "dozens of times" himself, and it would be fine.

As to the shocks, he said everybody gets the same dose: four milliamperes, but that people have different pain thresholds, so every-one reacts differently. "We don't actually measure the moments when you get shocked," he added. "We're only interested in anticipatory anx-iety before the shock."

In that case, I thought, he could start measuring now, because I was already anxious.

And whose hand, I wondered, would I be holding?

Jim said that according to the test protocol it would be an "anony-mous stranger" and he couldn't tell me anything more.

I signed a release, relieving the university of any liability for my experience in the scanner.

Fitted with electrodes, pockets emptied, release signed. Now there was a lull in the action while the technician fired up the machine. Sarah did some paperwork; Jim sat on a stool in the corner, checking messages on his phone.

The technician took a phone call. "Look, I'm about to put someone in the scanner," I heard him say, "but I'll call you back."

He hung up.

"We're all set," he told Jim.

"Okay," said Jim, looking up from his phone. "Good luck, Peter!"

Following behind Sarah, I left the control room and approached the MRI machine, which sat by itself in a larger adjoining room. Sarah instructed me to lie on my back with my head near the opening of the machine. She then put a cushion under my knees, clamped a re-straint on either side of my head to hold it still, fitted me with a pair of headphones, and covered my face with something like a hockey goal-ie's mask.

I thought of how fortunate I was to be entering this machine only to do research, not because I was ill.

I lay still for a few quiet moments in the silent, womb-like chamber and noticed I did not feel particularly uncomfortable; claustrophobia, it seemed, would not be a problem.

"How are you doing, Peter?" It was Sarah's voice from the control room coming through the headphones.

I said I was fine.

"Okay, great," she said. "We're about to start the anatomical scan in just a second. This is the one that will give us a three-dimensional view of the brain."

An image appeared in front of me—it must have been projected by mirrors onto a screen. It showed a forest scene with rivers and mountains.

"Okay, sir," said the technician, also through the headphones. "It's going to be about four and a half minutes."

Almost immediately there came loud, deep, repeating pulses of noise—*aaagh-aaagh-aaagh*—like a fire alarm.

I tried to picture hydrogen atoms in my brain being pulled toward the giant magnets surrounding me, but that was a hard image to sustain.

Aaagh-aaagh-aaagh.

For some reason, a phrase Jim had used at lunch about what makes "bad" day care came to mind: "if the people caring for your kid keep changing."

I should have asked Jim if he knew that John Bowlby himself experienced that as a young child. Bowlby and his siblings, raised in a traditional English upper-class home with parents who kept their distance, were cared for by a series of nannies and nursemaids. Minnie, the one who cared for him daily and with whom he bonded, left the family's employ when he was three. She was replaced by another, who was cold and strict, and with whom Bowlby never bonded. Years later, Bowlby's widow suggested John had "buried his grief" over the loss of Minnie.

Aaagh-aaagh-aaagh.

In that, Bowlby and I had something in common: the people who cared for us in childhood "had kept changing." In fact, from my mother's limited caregiving due to her polio, to the sudden death of Miss Kelly, the nurse who did care for me, to the woman who replaced her and who was in turn dismissed, I could draw a straight line to my interest in attachment theory and my being in that scanner.

I'd obtained a copy of Miss Kelly's death certificate and information on where she was buried. Never married, she died at age seventy,
on July 3, 1954, about three months after my first birthday. Cause of
death: acute myocardial infarction.

Recently, my sister and I had taken our dad out to lunch. After-
ward, he said he wanted to visit our mother's grave. I could have gone
with them, but I'd planned that afternoon to find Miss Kelly's grave, so
instead of visiting my own mother's grave, I visited hers. At Holy
Sepulchre, a cemetery I'd never been to before, I found her flat gray-
marble stone partially covered with fall leaves. Reaching down, I
brushed the leaves aside and read: "ALICE F. KELLY 1883–1954." I
bent down and ran my fingers over the raised metal letters that spelled
her name.

"How we doing, Peter?" It was Sarah's voice in the headphones.

They were ready to start the experiment.

"We're only going to do two runs," said Sarah, "the first with you
holding an anonymous experimenter's hand and the second with you
alone in the scanner holding no one's hand. In these runs you will be
the one that is getting shocked." She also reviewed the protocol: if you
see a blue circle, there'll be no shock, but if you see a red X, there'll be
a 20 percent chance that in the next few moments you'll receive a
shock.

Sarah said to extend my right hand and "the anonymous experimenter will come and hold it."

And then a new noise started, a kind of low, quavering tone—not
as loud as the earlier fire-alarm sound but loud enough and in its own
way unnerving. I reached my hand a bit outside the tube and felt another hand. It was soft. It was probably a woman's, and I suspected it
was Sarah's but couldn't be sure; it could also, I figured, be one of Jim's
grad students.

The panel in front of me, which had earlier displayed the forest
scene, now showed only a blue circle. Okay, I thought, blue circle
means no shock. Other than the annoying, quavering noise, this wasn't
so bad.

But then the circle disappeared and there was a bright, bold red X. I tensed, yet nothing happened. Jim and Sarah had said there's just a 20 percent chance that after the red X I'll get a shock, so maybe this—and then a huge jolt of electricity shot up my left leg, and not just for an instant but for what seemed like many seconds. I tried to pull my leg away from the pain but couldn't because the electrode was attached.

The shock finally stopped, and I was starting to breathe again when the blue circle appeared. A respite. I didn't want to feel that shock again. Could I calm myself? I remembered before my wife gave birth we learned a breathing technique, "pyramids of ten," to get through the pain of transition. You count in your head up to ten and then back to one and then one to nine and back again and so on until you're through the pain. I started: one, two, three, four—but then the red X appeared again. I braced myself, trying not to move, but I could feel my legs involuntarily twitch. I squeezed the hand—hard—in anticipation, but no shock came, and then the blue circle appeared. I hoped I hadn't squeezed too hard, but it was the only thing I could affect at all, because I was immobile and subjected to these shocks, which I figured were programmed by a computer and so not only out of my control but out of anyone else's too.

Another red X! I squeezed the hand. My legs twitched. The shock shot up my leg. Then there was the blue circle. I'd forgotten to do the counting. Then another blue circle. How long had it been? Maybe five minutes? I didn't know and then the red X—okay: one, two, three, four, five, six, seven, eight, nine, ten, nine, eight—I squeezed the hand harder.

Two more blue circles and another red X and a shock—like the finale of a fireworks display—and then the hand slipped away, and the screen went blank. The noise quieted.

"How you doing, Peter?" It was Sarah's voice in the headphones.

She told me to press buttons on a console to indicate the level of discomfort I'd experienced. Earlier, she'd shown me how to do it, but now I couldn't remember and pushed the wrong buttons.

"You can just tell me," she said. "On a scale from one to ten, with ten being the most painful, how would you rate the shocks you received?"

"Nine."

"Okay, Peter," she said, "for this next round you'll be alone in the scanner."

I didn't reply.

"Are you doing all right?" she asked.

I was thinking.

"Do you want to continue?" asked Sarah.

"I'd actually rather not," I said. "Do you have enough data from what we've already done?"

I could hear Sarah confer briefly in the control room with Jim.

"Okay, that's completely fine," she said. "We can take you out."

———

In the control room, Jim asked about my experience in the scanner.

"I didn't like the shocks at all," I said.

"Too intense?" Jim asked.

I told him they were more intense than I'd expected, and the anticipation of them was more unnerving than I'd expected.

Earlier, Sarah had said everyone feels the shocks differently, and some hardly respond at all.

"Sometimes I even have to check to be sure the shock box is working."

In fact, research shows that people experience and react to physical pain differently according to their attachment styles. In various studies, those with attachment insecurity—both anxious and avoidant— reported more intense pain during the early stages of labor, greater suffering after whiplash injuries, and more severe headaches after performing a distress-inducing task than those with secure attachment. And in controlled, laboratory studies in which pain was experimentally induced by having participants place their hands in a container of ice water for a full minute or more, those with attachment anxiety showed lower pain thresholds and reported greater suffering than those with either secure or avoidant attachment.

So perhaps—even before Jim analyzed data from the brain scan—the intensity of pain I felt from the electric shocks and my decision to end the experiment early was itself a confirming marker of my underlying anxious attachment.

I asked Sarah if it was her hand I'd been holding.

She said it was—her first time as a hand-holder, in fact.

As I debriefed with Jim and Sarah, I found I had trouble hearing everyone and holding on to thoughts—they seemed to flit in and out of my head before I could catch them.

"To be honest," I said, "my head feels a little fried."

"Yeah," said Jim, "it's very arousing. What happens is you get dosed with cortisol and adrenaline, and it'll make you feel a little jazzed up. It's also scary," he continued, laughing. "We're scaring you in there. In a sense, you were mildly terrorized, so you're coping with the fallout from that."

"And I really hated seeing that red X," I added.

Jim laughed loudly.

"Sorry, man! I relate. I relate. I've been seeing that thing for twelve years and I still hate it."

I was at least glad to hear that.

"The red X is abstract," said Jim, "but in fact it's getting at what Bowlby was most interested in, which is fear—and Bowlby got this part really right: the attachment behavioral system is largely about the management of fear and how we respond to threats."

The attachment behavioral system is largely about the management of fear.

Jim said that processing the test results might take a few weeks. "The probability that there'll be lots of concrete, usable information from this one scan is low, but we'll do our best," he offered.

I thanked Jim and Sarah, and left to walk back to my hotel. Despite the intensity of the experience in the scanner, I found myself thinking more about the earlier part of the day when Jim had raised some important questions: Can a romantic couple be "enough people" for each other? To help instill a secure attachment, who should care for children? Does it need to be one primary person or could it be more than one so long as they don't change? Of course I was curious about what the MRI would show—possibly confirming whether I was earned secure or not—but it was those other, bigger questions about romance and child-rearing that filled my cortisol- and adrenaline-flooded, jazzed-up brain.

And it was just as well that I'd found those other questions so compelling, because a few weeks later in a phone call, Jim told me the brain scan hadn't produced enough data to assess my attachment style. In that case, I could have done without the electric shocks.

Part II

Attachment throughout
Our Lives

CHAPTER 5

A Date for Coffee: Attachment and Dating

C eleste Sommers, a twenty-six-year-old student in the writing class I was teaching in Bethesda, Maryland, impressed me as thoughtful, kind, and bright. An anthropologist, she spoke six languages. In one of her papers, she wrote of traveling the world for a year on a Thomas J. Watson Fellowship to study remote, native tribes and how they use technology to preserve their cultures. One stop was in the Arctic, where she met a young Inuit man. Her paper included this marvelous description of Eskimo kissing, which, with her permission, I quote:

> Eskimo "kiss" is a misnomer, and it's so much better than the sanitized nose-to-nose rubbing they taught us as kids. It more closely resembles full-frontal face sniffing, the unsanitary smooshing of noses and mouths together.
>
> He tells me to try it. That night, I almost faint from huffing his round brown cheeks so hard; I'm afraid they might fall off. My skin burns with millions of these not-kiss kisses.

One evening after class, Celeste asked what I was working on. When I told her a book about attachment, she said, "Oh! My roommate just made me take an attachment quiz online. She said it might help me do better with dating."

Celeste's roommate was right.

"So how'd you score on the quiz?" I asked.

Officially called the Experiences in Close Relationships question-naire, the quiz measures attachment avoidance and anxiety on a 1–7 scale (see the quiz in the appendix). In the quiz, one is asked to agree or disagree with statements such as "My desire to be very close some-times scares people away," and "I prefer not to show a partner how I feel deep down."

"I was about a 4 on the anxious scale," said Celeste.

That would be an insecure anxious attachment.

And that's when the thought occurred to me: knowing Celeste's attachment style, I could introduce her to someone who—at least in terms of attachment—might be a suitable mate.

And, actually, I had someone in mind. In theory, he might be per-fect.

I hesitated, though; fixing anyone up is risky and faces long odds.

In the Midrash, a commentary on part of the Hebrew Bible, there's the story of a woman who goes to an old rabbi and asks: "Rabbi, the Torah says God made the heavens and the earth in six days, but what's He been doing since?"

"Trying to make matches," answers the rabbi.

"It's that difficult."

> *Romantic love is an attachment relationship.*

Still, knowing Celeste's attachment style gave me an important tool to improve those long odds. That's because romantic love is an attachment re-lationship.

John Bowlby wrote: "The formation of a bond is described as falling in love, maintaining a bond as loving someone, and losing a partner as grieving over someone." To be sure, adult romance is not *only* about attachment—other factors come into play—but attachment is an essen-tial part. Research shows no difference in attachment influences due to gender or sexual orientation. From flirting and dating all the way through marriage, "attachment issues are ubiquitous in couple relationships," note researchers Mario Mikulincer and Phillip Shaver. Attachment styles, therefore, "will affect both the quality" of romantic interactions "and their ultimate fate." Therefore, understanding one's own attachment style—and the attachment style of a potential partner—can increase the chances of a successful match and an enduring relationship.

Some combinations of attachment styles tend to work better than others in producing relationships that are satisfying and stable. But any combination where one partner is secure will have a fair shot at success. As Harry Reis advised his students: "If you can meet someone who's secure, you're five steps ahead."

"If I could introduce you to someone with a secure attachment, would you be interested in meeting him?" I asked Celeste.

She said sure, possibly.

"And what if he not only has a secure attachment, but he's actually known *nationwide* among attachment researchers as 'the poster child for secure attachment'?"

"The poster child?" she asked. "What does that even mean?"

"When researchers think of someone who as a young child had a nearly perfect secure attachment, they think of him!" I said.

I wasn't even sure the poster child was available, but if he was, would she be interested in meeting him?

"He's not in a relationship?" she asked.

"I don't think so," I said. A few weeks earlier I'd run into him at a coffee shop. He was with a woman, but I couldn't tell if they were together or not.

"He's about your age," I added. "And he works in data graphics."

Celeste thought data graphics sounded interesting.

"And he's good looking," I added. "Tall, dark hair, slim. Clean cut."

"Tall is good," she said.

Truth be told, they were both attractive.

"So what do you say? If I can reach him and he's available, would you be willing to meet him for coffee?"

"Sure," she said. "I'll give the poster child a try."

And with that, I'd committed myself to trying something at which God had labored since Creation.

Pairing Attachment Styles

Two secure partners offer the best chance for maintaining successful and stable couple relationships. People with a secure attachment, note authors Amir Levine and Rachel Heller, are

> programmed to expect their partners to be loving and responsive. . . . They feel extremely comfortable with intimacy and closeness and have an uncanny ability to communicate their needs and respond to their partners' needs.

As noted, any combination where one partner is secure will have a good chance of success. Indeed, being in relationship with a secure partner can, over time, help the insecure partner become more secure.

But people with insecure attachments can also be successful in relationships; the challenges are just greater.

People with avoidant attachments believe strongly in self-reliance and therefore tend to be less invested in relationships, and when conflict occurs in a relationship, they tend to distance themselves. In practice, they tend not to pair up with each other, often preferring a partner either who is secure or whose attachment anxiety, by comparison, lets them feel strong and self-reliant. If avoidants do pair up, they are likely to withdraw when problems arise.

Anxious people want to be close to their partners, even to merge completely. They are capable of great intimacy and—especially in the early stages—very intense positive emotions. But they also have difficulty trusting relationships and have a push-pull quality to their desire for closeness, reflecting an intense need to be in relationship but at the same time resentment at feeling insecure without one. The dynamic of two anxious partners can be one of mutual clinginess and control, neither promoting the other's full potential.

The prize for the worst combination of attachment styles goes to what authors Amir Levine and Rachel Heller have termed the anxious-avoidant trap. This is when one partner is avoidant and the other is anxious. Each needs different degrees of intimacy: the anxious one tries to get close while the avoidant one pulls away. When those needs are not met, they have opposite ways of responding, thus creating a vicious cycle that further stresses the relationship.

Given the distribution of attachment styles in the general population (55 percent secure, 25 percent avoidant, 15 percent anxious, and the rest disorganized), the number of people who fall into the anxious-avoidant trap is larger than we might expect, and for several reasons.

First, at least beyond early adulthood, secure people tend to pair up and stay in their relationships, so past age thirty or so, the insecure mostly make up the dating pool.

Past age thirty or so, the insecure mostly make up the dating pool.

Second, avoidant people's relationships tend to last for a shorter time and after a breakup they don't get sidelined by grief for as long as those who are secure or anxious— because they were never as vested in the relationship in the first place—so they seem to recover more quickly and put themselves back in the dating pool. Authors Levine and Heller note that when you meet someone new later in life, the probability that they have an avoidant attachment style may be higher than that style's relative share of the population.

Finally—and somewhat perversely—anxious people and people with avoidant attachment styles are often attracted to each other. For those with avoidant attachment, an anxious partner confirms their belief in themselves as strong and self-reliant, as well as their view of the other as needy and dependent. And for the anxious partner, an avoidant mate confirms the belief that one cannot trust a partner's commitment.

For the anxious partner, an avoidant mate confirms the belief that one cannot trust a partner's commitment.

Plus, anxious people may be so eager to be in a relationship that they're willing to take a less desirable mate. Either way, each fulfills the other's expectations of how a relationship functions—a self-fulfilling prophecy, often with unhappy results. In one longitudinal study, couples that included an avoidant woman and an anxious man were "highly predisposed" to break up within the three-year study period.

Still, no combination of attachment styles is doomed. Even with the more problematic pairings, a satisfying and stable relationship is possible, particularly if a couple understands how their attachment styles affect them and if they work—perhaps in counseling—to address the challenge.

―――――

Chris Wilson lived on the third floor of an apartment building near the trendy U Street corridor of downtown DC. I thought he was the same age as my writing student Celeste Sommers, but I was mistaken: he was thirty-two, six years older than Celeste. But I had remembered his appearance correctly: six foot three, slender, with dark hair, a squarish face, hip glasses, and a deep voice. The smart, clean-cut look reminded me of Clark Kent played by George Reeves in TV's *Adventures of Superman.*

I told Chris a little about Celeste, including that she was an anthropologist and spoke six languages. It turned out he was not in a relationship and, yes, he'd like to meet her.

"I should tell you, though," he said. "I'm married."

Oh.

About eight months before, after a brief marriage of less than two years, he and his wife had separated. A divorce was under way.

Secure attachment is no guarantee, of course, of long-term relationship happiness. I didn't know what Chris's wife's attachment style was, and Chris said he preferred not to speak about her publicly.

"Any chance you'll get back together?" I asked, hoping there wasn't.

"I would say there's an approximately zero percent chance we're going to reconcile," he said.

In fact, he'd already started dating. Over the summer he'd seen someone for a few months but then ended the relationship. "I feel an obligation not to waste people's time if I know in my heart it's not going anywhere," he said.

That struck me as something a secure person would say.

I told Chris more about Celeste and asked if he'd like to see a picture.

He said no. He didn't need to see a photo. I wondered if that, too, was the trait of a secure person, but later he told me he looks for no particular physical type in a woman so a photo simply wasn't necessary.

Is there any particular personality type he looks for? I asked.

"Only that they not be a nurturer," he said. "It drives me bonkers; it's a turnoff. I don't need someone to be my mother; I still have the real thing."

"So when you go on dates, Chris," I couldn't help asking, "do you ever mention that you're the poster child for secure attachment?"

"To be honest," he said, "I actually know very little about attachment theory beyond some of the experiments and the vocabulary." Although his dad chaired the psychology department at the University of Virginia where Chris did his undergraduate work, Chris majored in English and never took a psych course. "Until recently, I hadn't even realized I was a minor celebrity in the attachment field. Anyway, I don't know exactly how I'd bring it up on a date, unless I tried something like, 'You may remember me from such films as 'Christopher, Age 3.'"

The films Chris referred to were made when he was a young boy as part of research to find ways of measuring attachment in children. That work was done by Jude Cassidy, then a University of Virginia graduate student. She studied with Mary Ainsworth, inventor of the strange situation, the laboratory procedure used to assess attachment in very young children. Exploring how the strange situation would work with older children, Dr. Cassidy recruited local mothers and their kids as volunteers. Chris's mother agreed to participate, and that's how Chris came to be filmed.

Years later, after she had become a leading figure internationally in attachment research, Cassidy invited me to visit her University of Maryland lab on the day she was showing graduate students the films of Chris.

"Most of you know about Chris," she began, "as do most attachment researchers around the country." That's because in the nearly thirty years since she made the films, Cassidy had shown them at seminars and conferences throughout the world.

In the last of the strange situation's eight episodes—when the mother returns to the room—a toddler who is securely attached will run to his mother and want to be picked up, Cassidy told her students. "But with a three-year-old," she said, "even though the mother's physical presence is still desired, there's less need for physical contact. There's a study with babies showing that secure babies will smile at their mom, show her what they're doing, and then also vocalize about what they're doing. Insecure babies will do only one or two of those things, but not all three. But look, isn't it interesting here, with Chris at age three, that he's doing all three?"

"Now, let's look at Christopher at age three," she continued. In the film, three-year-old Chris, dark haired and happy looking, stands playing with a box of toys. He smiles broadly and often. "No child smiles more than Chris," Cassidy observed. "It's a real, genuine smile." During the early episodes, while Chris plays, his mother sits nearby. It's evident how attuned she is to her son. "She follows his lead," Cassidy noted. "She's attentive but not overbearing. She doesn't say, 'Oh, you're so wonderful. You're so bright!' Instead, she's gently encouraging and gives him space to explore."

And then in the final episode, when his mother returns, little Chris smiles at her, shows her his toy, and then describes in a few words his play—thus hitting all three responses that characterize a secure infant. In both that tape and another done when he was six, Chris was coded B-3—the most secure measure of childhood attachment.

And that's how for generations of attachment researchers the little boy with the dark hair and winning smile became, in Cassidy's words, the "poster child" for secure attachment.

———

In his apartment, after we viewed the films of his three-year-old self, Chris told me he looked forward to one day being a parent.

"I think I would make a good father," he said, "and I'd like to be married again—not sure how soon."

Three-quarters of us go through life with the same attachment style with which we came out of early childhood, and I suspected that was the case with Chris. But I felt an obligation to Celeste to be sure, so that evening, at my request, Chris agreed to take the same online attachment quiz that Celeste, at her roommate's urging, had taken.

While Chris answered the questions online, he invited me to look around his apartment. Against a set of windows facing busy 14th Street sat an electric upright piano. Later, he told me he'd bought the piano as a gift to himself after his marriage broke up. There was also a saxophone, guitar, and trumpet. Framed album covers of jazz artists John Coltrane and Miles Davis adorned one wall; on another was an oil painting of Russian composer Dmitry Shostakovich. Chris said he'd painted it himself from a photograph. On the dining table was a thick sheaf of papers, a ninety-thousand-word novel, as yet unpublished, Chris had written; nearby sat the manual typewriter he'd written it on. Later, when I asked why someone in an advanced field like data graphics would choose to type a ninety-thousand-word novel on an old typewriter, Chris said he just liked the aesthetics of the machine.

On the attachment quiz, Chris scored a 2.9 on the avoidant scale and 2.7 on the anxious scale. The scoring is on a scale of 1–7, so this still placed him solidly in the secure range. "Had my wife not left eight months ago," he said, "my guess is I would have been more fully in the secure zone."

Our conversation came around again to Celeste.

"So, would you want to ask her out for coffee?" I asked.

He said he'd be glad to and would contact her to set up a time. It would have to be soon, though—over the coming weekend—because the following week he'd be going into the hospital for surgery. "Nothing too serious," he said.

The timing would work well: Celeste had told me she'd be leaving about a week later for twelve days in Uganda, to train forest rangers to use technology to better protect chimp habitats.

"Are you going to be there at the coffee place observing us?" Chris asked. "Will we see you in Groucho Marx glasses at the next table?"

I didn't need to observe their date, I said, but I would like to talk with each of them separately beforehand. Their different attachment styles—he secure, she anxious—would likely give them different expectations and strategies for a first date, and it would be interesting to me, and possibly useful to them, if we could talk about it in advance.

Before I left that evening, Chris agreed to play a little music for me. The sheet music on the piano was the second movement of a Shostakovich concerto. Chris had done the arrangement for solo piano. He played the gentle, melodic piece sensitively and with confidence.

———

Setting up Chris and Celeste made me consider how helpful it would have been to understand the influence of my own anxious attachment when I was young and dating. Anxious teens (adults too)—feeling the need for a romantic partner as a secure base—tend to fall in love easily and often, and I certainly did. I can think of few times between my first crush at fourteen until my marriage at twenty-nine when I was not in a relationship. This was especially so when I lived away from home. In college I took a year abroad, traveling and living entirely on my own. Looking back, I can see how in that situation my intense need for attachment security led me to pull someone close too soon.

Had I understood that then, I might have skipped the year abroad or chosen instead a university-sponsored program with more built-in support.

A knowledge of attachment would also have helped me understand other issues in my earlier relationships, such as sexuality and my response to breakups.

How Attachment Affects Our Sex Lives

Knowing how the mind of a person with a different attachment style works can "give a framework for understanding" their sexual behavior, writes Israeli psychologist Gurit Birnbaum. Birnbaum has done much of the major work on the issue of attachment and sexuality.

While secure people generally seek fulfillment of sexual needs within committed relationships and are comfortable with intimacy, avoidant people, explains Birnbaum, tend to separate sexual activity from emotional closeness. Instead, they may use sex to avoid emotional intimacy by pursuing short-term relationships to confirm their self-worth and independence. As such, they are more likely than secure or anxious people to engage in one-night stands and short-term couplings. They are also more likely to respond favorably to attempts at "mate-poaching"—i.e., attempts to lure them away from their current partners. When they do have sex with their partners, they tend to focus on their own sexual needs more than their partner's needs. Their sexual fantasies often involve scenes of emotionally distant partners as well as some hostility. And couples where both partners have avoidant attachments report having the lowest rate of sexual frequency.

Anxious people, on the other hand, tend to use sex to alleviate their insecurities and promote intimacy. They sexualize their desire for affection, notes Birnbaum, and use sex to gain a partner's reassurance. Unfortunately, this may lead them to succumb to unwanted sexual advances and to engage in unprotected or unwanted sex. While having

Couples where both partners are anxious tend to have the highest rate of sexual frequency.

sex, they tend to try to please their partners while failing to achieve their own desires, and their worries about the relationship can sometimes cause performance anxiety. Couples where both partners are anxious tend to have the highest rate of sexual frequency, although some anxious people may prefer the affectionate aspects of sex (holding, cuddling, kissing) to actual sex. Their sexual fantasies often include submission themes that, as Birnbaum notes, "serve their desire to be irresistibly desired."

Breakups

People with a secure attachment tend to be better at achieving a resolution after a breakup than those with insecure attachments. They are more likely to accept the loss, deal with anger and sadness, and move toward recovery. (Avoidants may appear to recover more quickly—they get back into the game sooner—but there may be a large dose of denial in their response so they may not be truly recovered.)

Chris Wilson, it seemed to me, had shown such resilience. After the breakup of his brief marriage—a split initiated by his wife—Chris bought himself a piano. And after some months of grieving, he'd begun dating. Both actions struck me as healthy ways to cope.

People with anxious attachment generally have the toughest time with breakups. For them, the loss of a partner who represents the security they crave is difficult to bear. What causes sadness for those who are secure can cause desperation for those who are anxious. In a survey of five thousand respondents, anxious partners who were broken up with reported reacting with "angry protests, heightened sexual attraction to the former partner, intense preoccupation with the lost partner, and a lost sense of identity." And, somewhat surprisingly, it's the anxious partner who in the aftermath of a breakup is most likely to engage in violence. Unable to accept the loss of a secure base, the anxious partner may stalk or even strike out aggressively—and counterproductively—as a way to regain proximity to the partner.

"Those who miss out on an early secure attachment," write psychiatrist Thomas Lewis and colleagues,

> find that in adulthood, their emotional footing pitches beneath them like the deck of a boat in rough waters. They are incomparably reactive to the loss of their anchoring attachments—without assistance they are thrown back on threadbare resources. The end of a relationship is then not merely poignant but incapacitating.

———

Among the first things I noticed in Celeste's apartment, on a shelf just off the kitchen, was an old manual typewriter—just like the one in Chris's. The second thing I noticed was an electric keyboard with sheet music for a Beethoven piano sonata. Later, Celeste told me she also played banjo and ukulele. What were the odds, I wondered, of finding two young people with manual typewriters, keyboards with classical music, and who between them play at least six instruments?

Celeste's apartment was in downtown DC. I recalled from a paper she'd written in class that she'd been raised in a small town in central Texas, and I marveled at the cultural distance she had traveled.

Celeste told me, with a smile, that Chris had e-mailed her, and that they'd be meeting for coffee in a couple of days.

Since this whole matchup idea had started with the online attachment quiz, I asked Celeste whether particular questions on the quiz seemed to her to reflect her anxious attachment.

Celeste pulled up the quiz online, scrolled through the questions, and picked out two right away: "I'm afraid when my romantic partner gets to know me he won't like who I am," and "My desire to be very close scares people away."

Those were both classic statements reflecting anxious attachment.

Any others?

"Yeah, this one: 'I often worry my partner doesn't really love me.'"

Hearing Celeste read those statements made me realize how much courage it must take to go on a date, especially a blind date.

She said it had been a couple of years since she was in a serious relationship. Since then, she'd been "underwhelmed" with the dating pool in DC. Online dating had been so bad, she said, "I deactivated everything."

What would make a guy worthy?

"Someone who's emotionally mature. Men who can talk about their emotions. I need someone who's able to talk about hard things and sit with discomfort and talk about it. And intellectually curious. It's certainly not guys whose lives revolve around their jobs, or working out, or real estate. I prefer a wider view of life."

Chris Wilson, at least from my knowledge, drew a check in all those boxes.

"Chris sounds smart and has many interests like mine," agreed Celeste. "It definitely sounds from what you've told me that he has a few neurons firing."

Still, Celeste was curious about a few things.

"I wonder how it affected his life—or not—to be held up as a poster child for secure attachment," she said. "I'd always be conscious of it and imagine it would be stressful. I'd find it hard to live up to that.

"Also," she continued, "he seems young to have married and separated, especially given his secure attachment. I'd like to know more about that.

"And, finally, how does he have time to arrange music, write novels, and paint—and have a full-time job?"

Celeste got up to make tea for us, and I took the opportunity, with her permission, to look around. Throughout the apartment artifacts, masks, and posters ("Indigenous Women Defending Land and Life") reflected her world travels.

Viewing those items, Celeste's round-the-world adventures suddenly seemed more real to me and also left me wondering, given her anxious attachment, how she'd handled it emotionally. Her travels had taken her to the Canadian Arctic, Ecuador, the Brazilian Amazon, Borneo, and the Australian outback. On my year abroad, I'd had a tough time just being alone in one university town, but she had lived on her own in all those places. She mentioned having had a couple of relationships—including the Eskimo-kissing one—but even so I wondered how she had managed being alone.

"Oh, it was cool to travel alone for a year!" she said. "I'm a fiercely independent person, and I don't like ever being too comfortable."

Still, I was puzzled about how a person with anxious attachment could travel like that, especially at a young age, and not have a difficult time with loneliness or lack of a secure base. How had she maintained her emotional balance?

"Well, I'd seek out friends very quickly each place I went," she began, "to make myself part of the community." Sometimes she did this too quickly, she conceded, trying too hard to get people to trust and like her.

Seeking intimate relationships too quickly would be consistent with anxious attachment.

"But how'd you handle the loneliness?" I asked.

"Of course there were periods of loneliness," she said. "And sometimes it was hard to accept where I'd put myself." Celeste reached for her travel journal and quoted a brief entry: "I'm in the Arctic alone! What am I doing here?"

Then she told me of a system she'd devised for coping with loneliness.

Before she left her Texas hometown, she had asked family and friends—parents, parents' friends, even ex-boyfriends—to write letters she could take with her. The envelopes were marked to be opened at different times, such as "Open This on Your Birthday," and "Open This When You're Lonely," and so on.

Celeste left home with more than eighty letters waiting to be opened. "It worked pretty well," she said. "I looked forward to reading every one."

She still had the letters; they were in a box in a closet in her bedroom.

Celeste was just twenty-one when she left on her world tour. Her letter-writing plan displayed an impressive degree of self-knowledge for someone so young. In effect, she'd created a way to work around an insecure attachment—even to turn it to her advantage, because I suspect some of the empathy that compelled her to study native tribes and how they defend their culture probably sprang from that same strong desire to connect with people that is often inspired by anxious attachment.

So you came up with an ingenious way of coping with the stress of solo travel, I told Celeste. "Any creative ways you deal with the stress of a first date?"

"Going on a date definitely evokes anxiety," agreed Celeste, "and also a deep sense of fatigue, 'cause it's like, 'Oh, this again!' But, yes, I do have a way to deal with it: I consciously focus on the other person, asking them about their life. In other words, I frame it as getting to know another person, which as an anthropologist I'm well versed in doing."

"So, assuming the stress is under control," I asked, "what would make a first date successful?"

"If we can get through the first twenty minutes without talking about work," she said. "That's hard in DC, where everyone is so defined by their job."

I had a final question I didn't want to forget to ask.

"How about nurturing?" I asked. "In a relationship do you tend to be a nurturer?"

"Yeah," she said, and remembering Chris's attitude about nurturers, my confidence in the matchup quickly dropped—but then just as quickly Celeste changed her answer.

"No. No, I don't tend to nurture, actually," she said, correcting herself. "I mostly don't do that nurturing role."

Before I left Celeste's, I asked if she'd play some music. She took a seat at the keyboard and arranged the sheet music to the first page of the second movement of Beethoven's *Sonata Pathétique*. Celeste played beautifully, just as Chris had, and as I left the apartment I allowed myself to feel a bit more confident that I might have made a good match.

First Dates

I'd set up a situation with Chris and Celeste so that, going in, both knew the other's attachment style. But that's rare. More often, people going on a first date—particularly a blind date—will not know anything about the other's attachment. Yet knowing a prospective partner's attachment style can be useful. Not only might it provide clues as to how best to converse, but more important, it can help one avoid becoming involved with a partner whose attachment type is not compatible—most obviously, the anxious-avoidant trap.

First dates, write researchers Mikulincer and Shaver, are likely to activate the attachment system and evoke the "purest effects" of one's attachment style. "They are emotionally charged and can arouse hopes of care and support, as well as fears of disapproval and rejection."

Would it be possible, I once asked Harry Reis, to tell a person's attachment style on a first date?

"On a first date?" he mused. "I don't know. I'm sure a person could fake it. On the other hand, most people are not trying to fake their attachment style. So maybe there would be some clues."

And what might those be?

"Well, in a first conversation," he said, "and just as a general rule, I think you'd find that secure people would be relaxed, pleasant to converse with, easy company." Mikulincer and Shaver concur: on a first date, they write, secure people "manage tension and uncertainty constructively, transforming potential threats into challenges." When meeting someone new, they remain "upbeat and fairly relaxed" which in turn can help the other person relax and enjoy the experience.

And would there be clues to people with insecure attachment styles?

"Anxious people would be worried about rejection," Harry said, "but they can also be funny, engaging, and show interest in the other person. Of course, some anxious people aren't really interested in the other person. They're interested in the other person *liking* them and offering them security. It's like that Bette Midler line, 'Enough about me. Let's talk about you. What do *you* think about me?' That's an anxious person talking."

And how about those with avoidant attachment?

"Avoidants would be uncomfortable talking about feelings," Harry explained. "In fact, it might be easiest to spot avoidants. They wouldn't talk about personal things much but would focus on things they do— their jobs, their favorite sports teams, and so on. Nothing personal or deep, though."

People with different attachment styles, research shows, also vary in how self-disclosing they are willing to be on a first date.

People with avoidant attachment tend to reveal little and, consciously or not, may communicate that they really do not need a partner. Anxious daters, in contrast, tend to disclose too much too soon, often before the other person is ready for such intimacy, causing them to seem needy or overeager. Their urge to disclose, note Mikulincer and Shaver, can reflect a "wish to merge with another person, to quell anxiety, to perceive deep interpersonal similarity where no such similarity has been explored or established." Securely attached individuals, on the other hand, tend to do disclosure "just right," like the porridge in "Goldilocks": not too much, not too little, and attuned to what's going on between the two people at the moment.

In sum, Mikulincer and Shaver note, "Too much [self-disclosure] early on can signal excessive neediness, and too little in a later stage can signal lack of interest or commitment to the relationship."

———

Dressed for work at Time Inc., Chris Wilson looked even more like Clark Kent than he had at home: button-down checkered shirt, khaki pants, horn-rimmed glasses. In a corner office on a high floor, he sat behind a desk with two large computer screens. The window behind him, and also the window to his side—which overlooked busy Connecticut Avenue—were covered in doodles made with blue and black markers. Chris explained that this was his way of brainstorming how to visualize data—his specialty. On one window he'd drawn graphs showing the electoral strength of six presidential candidates. On the other were x- and y-axes, sine curves, decimals, and boxes.

"So I spoke with Celeste, and she said you'd been in touch to set up a coffee date," I began. He said he had, and added that it would be "a hell of a meet story" if things actually worked out.

"Would it surprise you," he asked, "if I said I get very nervous meeting someone on a date? I mean, given that I'm secure?"

He went on: "This might be the first genuine blind date I've ever been set up on, and I do have some anxiety. It's not crippling, but I am a bit of a socially nervous person." Chris said that growing up he had been shy around kids at school and at camp. "Secure is a big thing," he added, "but it's not everything. People can be securely attached and shy at the same time."

Chris said he tries to keep in mind that none of his dates was ever a disaster. "Some have been lackluster—but no one's ever gone to the bathroom and not come back."

That, to me, was another sign of Chris's secure attachment: even while feeling anxious, he could calm himself by recalling facts and keeping perspective.

He was feeling, he said, a mix of "intrigue" and the challenge of finding what it was he and Celeste might have in common. "Most randomly paired people can have interesting and engaging conversations, and to me it's fun to find what that is."

That, too, would be a mark of security—seeing a new situation not as a threat but as a challenge.

And what would make it a successful date?

"For me to leave with an intense feeling of excitement to see her again—even if she's in Africa for a while—and that we have a genuine spark and easy rapport."

"Well, the spark or chemistry I can't do anything about," I said. "It's a mystery. I don't know what makes the spark."

"Nobody knows," he agreed.

———

By Sunday evening, I hadn't heard from either Celeste or Chris about their date that afternoon. Monday evening, unable to wait any longer, I called Chris, and he told me what had happened. The next evening, before our writing class, I sat for a few minutes with Celeste, and she also filled me in. Putting together their two accounts, this seems to be what happened on Chris and Celeste's first date:

"Thirty minutes before we were supposed to meet," Celeste recalled, "I asked myself, 'Do I want to do this?' I felt very tense. 'Maybe I'm not ready to meet people,' I thought. 'Anyway, this is a weird way to meet someone.'"

For Chris, the date began as "a comedy of errors." He hadn't understood that a second, new coffee shop with the same name had opened in Chinatown and instead went to the old one. Meanwhile, Celeste's bus got stuck in traffic. She thought: "Now I'm more stressed out because the guy doesn't know me and I'm late." Realizing his own mistake, Chris texted Celeste: "Oh, crap, I went to the wrong coffee shop." Celeste, who by then was in a cab, redirected the driver to the correct coffee shop.

"When I got there he'd already grabbed a table outside," she said. "He stood up and shook my hand. I thought that was courteous and immediately stopped worrying."

Was there chemistry?

"I think so," she said.

They talked about music, about typewriters, and about Chris being separated.

"She just kind of threw it out there," recalled Chris. "And I appreciated that."

And they avoided talking about work for more than twenty minutes—exceeding Celeste's goal.

Had one of them been more self-disclosing than the other? I asked Chris.

"I'd say Celeste was," he said, "but not dramatically so. I think we did a reasonably good job of playing ping-pong, back and forth, with questions about each other."

The date lasted about an hour and a half.

"At the end," said Celeste, "he hugged me and said he'd be in the hospital for six days so wouldn't be in touch during that time."

A couple of hours later, Celeste texted Chris that she'd enjoyed the date and, when she returned from Uganda, would be glad to get together again.

Chris texted back that he'd also had a great time.

On a scale of 1–5, with 5 being the best, how did Chris rate the date?

"At the least, we could be very good friends," he said. "I'm glad I know her. I'd give it a 4."

Celeste rated it 3.5.

A couple of days later, after Chris had gone in for surgery, Celeste went to the hospital and left a plant and a note at Chris's nursing station. Before she left the hospital, Chris texted her: "I love what you wrote and the plant. Come back."

They met in the lobby. He had an IV and feeding tube.

After visiting for a while, Chris wished Celeste a good trip to Africa.

Celeste later told me, "I guess we already had our second date, and it was in the hospital."

———

I wasn't in touch with either Chris or Celeste for several months when finally curiosity got the better of me. Had they continued dating?

"I very much enjoyed meeting Celeste," Chris replied to my e-mail, "and wished that spark that none of us can define had been more present." But he hadn't felt a "strong enough connection" and so had written Celeste to let her know. "I'm sensitive to hurting people's feelings," he told me, "so I felt good about doing everything aboveboard and not ghosting." He said he still has the plant she gave him.

"He might be right about us not having enough of a connection," Celeste told me. "I didn't feel like I'd spent enough time with him to really know. Alas, this was all an experiment, so no love lost."

I asked Harry Reis what he made of the apparent lack of chemistry between Chris and Celeste. "With any potential matchup," he said, "the odds are still very much against success. Having compatible attachment styles can improve the chances of a hit—that is, finding a relationship—but we still don't know what makes two people feel like they have chemistry and two others like they don't. It's a mystery. Some researchers suspect it may just be a matter of chance and timing. So while attachment is important and can improve the odds, it doesn't answer all of life's great questions."

And so, even armed with knowledge of attachment theory, making matches—like creating the world—remains a difficult labor, but a labor of love.

CHAPTER 6

Raising a Human Being:
Attachment and Parenting

S ome years ago I'd seen, as had millions of others, a *Time* magazine cover story on "attachment parenting." It wasn't so much the content that disturbed me; it was the cover photo: it showed a three-year-old boy, in camouflage pants and sneakers, standing on a chair with his mouth at the naked breast of his young, attractive mother.

The article profiled a pediatrician, William Sears, who with his wife, Martha Sears, a nurse, coauthored *The Baby Book*, which popularized attachment parenting. In that and subsequent books, the Searses urge child-rearing practices that keep parents physically close to their babies, including "babywearing" (use of carriers and slings instead of strollers), breast-feeding (sometimes into toddlerhood), and cosleeping (having babies and young children sleep close to one or both parents instead of in a separate room).

Attachment parenting, as a movement, has attracted many followers but also ignited a philosophical battle. Is it a good way to help give babies a secure attachment or is it "a misogynist plot"— as some critics claim—to take women out of the workplace and confine them to the home?

Nearly all the attachment researchers I met rolled their eyes when I mentioned attachment parenting. Jude Cassidy, the attachment expert, who did the early research with Chris Wilson (aka poster child for secure attachment), told me, "Attachment parenting is a belief system about parenting and not something that attachment scientists do research on." James Coan, who scanned my brain at the University of

Virginia, said people who follow attachment parenting are not only "wrong," but "dangerous."

I could understand the concerns of Dr. Cassidy, Dr. Coan, and other researchers. Some who follow attachment parenting go overboard, adhering slavishly to practices that keep them physically close to their offspring for years, perhaps to the child's detriment. Others seem to shame mothers for working outside the home or for using babysitters or day care.

And yet, as I read more about attachment parenting, it seemed the core practices—babywearing, breast-feeding, etc.—were really just means to the same ends as those promoted by attachment theory. "In a nutshell," writes Dr. Sears, attachment parenting is "learning to read the cues of your baby and responding appropriately to those cues." That seemed in keeping with what Mary Ainsworth, inventor of the strange situation, advocated when she devised a "maternity sensitivity scale" based on three precepts: that the mother perceives a baby's signals, interprets them correctly, and responds appropriately.

Looking back, I realize that when my former wife, Marie, and I raised our kids—mostly in the 1980s and early '90s—we had intuitively found our way to at least the core practices of what would later become known as attachment parenting. We mostly used a stroller but also had a Snugli, an early form of baby carrier. ("It was helpful to have my hands free in the kitchen," Marie later explained.) Marie breast-fed for as long as the kids wanted, from about one to a little more than two years. We didn't "cosleep"—the kids each had their own rooms—but we did have what we called "open bed": anytime the kids wanted to come into our bed, they knew they were welcome.

I think what brought us to these practices was the insecurity we each felt from our own early childhoods and a desire to raise our children differently. We consciously made parenting our priority and found like-minded friends and neighbors to create a supportive community. As with all parenting, sometimes it was exhausting, but it was also exhilarating and remains the most rewarding and happiest part of both of our lives. Indeed, Mauricio Cortina, the psychiatrist who gave me the Adult Attachment Interview, suggested parenting had been "enormously useful" toward my becoming earned secure. I can't say for sure that our kids all grew up with secure attachments, because they've never been assessed, but it's my sense that they did. And when they were a bit older and our marriage hit a rough patch we were unable to overcome, I like to think their early attachment security provided some resilience to help them cope.

My parenting days were long over, but I was curious what I might learn if I could observe a young parent who was both knowledgeable about attachment theory and consciously trying to raise a child with secure attachment. I wasn't interested in the extreme form of attachment parenting, but someone who was moderate in their approach and who could articulate what they were doing and why it would be ideal. So, putting aside the disdain of the attachment researchers, I decided to search for a mom engaged in attachment parenting.

Online, I quickly found Alexa Weeks—in my hometown of Rochester. Alexa was raising her children—including an eighteen-month-old son—according to attachment parenting principles, and she had a relevant academic and work background: a bachelor's in sociology, a master's in social work, and she was currently enrolled in an accelerated nursing program with the aim of becoming a maternity nurse. She'd worked as a doula—an aide who assists a woman before, during, and after childbirth—and now also taught a babywearing class.

In response to my request, Alexa invited me to visit her next babywearing class.

———

The class was held in a suburban mall at the whimsically named Baby Bump Academy. Alexa, thirty, was petite with straight dark hair that fell to her shoulders and bangs that reached to the black frame of her eyeglasses. She wore a plaid flannel shirt and corduroys. On a mat in the center of the room, she sat on her heels, back straight as in a yoga pose, facing her students: ten moms and two dads, with at least a dozen babies and toddlers.

In her introduction, Alexa noted that babywearing is not new. In most non-Western cultures, she continued, mothers have long found ways to strap their children to their bodies. In her book *Babywearing*, Maria Blois notes that indigenous cloth carriers include the Mexican rebozo, the African *kanga*, the Indonesian sarong, the Peruvian manta, the Tahitian pareu, and the South Asian sari. Babywearing was once common in North America too: the US one-dollar gold coin shows the Native American woman Sacagawea carrying her child on her back.

In her class, Alexa covered safety rules: "Slings and carriers should be tight." "Keep baby's chin off the chest so the airway is not occluded." "Baby's face should be in view at all times."

"And finally," she cautioned, "don't wear anyone else's baby, and don't drop your baby."

She demonstrated different types of carriers. "If you're just starting out with babywearing," she advised, "soft-structured carriers can be easy to use for front, back, or hip carries." From a suitcase, she pulled a few samples. Next were the slings: lengths of fabric, many hand woven and dyed in colorful patterns. When worn correctly, they use dynamic tension to hold a baby. Alexa gracefully wrapped one around herself, from one shoulder to her opposite hip and then back up to the shoulder, threading an end through metal rings to create a buckle effect.

"Some babies want to be in a molded position," said Alexa, pulling herself into a sort of fetal position as if she were a baby lying close on her mother's chest, "but some want legs out—the 'froggy' position. You just have to watch and see the natural position your baby assumes once you put them up against your chest."

Alexa's mention of a "molded position" reminded me of Susan Paris, the strange situation coder, who said that in assessing a child's attachment she looks for whether there's complete relaxation, "heart to heart," when a mother holds her baby.

I could see how carrying an infant in a carrier or sling could produce a "mold," something not possible with a stroller.

Alexa then encouraged parents to get up and try on the different carriers. They walked around in them, much as you might in a shoe store when trying out the feel of new shoes.

———

"Woof-woof!" said Wyatt.

Eighteen-month-old Wyatt had a soft, pale complexion—like his mom—and large chipmunk cheeks. He and Alexa sat at a wooden table in the living room of their cozy home, playing with picture cards.

Alexa had invited me to visit and talk about how she was raising her kids to have secure attachment. Minutes earlier, her husband had left for work at a tattoo parlor.

"Woof-woof!" said Wyatt again.

"No, honey, not a woof-woof," said Alexa. "That's a picture of a cat."

Alexa explained: "We have a neighbor with a dog that barks a lot. 'Dog go woof' were actually Wyatt's first words."

I thought of Isaiah, the boy I'd observed at the foster care visitation center, who even at two could not, or would not, say so much as "woof-woof"—possibly due to early neglect.

At the table, Wyatt put down the picture cards. From a roll of masking tape he tore off small pieces and stuck them to the table edge. He smiled and made happy, babbling sounds.

I asked Alexa if she'd ever studied attachment theory.

Yes, she said, for her social work degree, and in college she'd taken courses in child and family development.

"It's not that complicated," she said, as we watched Wyatt play with the tape. "The essence of it is just about responding to your baby, and these specific things—the babywearing, breast-feeding, and cosleeping—they're just ways to keep you close enough so you can learn your baby's language and be aware of his needs and respond."

I wondered if her interest in attachment parenting had been, like mine, in any way a reaction to her own upbringing.

"A reaction?" she asked. "No, I grew up with sensitive parents interested in my development." Her mother was a clinical social worker who directed a group home for developmentally challenged adults. Her father was a city firefighter. "They were both very busy, and sometimes I did have a sense of being along for the ride—Mom would take me to lunches with her colleagues, and Dad would let me hang out at the firehouse—but there was nothing inherently negative. And I never went to school on my birthday!" she added, proudly. "Mom always took the day off and did something with me."

She'd never had her attachment style assessed, but she guessed she was secure.

So why, I asked, did she think some people have such negative views of attachment parenting? I mentioned the *Time* cover story.

"I know what people think," she said. "This attachment parenting stuff is all about perfectionism, and to be honest there is an extreme where you do have moms—the more neurotic types—where everything for them is just do or die. That's what the media focuses on, this sensational idea of moms who never leave their babies and breast-feed them until age seven and keep their babies in their beds."

But you do it differently? I asked.

> *"It's not about being a perfect parent—it's just about paying attention to my children."*

"Yes, I do," she said. "I embrace the principles of attachment parenting but in a more realistic way because it's not about being a perfect parent—it's just about paying attention to my children."

Her children included Wyatt, his four-year-old brother, and an eleven-year-old stepdaughter from her husband's first marriage.

"It's about understanding that these early years matter," she continued, "and trying to be in tune with my children."

Attunement

Being in tune, or "attunement," does not mean hovering or always being attached to a child. Instead, it means—in attachment terms—being sensitive to a child's cues. "Children don't come with an instruction manual," Glen Cooper, a clinician who works with children and families, has observed. "They *are* the instruction manual, and behavior is how they communicate their needs."

For a baby, aspects of attunement might include timing of feeding, minimizing intrusive touch, moving with and gazing at the baby in predictable patterns, and interacting playfully and in harmony with the baby's mood and at the baby's own timing, not the caregiver's.

The purpose of parental sensitivity is, researchers note, "to provide a secure base from which the child can explore in the secure knowledge that the caregiver will be physically and emotionally available in case of distress, and will alleviate this distress."

Being physically close to an infant can help a caregiver learn an infant's signals and become better attuned, but attunement is not about how much time one spends with an infant, and it is not about hovering; a caregiver could be with a baby 24-7 but still not be attuned. Instead, it's about paying attention, learning to read the baby's signals, and responding appropriately. A parent could "wear" his baby but if at the same time he's staring at his phone and texting, he's not likely to perceive his baby's signals. On the other hand, a parent could have his baby in a stroller and—particularly if the baby is facing backward—pay attention to the baby and be attuned.

Reflecting on research into maternal sensitivity done by Mary Ainsworth, Thomas Lewis and colleagues have written:

> Ainsworth found no simple correlation between the length of time a mother spent attending to her child and his ultimate emotional health . . . [instead] secure attachment resulted when a child was hugged when he wanted to be hugged and put down

when he wanted to be put down. When he was hungry, his mother knew it and fed him; when he began to tire, his mother felt it and eased his transition into sleep. . . . Wherever a mother sensed her baby's inarticulate desires and acted on them, not only was their mutual enjoyment greatest, but the outcome was, years later, a secure child.

Attunement also means encouraging a child to explore. The attuned parent will know when it is okay to let a child struggle to solve a problem on her own and when it's time to help. That balance between allowing a child to develop his own skills and resources and stepping in to prevent failure is another aspect of attunement.

Aiding a parent's ability to provide attuned care are aspects of what researchers call "family ecology": parents' good mental and physical health, a stable marriage, supportive grandparents, and quality day care. Yet these same factors, if negative—parental depression, marital discord, nannies or day-care workers who are neither consistent nor sensitive—may detract from the positive effects of a parent's attuned care. The presence or absence of these factors may help account, in part, for siblings in the same family developing different attachment styles.

———

As Wyatt continued playing at the table, Alexa added, "Attachment parenting is not about being perfect. In fact, I fail at it on a daily basis."

Fail how? I asked.

"I have days when I get frustrated," she said, "and react to Wyatt in a way that I look back on later and say, 'Well, that really wasn't great.' I mean, there's so little time and only so much you can do. I have to make dinner, do laundry, go to class, clean house."

So how do you handle all that? I asked.

"Well, when Wyatt's awake I don't clean house or do laundry," she said, "unless I absolutely have to, because I'd rather spend time with him and give him my attention. When it's just me and Wyatt, by the end of the day there's stuff everywhere."

I could accept Alexa's admission that she sometimes failed, but what I saw suggested she more often succeeded. She was participating in an on-the-record interview—complete with running tape recorder—yet maintained primary focus on her son. Another parent might have parked their toddler in front of the TV, video game, or motorized toy, hoping he'd keep occupied while they did the interview. Instead, Alexa had set Wyatt up with two games—picture matching and sticky tape. Both games were tactile, letting Wyatt practice dexterity and fine motor skills, and nonstructured, to allow creativity. She stayed seated next to him and played along with him—but not all the time. I believe she was continually assessing whether he was fine playing on his own or whether he needed her—that balance between her being his secure base and giving him freedom to explore. Only when she was satisfied that he was happily playing on his own did she shift her attention to me.

Alexa pulled a piece of tape off the roll and handed it to Wyatt to stick to the table edge.

I wanted to ask Alexa about some of the roughest criticisms of attachment parenting I'd heard and read, and hoped she wouldn't be offended.

"How would you respond to criticism," I asked, "from feminists and others who say attachment parenting chains a woman to her house and kids?"

"I consider myself a feminist," she said. "I have a career and I have a life, but I chose to have children. Taking the time to foster secure attachments for our children, I think, promotes autonomy and promotes feminism in a sense too, because if I'm taking the time to raise my daughter to be secure and confident, that's important. And I want sons to have that security because I want them to grow up to be respectful and mindful of how they interact with other people. I want all my kids to be secure, happy, good people."

"But even if kids are raised with secure attachments, is it a sure thing they'll actually end up being 'good' people?" I asked. "Couldn't a child be secure and still turn out to be a wife beater or serial killer?"

"A secure child can still be buffeted by other experiences or personality traits that will lead to problems in adolescence or adulthood," said Alexa, "so parenting isn't all the equation. But starting off with a secure attachment gives a child the best possibility of developing in a healthy way. I think if you look at the research, you'll see it's individuals with insecure and disorganized attachment who are far more likely later on to end up with psychopathology."

Alexa was pretty much on the money there. Early attachment security, studies show, provides resilience for managing distress and coping with life's problems, thus making it less likely a person will later succumb to "maladaptive emotional states and psychopathology," write Mario Mikulincer and Phillip Shaver. Other studies show that it's adolescents with insecure attachment who are more likely to engage in delinquent behaviors like stealing and assault; smoking and abusing alcohol and drugs; and committing crimes, including sexual offenses and domestic violence.

Wyatt, done with the masking tape, reached for a container of colored markers. Alexa gave him a piece of blank paper, and he began coloring.

She wanted to get back to the "feminism thing."

"People always want to dichotomize things—make them all or nothing," she said. "Like if you're not home all the time, you can't raise a secure child."

Alexa had not had Wyatt with her at the babywearing class, I recalled, and asked her where he was. Her mother had watched the boys that morning, she said, adding, "I can't have someone as active as Wyatt with me when I'm teaching.

"Look, I believe you should be focused on your kids," she continued, "but you don't have to sacrifice all your life for that, and it's unrealistic to be with them 24-7."

In a typical week, she said, between work and school she was out of the house three days "from 7:00 a.m. until like 4:30 p.m." On two of those days either Alexa's mother or a babysitter came to the house, and on the other day Wyatt went to preschool.

So she wasn't against day care? I thought immediately of Jim Coan, the University of Virginia professor who'd assumed people who did attachment parenting would oppose day care. He had extolled it—as long as it provided consistency of caregivers.

"I would absolutely agree with that," said Alexa. "Day care can be fine if the caregiving staff is consistent, but I'd push it a little further and look for more specifics, because if the caregivers are not attending to the babies, so the babies end up sitting half the day in cribs or exercisers or swings, then I don't think that type of interaction does much to foster attachment, even if it's the same day-care worker all the time."

Back in the 1970s, women's rights advocates attacked John Bowlby—some even walked out of his early lectures—for his claim that children did best when cared for by their mothers, especially in the first years. But Bowlby later came around to Alexa's point of view: when combined with sensitive parenting, day care is okay as long as the quality is good and the caregivers are consistent.

In 2001 a study sponsored by the US government largely confirmed this position. Children from more than thirteen hundred families were measured for attachment security, using the strange situation, at fifteen months and again at thirty-six months. Measures were made of maternal sensitivity and of each child's experience, if any, in day care. The results showed that children's development of attachment security was more tied to maternal sensitivity than to whether they had been in day care. (Less sensitive mothering, however, in combination with long hours in day care did correspond with a greater likelihood of insecure attachment than just day care alone.)

Today many experts, while still wary of day care in the first year, seem confident that day care for toddlers and older children can be okay—even beneficial in promoting development—as long as workers are of high quality (able to correctly interpret a child's signals), the staff-to-child ratio is high (one to three for infants and one to four for children under three), children are assigned a particular caregiver, and there is low turnover. Unfortunately, much day care available in the United States today falls short of these standards, particularly for poor children.

As an alternative to commercial day care for Wyatt, Alexa knew other stay-at-home moms who took care of kids and followed attachment parenting principles. "You can surround yourself and your kid with like-minded parents—a kind of stay-at-home mom kids' swap," she said.

Saying, "Wyatt wants to nurse now," Alexa picked him up and carried him to the living room sofa.

I hadn't heard Wyatt cry or fuss. Was it Alexa's acute attunement that told her he was hungry?

"How'd you know he wanted to nurse?" I asked.

"He stuck his hand in my shirt," she said. "He's not shy about it."

Somehow I'd missed that.

On the sofa, Wyatt cuddled against his mother and began to nurse. After a minute or so, he stopped, sighed, said, "More," and continued nursing.

It struck me as yet another perfect "mold."

Breast-feeding is a "built-in" attachment tool, write the Searses. Citing health benefits to both mother and baby, the American Academy of Pediatrics encourages breast-feeding for at least the first year and longer if both mother and child desire.

Though she advocates breast-feeding, Alexa said, "You make the accommodations you need." If she needs to be out during the day, for example, she'll express or pump milk and let her husband, mother, or nanny give Wyatt a bottle. She also was doing "baby-led weaning"— introducing regular food to Wyatt as he seemed ready.

And she still nursed him at night. "It's nonnutritive," she said, "but that depends on how you define 'nutritive.' Wyatt needs that nurturing to go back to sleep. No harm at this age; it's part of setting up a secure base—that's what I'm supposed to be for him when I can do it, even if it takes getting up once at night at eighteen months."

While Wyatt continued to nurse, I told Alexa about my conversation with Jim Coan and his belief that by nature human babies should have multiple caregivers.

She didn't disagree.

"Look, I'm Wyatt's mom. He developed inside of me and I'm always going to be his primary attachment. But, yes, it's developmentally appropriate for children to have attachment bonds with other caregivers. For example, my husband is also a caregiver, and Wyatt is exposed to other caregivers as well, because I have other things that require my attention, such as school and work. What is important is not that he be with me all the time, but that with whatever caregiver he's with, the nature of the care be consistent with the way we're rearing him."

But would Alexa be able to care for her kids that way, I wondered, without her husband's help, without the nanny, without her having studied sociology, social work, and nursing? Some charge that attachment parenting is a luxury of the elite.

"I don't consider myself elite!" she declared. "We function on one income for the most part and we do okay, especially given that there are five of us, but we're not by any means well-off. My husband and I—after we'd had our older son—went through a rough time, when we took a break from our relationship. We didn't live together for close to a year. I lived alone and worked, and had to juggle child care, so I'm well aware of what that's like financially."

Wyatt pulled back from the breast—he'd nursed for less than five minutes—babbling softly, eyes half-closed.

"Want to go to sleep?" Alexa asked.

She cradled him in her arms.

"Want to take this with you?" she asked, gesturing toward a pillow she'd used to help position him while he nursed.

"Dis," said Wyatt, meaning the pillow.

"Can you show our guest your room?" asked Alexa. "Where's Wyatt's room?"

Alexa gently carried Wyatt from the living room and down a short hallway.

"Here's baby's room," she said quietly.

She carried him in and laid him on a changing table.

Wyatt began to cry.

Later, putting him in his crib, Alexa cooed to him and then put on a recording of lullabies.

"Want to sleep? Want me to wrap you up? Or just want to sit and look at a book?" she asked.

Wyatt cried a little louder.

Alexa said, "He's crying because he's protesting—he wants to stay and play more—not because he's needing comfort right now. At eighteen months, that's okay; I let him cry. But if he was five or six months, I'd hold him, nurse him more, soothe him. I wouldn't let him cry. At that age, you're not teaching them self-soothing or discipline—it's just harmful."

Not letting a baby "cry it out" is another core practice of attachment parenting. Babies, write the Searses, "cry to communicate, not to manipulate. The more sensitively you respond, the more baby learns to trust his parents and his ability to communicate."

I wondered if my presence was distracting Wyatt.

"Maybe it's better if I'm not in here," I said, and quietly left the room.

After a few minutes, Alexa returned to the living room with a mug of coffee. From the bedroom, I could hear Wyatt still crying softly.

"He's just playing," said Alexa, sipping her coffee. "That's a playing cry. As long as he's happy, it's fine with me. He'll fall asleep."

I asked about Wyatt sleeping in a crib in his own room. Another tenet of attachment parenting is that babies should cosleep or at least share a room with their parents, a practice that, while rare beyond the first months in the United States, is widespread elsewhere. "Almost all the world's parents sleep with their children," Thomas Lewis and colleagues note.

Alexa said she and her husband had done a modified version of that. They had Wyatt sleep in a "sidecar crib," a crib open on one side and placed next to their bed. Later, as Wyatt became more mobile, they switched him to a floor bed that was like the sidecar but on the ground to avoid danger from crawling or rolling off. "He almost always sleeps in his crib now," she said, "unless he's sick or uncomfortable."

After several minutes, Wyatt had fallen asleep.

I had a few more questions based on common criticisms of attachment parenting.

"How about all those researchers," I asked, "who dismiss attachment parenting as an ideology grafted onto attachment theory and without any basis in science?"

"What's not science based?" she asked, sounding a little annoyed. "You have the science behind attachment theory—you know that these early experiences matter."

But I'd met researchers, I continued, who turn up their noses at attachment parenting. They call it excessive and instead encourage what they call "good enough" parenting, a notion popularized in the last century by English pediatrician and psychoanalyst Donald Winnicott. Parents need to be mostly responsive and mostly available, he advised, but not perfectly so and not all the time.

"So how about this notion of 'good enough' parenting?" I asked Alexa.

This, finally, got her back up.

"I find that offensive!" she said. "I'm frustrated with this pervasive sense of mediocrity in the culture, like 'How can I do just enough to get by?' That's not what we should aim for with our children—especially not scientists who supposedly know this stuff. Not with children. With raising children, we should never choose to half-ass it. I'm sorry, there're a lot of things we can be satisfied with that are 'good enough,' but not parenting. C'mon, I'm raising a human being!"

———

A few days later, I tagged along with Alexa and Wyatt as they did their Saturday-morning shopping at the public market.

"You want a little apple?" a vendor asked Wyatt.

"Dis!" he said, and the woman handed him the apple.

Alexa carried Wyatt in a Mei Tai, a carrier of Asian design, hand woven in Guatemala. It was a long rectangle of colorful cotton with a strap coming off each corner and held Wyatt, chest to chest, against her. His tiny white sneakers dangled below. Though held against his mother, Wyatt was able to look all around, taking in the sights and sounds of the market.

When we passed a booth selling live chickens, rabbits, and two goats stacked in tiny cages, Wyatt, wide-eyed, said "Woof-woof!"

"No, not woof-woof," Alexa corrected. "That's not a doggie. It's a goat."

Cruising easily among vendors' stalls, Alexa filled shopping bags on her right and left shoulders with vegetables and fruits as Wyatt rode in between, in the carrier.

"You're really loaded up," I observed.

"But he feels weightless," she said. "I actually feel the veggies and fruits more than him."

Watching her move so agilely among the stalls, I couldn't help but contrast it to what I so often see at the supermarket: parents ponderously pushing their kids in enormous plastic strollers, provided by the store, that are made to look like cars or trains and that take up most of an aisle.

Done with shopping, Alexa headed to her car. On the way, she noted that babywearers had outnumbered strollers at the market that day. "Maybe it's a turning of the tide toward more people choosing to wear their babies," she said.

Untying the straps on the back of the Mei Tai, she gently lifted Wyatt out of the carrier and into a car seat.

Through this whole process, Wyatt remained quiet. And then it occurred to me that during the whole shopping trip Wyatt had been quiet. We'd been maneuvering among stalls, passing what other children might find irresistible, such as colorful foods and cute bunnies, or scary, like caged goats, bustling shoppers, and shouting vendors—yet Wyatt had been quiet and seemingly content. There'd even been a stranger—me—shadowing him and his mom, interrupting with questions, yet throughout he'd munched his apple and shown a quiet serenity. His composure had required no continuous chatter from Mom, no video screen to distract, no big stroller made to look like a train. I could be wrong, but it seemed that all it had taken was a parent who'd paid attention to him and a long piece of cloth that created a space for him to be held, chest to chest, against her.

I'd noticed the same thing the previous week at Alexa's babywearing class: ten mothers and a dozen kids, but not a single baby or toddler had cried or even fussed much; they had seemed content and were quiet.

The tools of attachment parenting, write the Searses, "lessen a baby's need to cry." A caregiver's attunement, note child-development experts Robert S. Marvin and Preston A. Britner, helps minimize "the frequency and intensity" of an infant's crying.

Alexa folded the Mei Tai and put it—along with the bags of fruits and veggies—in the hatchback. Then she and Wyatt headed home.

———

I liked how Alexa had taken the essence of attachment parenting—the practices that help keep her close and attuned to Wyatt—and made it work for her and her family, without sacrificing her career. To be sure, she had "family ecology" factors working in her favor: her studies of child development and support from her husband, her mother, and like-minded parents.

But Alexa had also confided that she and her husband had gone through a rough patch—actually lived apart for a year. She hadn't mentioned it and maybe she didn't know about it, but, as I was soon to learn, attachment theory can also help troubled couples repair their relationships. And just as I'd felt lucky to have found Alexa, I was about to find a generous couple who would let me see, up close, how attachment-based counseling had helped them preserve their marriage.

CHAPTER 7

Dancing Close: Attachment, Marriage, and Couples Counseling

A relationship is like dancing close; we're all drawn together in the beginning because of the attraction but later we start stepping on each other's toes.

If we don't have a secure attachment, instead of continuing to dance close, we'll both step back—arms out straight like kids at a middle school dance.

Eventually we'll get very far back. That's when affairs happen. And that's when most couples walk through my door.

—DAVID SCHWAB, FAMILY COUNSELOR TRAINED
IN EMOTIONALLY FOCUSED THERAPY

Tiffany and Edgar, both born and raised in the Washington, DC, area, met in elementary school. In high school they briefly dated. Later, while attending the same community college, they dated again, and after living together for five years, they married, at age twenty-seven. Parents and friends attended the ceremony at the courthouse the day before Valentine's Day. A few months later, Tiffany learned of Edgar's affair.

I met Tiffany and Edgar (they prefer to be identified by first names only) at a coffeehouse—named, ironically, Tryst—in DC's Adams Morgan neighborhood. The first thing that struck me was how similarly they were dressed: both wore pullover shirts with almost matching stripes—as if they were on the same team. He had a short, neatly trimmed beard and mustache; she wore her dark hair pulled tightly back in a ponytail.

Holding hands, their wedding bands caught the room's light. They were eager to tell me their story. They wanted me to understand how they'd moved from the wrenching discovery of Edgar's infidelity, less than a year before, to where they were that day: happy, committed, and confident of their future.

———

When I'd first learned of attachment theory I was fascinated because it seemed to explain why a lengthy relationship I'd been in had been so tumultuous and—despite great passion—ultimately unworkable. In attachment theory, I felt I'd found a Rosetta stone: the key to the mystery of why some relationships work and others so spectacularly fail, in a protracted way. Even so, it didn't occur to me that attachment theory might also offer a key for improving and even saving troubled relationships. That realization would come only when I discovered the work of Canadian psychotherapist Sue Johnson.

As a young practitioner, Johnson had worked successfully with both children and adults. Yet, as she recounts in her popular book *Hold Me Tight*, when she worked with couples she often felt "defeated." Warring partners, she realized, "didn't care about insights into their childhood relationships. They didn't want to be reasonable and learn to negotiate. They certainly didn't want to be taught rules for fighting effectively."

Johnson's lament about the difficulty of helping "warring" couples rang a bell. Before my wife and I separated and divorced, we saw several marriage counselors together. None of it helped. We both felt vulnerable, although I don't recall any of the counselors probing into what deeper emotions were at play or why. They mostly seemed focused on how we communicated—interesting but ultimately not helpful.

Sue Johnson sensed that the problem with traditional couples counseling was that it lacked a clear, scientific understanding of the core issue: love.

So, what is love? And when it breaks, how do you fix it? Answer those questions, Johnson reasoned, and you'd have the basis of a more successful therapy.

It took many frustrating years of working with couples and doing research but Johnson—who as a child "watched helplessly" as her parents "destroyed their marriage and themselves" with their endless arguments—finally found her answer in attachment theory. Drawing on the writings of John Bowlby, she concluded—as had other leading researchers—that romantic love is an adult form of attachment. As such, love exists for the same reason the infant-parent bond exists: when we emotionally bond with loved ones, they become our safe havens and secure bases.

Love is "the best survival mechanism there is," Johnson has written. It "drives us to bond emotionally with a precious few others who offer us safe haven from the storms of life." This need for safe, emotional connection is "wired into our genes" by millions of years of evolution and is as basic to health and happiness as the drives for food, shelter, or sex.

Couples in a loving relationship depend on each other, not only as each other's secure bases and safe havens, but also to help regulate each other's emotions and physical selves. Loving partners become linked in a "neural duet" in which one sends out signals that help regulate the hormone levels, cardiovascular functions, body rhythms, and even immune system of the other. "Our bodies are set up for this kind of connection," Johnson notes.

The hand-holding experiment conducted by Jim Coan (see chapter 4) is an example of coregulation. There, people in an MRI machine, put under threat of electric shock, reported lower stress and pain when holding the hand of a loving partner. "The people we love are the hidden regulators of our bodily processes and our emotional lives," notes Coan.

Other studies have shown that men and women in satisfying marriages generally live longer and more healthfully than do their single peers.

"Science from all fields," observes Johnson, "is telling us very clearly that we are not only social animals, but animals who need a special kind of close connection with others, and we deny this at our peril."

Withholding that safety and security from partners—failing to meet each other's attachment needs—is what threatens relationships.

Fights are really protests over emotional disconnection, says Johnson. "Underneath all the distress, partners are asking each other: Can I depend on you? Are you there for me? Do I matter to you?"

In too many relationships, she concludes, attachment needs and fears are hidden agendas, "directing the action but never being acknowledged." When partners feel unsafe, they become defensive and blame each other, she says. But most of the blaming "is a desperate attachment cry, a *protest against disconnection*. It can only be quieted by a lover moving emotionally close to hold and reassure. Nothing else will do."

At other times, other researchers have suggested, it can also be a protest against *too much* connection.

Either way, the goal in therapy is to draw a couple back into an emotionally appropriate bond and reestablish a sense of safe connection.

To do so, partners must acknowledge their attachment needs and their dependence on each other. This can be difficult. Not only do most adults not understand their attachment needs but to acknowledge them runs counter to the American idea of adulthood: that the height of maturity is to be independent and self-sufficient. Dependency, in popular culture, is a weakness. Bowlby, however, saw "effective dependency" (we might also call it "mutual dependency" or "interdependency") and the ability to turn to others for emotional support as "an innate part of being human" and both a sign and a source of strength.

From these insights, Johnson aimed to develop a new approach to couples counseling.

Johnson called her new approach emotionally focused therapy (EFT). Its core message is straightforward: "Recognize and admit you are emotionally attached to and dependent on your partner in much the same way that a child is on a parent for nurturing, soothing and protection." And to strengthen that emotional bond, "be open, attuned, and responsive to each other."

Early work with EFT pointed toward success.

"My clients had to learn to take risks, to show the softer sides of themselves. . . to confess their fears of loss and isolation" and to talk about their "longings for caring and connection."

It is this form of *healthy* dependence, she wrote, that is the essence of romantic love. A key shift in a couple's relationship occurs when both partners can "hear each other's attachment cry and respond with soothing care."

In the years since she developed EFT, Sue Johnson has trained other therapists to use it. They, in turn, have trained thousands in North America and around the world. Compared to more traditional forms of couples counseling, EFT works exceptionally well. In several studies, 70–75 percent of couples working with EFT-trained counselors reported reduced distress and increased happiness in their relationships.

(To locate an EFT-trained couples counselor near you, see the website of the International Centre for Excellence in Emotionally Focused Therapy: iceeft.com. Many of the counselors listed also see individual clients and will use the same principles of attachment theory in their work with them. In fact, Sue Johnson and colleagues have recently developed emotionally focused individual therapy—a form of EFT specifically for use with individual clients.)

EFT's effectiveness on a neurological basis is demonstrated by Jim Coan's MRI-hand-holding study. Twenty-four women who reported their marriages as *unhappy* were put alone into the MRI scanner. When threatened with electric shock, their brain activity was the same whether they held a stranger's hand or their husband's hand. But after several months of EFT counseling, when the women were again put into the scanner and held their husbands' hands, their brains were quieter; they reported the shocks as "uncomfortable" but not painful. The researchers concluded: "EFT can alter the way the brain encodes and responds to threats in the presence of a romantic partner."

Notes Sue Johnson, "Love is a safety cue that literally calms and comforts the neurons in our brain."

———

When his affair became known, Edgar pushed for counseling, but Tiffany was reluctant. She'd seen a therapist for anxiety and depression and hadn't found it helpful. But Edgar persisted. Cost, however, was a concern. Both Tiffany and Edgar were working—he as regional manager for a janitorial services company and she doing part-time sales and office work for a dog-walking company—but finances were tight. Tiffany was already raising two children from previous relationships and was pregnant with her and Edgar's first child. To save money, they were living with Tiffany's parents.

Edgar found a Maryland nonprofit, the Pro Bono Counseling Project, that connects people with limited resources with mental health professionals who volunteer to provide services at no cost. They referred Tiffany and Edgar to a licensed marriage and family therapist, Reena Bernards.

With Tiffany and Edgar's permission, I met Reena at a restaurant in Silver Spring, Maryland.

EFT was challenging to learn, Reena told me, but over eight years of practice and several dozen cases, she had found it effective, particularly with the most difficult relationships. "It's especially effective with 'escalated' couples," she said, meaning those in a "negative cycle of behavior, blaming each other, feeling hopeless, including couples having affairs."

In her practice, EFT counseling typically lasts twenty to thirty sessions over six to ten months. Tiffany and Edgar finished in just fourteen sessions, the fastest she's seen. "And not all couples finish," she noted. "Some get better, and some decide to split up, although that's rare."

The sessions generally move through three stages of therapy:

Stage One: De-escalation

In the first two EFT sessions, Reena familiarizes couples with the process and begins to get to know them. Recalling her first impression of Tiffany and Edgar, she said, "I felt a lot of love and caring between them, but I was concerned about the affair and what the implications would be. It was a real breach, and I didn't know if we'd be able to repair it." Her other goals are to identify the couple's cycle of negative emotional behavior, interrupt it, and begin to help them de-escalate.

One of the first steps is to meet individually with each partner to ask questions about their families of origin and their experiences growing up. These questions are taken from the Adult Attachment Interview (see chapter 2) and are meant to reveal each partner's attachment style. With this information, the therapist can gauge patterns of trusting and not trusting, of how emotionally open each person is comfortable being and how much they are willing to rely on others.

"Growing up, I really didn't trust anyone," Tiffany had told Reena in response to the AAI questions. "I didn't trust people and that made me feel I couldn't rely on them, though I wanted to." In her relationship with Edgar, she continued the same pattern. "I'd raised two kids before Edgar came along and needed his help but didn't feel I could rely on it."

Edgar, for his part, answered the AAI questions by acknowledging that in his relationship with Tiffany he repeated a pattern from growing up: "Tiffany didn't trust me to help with anything, so that left me on my own and not feeling very useful."

From their opening sessions, Reena concluded, based on the AAI questions and further conversation with both Tiffany and Edgar, that Tiffany's attachment style was anxious and Edgar's was avoidant. "It's always a continuum," she cautioned. "No one's all one thing or all the other. But in general these are their attachment styles."

As such, Tiffany and Edgar fell into the dreaded anxious-avoidant trap. "For avoidants," explained Reena, "relationships and closeness can be dangerous, but the more the avoidant partner withdraws, the more the anxious one pursues, so you get the anxious-avoidant trap." (For more on why this combination of romantic partners is problematic, see chapter 5.)

Among the couples she'd seen in counseling, Reena consistently found an overrepresentation of attachment insecurity. "I have sometimes had a couple where one partner is somewhat secure, and that does help things move forward. But I've never had anyone who's 'right on the money' secure. If they were, the couple probably wouldn't stay stuck so long on whatever their issue is, and they'd be unlikely to end up in therapy."

Among her clients, the anxious-avoidant combination is common, said Reena. She's also seen couples in which both are anxious, and in which one was anxious and one disorganized. She's never had a couple in which both were avoidant.

In these early sessions, Reena explores how anxious and avoidant styles play out in a couple's relationship. An anxious person, for example, may feel an intense need for his or her partner but at the same time may never fully trust that those needs will be met. For some, this can trigger behavior that is critical and complaining. For example: "You're not really there for me; you're going to disappoint me again!" Or it can be expressed as an extreme form of self-reliance that is really just a defense mechanism. On the surface, anxious people will often blame their partner, but underneath they're really looking for closeness and connection.

Avoidants, on the other hand, may be unable to figure out how to get their needs met in a relationship and, rather than pursue their partner, will just withdraw. And sometimes a way to withdraw—to exit the relationship—is to have an affair.

In contrast, when the anxious partner has an affair, it's often from a feeling of having tried to get needs met and having failed and being burned out. "We call that a 'burned-out pursuer,'" Reena explained.

Risk Factors

During this first stage of EFT—particularly during individual sessions—a therapist might learn that either partner is engaged in ongoing behaviors that rule out use of EFT. These include substance abuse, domestic violence, and infidelity. (Screening out these most difficult cases, some researchers contend, may help boost reported EFT success statistics.)

In this case, Reena was satisfied that Edgar's affair wasn't a risk factor. "Edgar and Tiffany both told me it was over," she recalled, "and Tiffany said she wasn't suspicious."

From an attachment perspective, it is not surprising that Edgar rather than Tiffany had the affair: within a couple it is more often the avoidant partner who is unfaithful.

It is more often the avoidant partner who is unfaithful.

Compared to secure and anxious partners, avoidants tend to have a "low commitment to their primary relationship" and thus to engage in affairs. They are also more likely to respond favorably to "mate-poaching"—that is, attempts to lure them away from current partners.

The risk of relationship violence, on the other hand, is more prevalent in the anxious partner. The anxious person's strong desire for closeness can, under the stress of separation—and particularly the fear that a separation may be permanent—trigger a hostile reaction. Bowlby called this "anger born of fear."

This may seem odd because we usually think of the anxious partner as the one who needs closeness, but studies confirm that if there is violence within a romantic relationship, it is most likely to come from the partner who is anxious. "Viewed from an attachment perspective," note researchers Phillip Shaver and Mario Mikulincer, "couple violence is an exaggerated form of protest against perceived partner unavailability and lack of responsiveness."

(This is true, other researchers note, for what is sometimes called "common couple violence"—i.e., fights that escalate out of control—but probably not for more extreme violence, such as battering.)

Relationship violence was not an issue with Tiffany and Edgar, however, so their counseling with Reena proceeded.

Stage Two: Repairing Attachment Wounds

In this part of EFT, each person has a chance to say what emotions—such as fear, sadness, or loneliness—get stirred up by the other's behavior and to ask for what they need when they are feeling those emotions. This is the beginning of repairing attachment wounds.

Where there's been an affair, for example, the therapist will work to understand the emotions of the betrayed partner and what it will take to heal them, and also the emotions of the partner who strayed and what led to that behavior. "This is not condoning the behavior," Reena emphasized, "just understanding why it happened—but that's not saying it was okay to do it."

The first step here is what Reena calls "withdrawer reengagement." In this case, that meant asking Edgar, "When you get into that cycle with Tiffany where you feel bad about yourself, what does it really feel like?" Reena asked Edgar to describe it to Tiffany. As part of his response, he said it often feels like he needs a hug.

Next Reena asked Tiffany what it really feels like when she's feeling she can't trust anyone and that she's shouldering all the burdens of the family. She asked Tiffany to describe those feelings to Edgar and to tell him what she needs in those moments. Reena also asked Tiffany to talk about how bad Edgar's affair was for her and how it felt for her.

After listening, Edgar apologized and was able to say what disconnection in their relationship had led to the affair and what had changed over the course of therapy that would not allow it to happen again.

As it happened, during this stage of EFT, Tiffany's grandmother became ill and Tiffany helped care for her during her final days. This turned out to be an opportunity—albeit a bittersweet one—for Tiffany and Edgar to practice what they were learning in EFT. "Reena's focus was all about how Edgar and I needed each other emotionally in the relationship. That was new to me. I just never realized how much I needed him. So when my grandmother got ill, it helped me realize I could trust and I could turn to Edgar in a time of need.

"Later, when my grandmother died, I let Edgar hold me. He gave me so much comfort. Reena made me realize that I had never been willing to let that kind of comforting into my life. Before, I'd always been pushing it—and Edgar—away. I was scared to let him in because he might leave me—that had been the pattern of my life."

Edgar remembered it this way: "When Tiffany's grandma passed away, I was able to comfort her. I felt she let me in and let me be part of her life. I could comfort her and hug her, and finally she'd hug me back."

Stage Three: Consolidating Gains

There's always a danger that after therapy a couple will fall back into their negative cycle, so in the final stage of EFT the therapist encourages them to find ways to get out of negative patterns by using different "dialogues." For example, when a couple is hurt or disappointed, they can learn to express their underlying emotions, not just the secondary emotions like "I'm angry," but instead the more vulnerable feelings: I'm scared. I'm sad. I'm feeling alone. I miss you. It's a difficult thing to learn, but it can dissolve the negative pattern.

Tiffany recalled her and Edgar's final EFT session. "Reena asked us,

'So, what do you want to talk about today?' And I said, 'I think we're good.' We were done."

"She had taught us our whole fighting cycle," recalled Edgar. "All of it—piece by piece."

"We have way better communication now," said Tiffany.

For her part, Reena was impressed with the couple. "All in all, they took the process very seriously and took emotional risks to make it work. They're a lovely couple, and I saw their relationship change tremendously over the course of the half year I worked with them. They stayed with it and were brave. I'm hopeful they'll continue to grow and stay connected."

———

After becoming aware of EFT, and especially after learning of Tiffany and Edgar's good outcome with Reena Bernards, I found myself wondering whether the outcomes for many thousands of couples might be different if EFT were more widely used. Could they learn about their own attachment needs, and how to express the emotions that underlie anger, hurt, and distrust, and to forgive each other and therefore allow many more children to be raised in a stable, intact family?

———

One year after my meeting at the Tryst coffeehouse with Tiffany and Edgar, we had a chance to catch up by e-mail. Tiffany wrote: "Edgar and I had a baby boy back in December. His name is Lucas. He is now seven months old and is keeping us both very busy! Since we last met, we have both tried our best to keep working on ourselves to have a better relationship, and the baby has really brought us closer together as well."

Tiffany added that because she had needed to be on bed rest for much of her pregnancy, she and Edgar had spent the year living with her parents for some extra support and care. "But as wonderful as my parents are," she wrote, "it was a hard situation on Edgar and me as a couple. But everything we learned with Reena really helped us through that time. We ended up moving into our own place and are very happy now."

Tiffany closed her note: "We have not been in contact with the wonderful Ms. Reena, but we like to take that as a good thing."

CHAPTER 8

Sassy and Classy:
Attachment and Friendship

Hesitantly, I knocked at the apartment door across the hall. Some-one new had moved in, and I thought I'd say hello. A dog barked. The door opened a crack and a woman shouted, "Chief, quiet!" The door opened a bit more, and I saw my new neighbor: a young woman in her midtwenties, with long brown hair and a warm smile. She held her head at a slightly odd angle and wore a neck brace.

She invited me in.

The look of her apartment was not what you might expect for a young professional in Washington, DC. There were no displays of di-plomas, campaign posters, or photos with politicians. Instead, the fur-nishings were unpretentious, even cozy: lots of framed family photos, throw pillows and comforters, and stuffed toys for her dog.

One framed picture in the kitchen, however, hinted at my young neighbor's current situation: it said, "When Life Gives You Limes, Just Add Tequila." Jen, I would learn, had lately had more than her share of limes. (For reasons of privacy, she asked me not to use her last name.)

Four months earlier—on her twenty-fifth birthday—Jen had been injured in a car accident. She was driving her mother and sister in downtown Washington, DC, when she stopped at a red light and the car behind her plowed into them. Her passengers were not badly hurt, but "because of the way my neck was turned," she explains, Jen sus-tained neck injuries and head injuries and a concussion. She was taken to the hospital by ambulance.

The accident had come less than a year after the abrupt end of a brief, unhappy marriage.

And yet despite the physical and emotional challenges, Jen seemed resilient. The neck and head injuries left her tired and often unsteady on her feet: one time, she told me, she fell in the shower; another time I saw her fall as she got into the elevator, spilling a full cup of hot coffee. But every day she got up, dressed, and kept her appointments with doctors: among them a neurologist, neuro-optometrist, chiropractor, and physical therapist. And daily, regardless of the weather, she walked Chief, her seventy-pound black Lab.

It would be a lot for anyone to handle, especially a single person recently divorced. Her family seemed close and supportive: her mother, father, and aunts often took turns staying overnight to help. But I wondered about the role of her friends as Jen dealt with her challenges. A conversation I'd had earlier with Harry Reis came to mind:

"Researchers talk sometimes as if only people who are married or have a romantic partner have attachment relationships," Harry had said. "But there are lots of single people, and they're not all walking around without secure bases and safe havens. So how are they getting their attachment needs met?"

Often, said Harry, it's through an especially close friend.

His point wasn't that most friendships are full attachment relationships but that close, supportive, and long-standing friends nevertheless can fulfill at least some of our attachment needs.

My neighbor, I learned, was blessed with such a friend.

My first view of Lucy was in a framed photo in Jen's living room. It had been taken a few years earlier, in happier times. In it Lucy's arm is draped around Jen's shoulder. Their heads are pressed together as they face the camera and smile. "She's beautiful, gorgeous, with red hair and freckles," Jen told me, describing Lucy.

They'd both been raised in the DC suburb of Bethesda, Maryland, but had gone to different schools. It wasn't until the summer after their junior year of high school that they met, while volunteering with the Red Cross at a military hospital.

They were essentially candy stripers, recalled Jen, organizing storage closets filled with donated video games and clothing for amputees.

"But we also met patients' families," she recalled. "We saw patients, some of whom later died. It was quite an experience to go through with someone at age seventeen."

Patients and hospital workers, seeing them always together, referred to them as "Sassy and Classy."

"Which one were you?" I asked.

"I think I was Sassy," said Jen. "Lucy was the classy one: reserved, very put together. She wore a lot of bows and lace. I was more sweatshirts and jeans."

During senior year, they continued volunteering. "It became our lives," said Jen. They ended up running the program together.

After high school, Jen went to college in Maryland, and Lucy in Rhode Island, but they visited and spent breaks together. When Jen flew to Arizona to see her grandmother, Lucy came along. "She became a part of my family," said Jen.

A photo of Jen's wedding party shows Lucy standing with other bridesmaids, each in a champagne-colored sequin dress. At the wedding dinner, Lucy sat with members of Jen's family.

"Lucy's the kindest, most compassionate, understanding, supportive person I've ever met," Jen summed up. "At other points in my life I've had other close friendships, but Lucy has been my steady best friend."

"Oh, and she texted yesterday to say she'll be in town next weekend."

Lucy lived in New York City, where she did marketing for an online magazine. Although they kept in close touch by phone and text, Jen and Lucy hadn't seen each other for a couple of months.

Could I see them at the moment they got together again? I asked Jen.

"Absolutely," she said, "as long as you don't mind hearing us scream when we see each other."

———

That in her teens Jen found in Lucy a friend who could fulfill some of her attachment needs fits a pattern recognized by researchers: as early as middle school and accelerating through adolescence, young people will begin to transfer some attachment needs from parents to same-sex peers. The first attachment need to transfer is often "proximity seeking"—that is, the desire to keep a friend physically close, or at least in close communication. During the teen years and into the early twenties, another need likely to transfer is "safe haven": leaning on a reliable friend for comfort and support when problems arise.

Note, however, that studies show the attachment need for secure base—finding in someone's rock-solid commitment the confidence to go out and explore the world—typically does not transfer until a young adult has a romantic partner or spouse. And some people, even after marriage, keep their parents as a secure base well into adulthood.

To help people identify who in their lives fills these needs, attachment researchers, including Cindy Hazan, now at Cornell University, have developed what is known as the WHOTO scale. It's a questionnaire designed to reveal whom we go to when we feel distressed or in need. A question that taps the proximity-seeking need, for example, asks: "Who is the person it is hardest to be away from?" Another taps the safe haven need: "Who is the person you want to talk to when you are worried about something?" Questions that tap the secure base function include: "Who is the person you know will always be there for you?" and "Who is the person you want to share your successes with?"

While a close friend may fulfill these selected attachment needs, it would nevertheless be unusual for a friendship among adolescents or young adults to be a true attachment relationship. For that, the friendship would need to fulfill all attachment criteria, including secure base and also "separation protest"—showing emotional upset over the actual or even potential separation from the friend. As noted by researcher Wyndol Furman:

> Individuals may seek proximity to their friends and some may turn to them as a safe haven, but most friends do not seem to serve as secure bases from which to explore the world, nor do individuals usually protest when separated involuntarily from their friends.

There are some friendships, however—most often found among adult siblings or the elderly—that do fulfill all these needs and thus may rise to the level of true attachment relationships.

————

For Jen, her first major reliance on Lucy as a safe haven may have come during the collapse of her short-lived marriage.

"I called Lucy sobbing," Jen recalled, "and she talked me through it. There are certain things you have to talk through a million times, and Lucy is perfect—amazing—at playing that role. Without judging, she reiterated what I was feeling. 'Yes, you're hurt,' she'd say. 'You have a reason to be hurt.'"

"I was young. Other friends didn't know how to handle my divorce," recalled Jen. "But Lucy did know.

"And she could understand the complexity. So one day I was, like, 'I've got to leave him,' and the next it was, 'I've come this far I can't quit now.' But either way she supported me. She coached me through it. She was my greatest supporter."

Jen recalled, "Shortly after I kicked him out, I went to stay with Lucy." Later, when Jen was back in DC, she and Lucy kept in touch by phone, FaceTime, and text, as well as repeated visits back and forth.

Ten months after the wedding, Jen's divorce was final.

The quality and stability of a friendship, studies show, will be influenced by the attachment styles of both parties and how the two styles mesh together. Some of the strongest findings in the attachment field show that an individual's attachment history affects the number of close friendships as well as their intimacy and stability.

As with romantic relationships, people with secure attachments will be best able to make and sustain friendships. This is because friendships are close relationships and thus are influenced by the "mental model" of relationships

> *People with secure attachments will be best able to make and sustain friendships.*

formed by an individual in early childhood, based on the caregiver-infant experience.

The effect is evident as early as elementary school. "Infant attachment security," notes Alan Sroufe, an internationally recognized expert on early attachment relationships, "is a clear predictor of peer competence at every age," forecasting later qualities of friendship. Attachment *insecurity,* on the other hand, predicts "more troubled relations" with friends later on.

The list of benefits that a secure attachment brings to one's ability to make and sustain successful friendships is long: in various studies, friends with secure attachments compared with those with insecure attachments have been found more willing to self-disclose (but to do so appropriately), more comfortable with emotional intimacy, more trusting and trustworthy, better able to commit to a friendship, better able to have smoother and more stable interactions with friends, better conflict resolution skills, and overall greater satisfaction with their friendships.

What about those with anxious attachment? They invest in friendships and are committed to them, and easily self-disclose—sometimes excessively so. But they sometimes may end up faulting their friends for failing to match their own intense need for intimacy. Also, among the highly anxious, a fear of abandonment may cause some people to pressure friends to show more commitment than they're willing or able to, thus pushing friends away.

In contrast, individuals with avoidant attachments, due to a strong desire for independence and self-reliance, show lower levels of self-disclosure, find intimacy in friendships less rewarding, and have higher levels of friendship conflict. In a study of 120 pairs of same-sex friends ranging in age from seventeen to fifty-six, those high in avoidance showed less commitment to, lower investment in, and were less satisfied with their friendships.

I had not yet met Lucy, but from Jen's description of her sensitive and unwavering support during Jen's marital crisis, I formed the impression that in Lucy, Jen had likely found a friend who was securely attached.

———

Two days later, Jen invited me to join her to walk her dog, Chief.

"Leash!" said Jen, as they prepared to leave her apartment, and the dog dutifully picked up his leash in his mouth.

Jen no longer wore the neck brace. She wore her dark hair in a bun and covered with a wraparound head scarf—her physical therapist said it might help with headaches. She also wore large, round tortoise-shell sunglasses to help with light sensitivity since the accident. The accessories may have been therapeutic, but the overall look—dark updo, head scarf, oversized shades—was decidedly fashionable and reminded me of a young and elegant Audrey Hepburn in *Breakfast at Tiffany's*. Years earlier, Jen may have been Sassy and Lucy, Classy, but that afternoon as we strolled among the embassies and mansions of downtown DC, Jen looked plenty classy too.

We had gone about a block and were standing near a grassy patch in front of a stately building with a historical marker saying it had once been the home of Alexander Graham Bell.

"Chief, get busy!" said Jen, and within moments he did.

Jen picked up after him with a plastic bag.

For such a large dog, he seemed remarkably docile and obedient.

She'd originally raised and trained Chief to be a service dog for a local nonprofit, to work with disabled veterans. But he failed the final exam when he barked too much, so Jen adopted him.

"So that's ironic that he ended up helping you," I commented.

"Yeah, everyone says that," said Jen. "They say he failed for a purpose."

As we walked, I noticed a lot of people in their twenties and thirties, about half of whom stared at their phone screens, perhaps checking in with "friends" on social media. It brought to mind a recent study

I'd seen comparing people with different attachment styles and how satisfied they are with online versus offline friendships. It's just one study, but the result is interesting: across all attachment styles, it suggests, people self-disclose more with offline friends than with online friends and, perhaps as a result, most people report greater satisfaction with offline friends than online ones. Except for one group: anxious people. In the study, anxious people showed no difference in rates of satisfaction between offline and online friendships—they turn out to be equally dissatisfied with both types of friendship. Apparently, the factors that often lead anxious people to be dissatisfied in relationships—notably a frustration that friends do not reciprocate the intense level of intimacy and commitment they crave—also apply to online friendships.

As we continued walking, Jen updated me on plans for Lucy's visit: she'd arrive in town tomorrow but still wasn't sure where or at what time they'd get together, but Jen was sure they would and I was welcome to be there.

From Jen's earlier description, Lucy clearly had fulfilled the attachment functions of proximity seeking (keeping a friend close or at least in close communication) and safe haven (using a reliable friend for comfort and support) during Jen's separation and divorce. I was curious, though, if Lucy had been able to fulfill those same attachment functions for Jen following her recent car accident. By then Lucy was living in New York, and after the accident I doubt Jen—given her concussion—was able to talk on the phone much or do much online, and she certainly couldn't travel.

"I didn't know it at the time, of course," Jen said, "but apparently my mom texted Lucy right after the accident, and within days she came to the hospital."

That would cover proximity seeking, I thought, but how about safe haven? Once she was in town, how had Lucy provided Jen with comfort and support?

"She bathed me," said Jen.

"Bathed you?" I asked.

"That's right. She came to the hospital and because I had an IV twenty-four hours a day, I wasn't allowed to shower myself. So Lucy walked me over to the shower and came in with me. I was naked and she rolled up her sleeves and shampooed me, washed me with a wash cloth, and then braided my hair."

That was about as poignant a description of a safe haven as I'd ever heard.

"In that moment, it didn't feel weird at all, and there was no other person I would trust to do it," said Jen. "That's how as a grown woman you know you have a best friend."

As Jen and I took Chief for one more loop around the neighborhood, it occurred to me that despite all she'd recently been through, Jen was in many ways a fortunate young woman.

I left Jen and Chief, that afternoon, thinking that from everything Jen had told me about Lucy, Lucy seemed to be blessed with a secure attachment.

But it could have been otherwise. Jen and Lucy had met by chance as volunteers at the military hospital. What if they'd become fast friends, but Jen later found that Lucy was not secure but instead highly anxious or avoidant?

How does one best navigate a friendship when a friend has an insecure attachment?

"Treat insecure friends in a manner consistent with their defenses," advises Harry Reis. In other words, if a friend is anxious, reassure him often of your availability and commitment. If a friend is avoidant, don't push for too much intimacy and instead give her space.

That approach may be doable but ultimately frustrating, because one is still left with a friend who cannot be an intimate, stable companion. And yet, now a groundbreaking study offers some hope for dealing with insecure friends, particularly those who are highly avoidant.

"It is not the case," researchers at a New Zealand university assert, "that highly avoidant individuals do not want or need care and support; they do. But they also want to protect themselves from the neglect and hurt they expect will occur if they reach for or rely on their partners."

The study was done with romantic couples but may also apply to friends. It found that with avoidant people, while *average* levels of support may only serve to trigger the person's fear of dependence, *very high levels of support* can break through those defenses and allow the avoidant person to respond positively to a friend's support.

Not all kinds of support work, however. *Emotional* support, such as expressing caring or saying you understand and empathize, doesn't help much. But when avoidant people consistently received very high levels of *practical* support—offering information, suggesting concrete action, generating solutions to a problem—their defensive barriers fell.

So if a friend is avoidant, in general don't demand too much self-disclosure or intimacy and give plenty of space. But if you genuinely desire a closer, more intimate relationship with that friend, try being highly supportive in a practical way: with information, advice, and help with problem solving. Over time, that may be enough to break through their defenses and allow your friend to open up, to trust, and to share in a closer, more intimate friendship.

Unfortunately, the same high level of support does not appear to work with friends who are anxious. Even high levels of emotional or practical support, researchers found, are not enough to meet the highly anxious person's "insatiable desire for closeness and care." Indeed, anxious people are liable to interpret such care as suggesting their own incompetence, thus triggering negative views of themselves and even more resentment and defensiveness. "Despite their longing for support, highly anxious recipients often fail to appreciate or be calmed by the support," the researchers found.

For an anxious friend, the best approach is simply consistent reinforcement of your availability and commitment. But, warns Professor Reis, the highly anxious person's need for reassurance can often be "so overwhelming it essentially can't be met." Moreover, some anxious people are "so desperate to keep a relationship that over time they will come to resent that very dependency—and the relationship, too—and back away or trigger a breakup." Overlooking such periodic emotional disruptions may be another good strategy; in many cases, the rupture will be only temporary.

———————

"Gonna walk to Nick's in Georgetown to see Lucy now," Jen texted me the next afternoon.

Jen, along with friends who were visiting at her apartment, would walk to see Lucy at the restaurant. They'd take Chief too, and I was welcome to come.

The walk to Washington Harbour took us through downtown DC. At one point, when we passed an active construction site, Jen momentarily lost her balance. Loud noises, she told me, trigger an acute stress response.

At Washington Harbour we saw the restaurant but not Lucy. Jen couldn't go in with Chief, so she texted Lucy to let her know we were outside.

While we waited, Jen reached to pull down the heel of her sneaker and look at what she suspected was a blister.

Then I saw a young woman walk out of Nick's. She was about the same age and height as Jen and even from a distance I recognized, from the photo in Jen's living room, the long red hair pulled back in a bun.

"Isn't that Lucy?" I asked Jen.

"Oh my God!" she shouted. And then instead of putting her shoe back on, Jen rushed toward the restaurant, hobbling as she went.

Holding Chief by the leash, I watched as Jen hugged her best friend, pulled back a bit to smile at her, and then hugged her again.

They walked back toward us arm in arm. Jen introduced me to Lucy, and then Lucy bent down to put Jen's shoe back and retie the laces. As she did, Jen talked without a pause, catching Lucy up on whatever had happened since they last spoke. It reminded me of a child come home from school with so much to tell her mother that she doesn't stop talking even to put down her backpack.

"I wish you hadn't come with the dog," Lucy said to Jen, "so you could come in the restaurant."

"I love you," Jen said in response.

"I love you too," said Lucy.

They hugged again, and Jen laid her head on Lucy's shoulder. Then Jen spun around so she and Lucy were back-to-back, and she linked their arms together. Lucy didn't seem surprised by the move. I imagined it might have been something they did for fun when they were younger.

"Hey, so who's Sassy and who's Classy?" I asked them.

"I'm definitely Classy," said Lucy.

"So when do I get to see you?" Jen asked Lucy, meaning for more than a brief chat outside the restaurant. Lucy agreed to join Jen and her other friends that evening. In the meantime, Jen's friends would watch Chief so Jen could go inside with Lucy.

And that's where I left them: walking together into the restaurant, Lucy holding Jen by the arm, steadying her.

Jen and Lucy's close friendship fulfilled—particularly for Jen in her challenging circumstances—essential attachment needs: a safe haven and close, even if not constant, proximity. When thinking of our own close friendships, we might ask ourselves: does our friend have some attachment needs that we might be uniquely able to fulfill?

CHAPTER 9

Getting Old:
Attachment and Aging

At seven on Sunday morning, the phone rang.

"Peter, it's Dora"—Dora was an aide who helped care for my father. "Come right over. I'm calling 911."

I was dressed and out the door in minutes. I figured we were going to the hospital.

At my dad's apartment, Dora walked toward me, shaking her head.

"He's gone," she said. When she'd arrived that morning, she told me, she'd found him on the bedroom floor.

I went in to have a look.

It's startling to see your father, even at ninety-six, dead. That thing you feared from when you first understood that someday your parents would die, now has happened, and all at once you know the end of the story—both the when and the where.

On the carpet, Dad lay, in beige pajamas, on his left side, facing the king-size bed where he'd slept alone for the six years since my mother died. A gash marked his forehead. I supposed during the night he'd gotten up to use the bathroom, had a heart attack, and fell against the glass-topped night table. Or, as the medical examiner later suggested, he may have had the heart attack in his sleep, then woke feeling ill, tried to get up, and fell.

I didn't expect that my father would die while I was working on this book, but so it happened. Looking back, I can see how his death and the period leading up to it illustrate many of the ways in which attachment style influences people as they age. This is because aging, and the illnesses that accompany age, threatens our well-being—indeed, our existence—and thus activates the attachment system.

As in so many other situations, people with attachment security tend to handle these threats and stresses better than those with insecure attachment. If there's a lesson here, it may be that when, as parents, we care for a newborn we might keep in mind that we are also caring for the older adult that he or she will ultimately become.

Retirement and Life Transitions

On a summer day in 1985, my father sold his commercial printing business. He was sixty-nine years old. He and his brother had started Great Lakes Press in their early twenties, in the depth of the Great Depression. By the time of the sale, the firm occupied several city blocks and employed more than four hundred people. The deal for the sale was a good one—the buyer paid all cash—but the sale would mean my dad's immediate retirement. I was curious how he'd handle that sudden change in status.

How people handle major life transitions, especially those that involve status and self-definition, is influenced by attachment style. In a study of older adults who had recently lost their jobs or had become empty nesters, those with secure attachments showed "greater coping efforts" and "less of a drop in well-being" than those with insecure attachments. This would be consistent with other studies showing that attachment security contributes to self-confidence, optimism, and trust in the future.

Interestingly, researchers have found that the percentage of older adults with insecure attachment changes with advancing age. Anxious attachment styles, for example, appear to decrease with age. This may be because some adults gradually become more secure due to the stabilizing effects of a long-term marriage, the experience of parenting, or other healthy long-term relationships over the course of their lives.

At the same time, however, avoidant attachment styles appear to increase with age. The deaths of so many friends and loved ones, researchers speculate, may gradually cause some older adults to lose their tolerance, or even desire, for relationships. If true, this might account for the stereotypical view of the curmudgeonly elder. See, for example, the *Seinfeld* episode "The Old Man," where Jerry is paired, through the Foster-a-Grandpa program, with old, crotchety Sid Fields, played by the late Bill Erwin. Jerry visits Sid at his apartment and says warmly, "I'm here to spend some time with you. Want to get a cup of coffee?" Sid yells back, "With you? I'd rather be dead. Now get the hell out of my house!" A very different explanation, however, is offered by Stanford psychologist (and my high school classmate) Laura L. Carstensen. Her well-accepted "socioemotional selectivity theory" suggests that as we age, we shed superficial relationships to focus on the important ones, so our interactions with others may become less frequent but emotionally richer. This approach strongly undercuts the Sid Fields stereotype.

I can't know for sure what my father's attachment style was, but many aspects of his life are consistent with a secure attachment: he had a stable sixty-six-year marriage; solid relations with his two brothers, with whom he was also in business; and an abundance of enduring friendships, many stretching back to childhood. As a youngster, he appears to have been resilient, with a positive attitude. For example, he once recalled enjoying starting kindergarten at age four, happy to spend all day with the teachers, while other kids cried and cried.

My dad also showed steady nerves throughout his life. I don't believe, even when challenged by business or family problems, he ever missed a night's sleep. In fact, being a good sleeper as we age can also be an indicator of attachment security. In a 2009 study, for example, researchers found that older adults with secure attachments had less difficulty falling asleep than those who were insecure. In contrast, those who were anxiously attached, perhaps due to "preoccupation with daily

Being a good sleeper as we age can also be an indicator of attachment security.

challenges," had more trouble getting to sleep, took more naps, and relied more on sleeping medication.

As possible further evidence of attachment security, throughout his life my dad seemed to accept whatever situation he was in and to trust in his own ability to cope. After my mother's funeral, for example, when I asked how he'd handle living in the apartment alone, he said, "What are my choices? This is the hand I've been dealt. I have to play it the best I can."

If my dad's attachment style was indeed secure, it would help explain how he handled the sudden transition to retirement so well. With his two older brothers, he took the proceeds from the sale and rented an office in a suburban office park. There, in what became a sort of clubhouse, the three of them—who as kids had grown up poor, sharing a bed—kept each other company, discussed the political and financial news of the day, and lunched with friends.

Health and Wellness

One morning nearly twenty years after his retirement, by accident I saw my dad in his cardio fitness class, to which he dutifully went three days a week. I'd come on an errand to the community center, and someone had left the door to the fitness room open. I couldn't recall the last time I'd seen my dad in shorts and a T-shirt. He wore an elastic bandage on his left knee—it had given him trouble since his youth and caused the army to reject him during World War II. Yet there he was, with a dozen other seniors, doing arm circles and high stepping in time to a disco beat and loud calls from a young female instructor.

That my dad had that discipline, not only to exercise, but also to watch his diet and otherwise take care of his health is another behavior influenced by attachment. People with secure attachments, studies show, are better at what researchers call "self-regulatory processes"— that is, the disciplines essential to healthy aging: staying physically active, following a good diet, keeping medical appointments and taking prescribed medications, and avoiding risks such as smoking, drinking, and drug abuse.

Insecure attachment, on the other hand, may interfere with these same behaviors. In studies, for example, older people with avoidant attachments made fewer needed health care visits; those with anxious attachments, while claiming their intent to lose weight, failed to take the necessary steps to do so.

Another part of healthy aging is maintaining a strong social network—it can even contribute to longevity. In a ten-year study of older Australians, for example, those who were able to foster and maintain a network of supportive friends lived longer than those who did not. And, here again, those with attachment security, who studies show are more outgoing and accepting of others, tend to be better at finding and nurturing a network of friends.

In my dad's case, when he was in business he worked mostly in sales, and he attributed his success to the relationships he built with his customers, many of whom he counted as friends. He took friendship seriously. "To have a friend, you have to be a friend" was among his favorite aphorisms. In retirement, he continued those relationships, inviting former customers and employees for golf and lunch, making sick visits to friends and attending their funerals and those of their family members, and receiving their phone calls and visits when he himself began to decline.

Older adults who are avoidant report fewer social exchanges, less effort to seek emotional support, and overall have a lower quality of close relationships. Those who are anxious show less emotional stability and higher rates of depression, both traits that may challenge the ability to maintain a supportive social network.

———

If older people whom we care about don't have secure attachments, how can we help them form and maintain social networks? Here are two initial ideas:

For someone with an avoidant attachment—a bit of *Seinfeld*'s Sid Fields, say—we could help them get started playing an online game, such as Words with Friends, with former friends or colleagues—an activity that offers social contact but with distance and some competitiveness built in.

For an anxiously attached person, we could access, through a community center or an apartment building's Listserv, a weekly card game where residents are looking for an extra player—an activity that offers close, face-to-face contact with the built-in security of repeated visits. There could be a hundred variations on these ideas; it just may take a little sustained effort and creativity—and it helps to have the insight of seeing the individual through the lens of attachment style.

Illness

Eventually, my father grew weaker and began falling—at the fitness center, at restaurants, and at home—often sustaining cuts and bruises to his arms and face. One night he was dizzy. My sister and I took him to the hospital. There an MRI showed he was bleeding internally and had become anemic from a colon tumor that soon was found to be cancerous.

Doctors said he had only a few months left and advised hospice care. But a young colorectal surgeon we consulted believed Dad was a candidate for surgery. Though he'd never operated on anyone so old— my father was by then ninety-five—he thought, given Dad's general strength, he'd have a good chance of surviving the procedure. In light of his age, however, there was also the chance he would not survive or that he would come through with his mental state impaired.

My sister and I presented our father with the two choices: hospice or surgery. Without hesitation, he chose surgery; he was confident it would succeed.

Illness is one of those events—like injury and distress—that threatens our well-being and therefore activates the attachment system. In other words, how we react to illness is colored by attachment style.

How we react to illness is colored by attachment style.

When ill, people who are avoidant may initially resist medical care, deny or downplay the illness, or try to deal with it on their own. On a more positive note, however, they may also resist the overtesting that can sometimes lead to overtreatment for conditions that might otherwise pose little or no risk.

Those who are anxious, on the other hand, may catastrophize—that is, assume the worst about their illness and become consumed with thoughts of the worst possible outcome. But, more positively, they are also more likely to aggressively seek care and therefore to detect disease, such as cancer, at an early, treatable stage.

An interesting study about how attachment style affects us during illness was done in an emergency room in Pretoria, South Africa. The aim was to measure the link between patients' attachment styles and doctors' perceptions of patients as difficult. In the study, 165 patients, ranging in age from fifteen to ninety-three, had their attachment styles assessed by the adult attachment quiz before they were treated. (As much as I like this study, if it was I in the emergency room, I'm not sure I'd be willing to take the time to fill out an attachment quiz.) Following treatment, twenty-six ER doctors were asked to rate "difficult personality traits" in the patients. The findings revealed that while doctors rated only 2 percent of patients with secure attachment as "difficult," they rated 17 percent of anxious patients and 19 percent of avoidant patients as difficult. Patients with avoidant attachment, note researchers, may have a communication style that "underemphasizes distress" and so may interfere with the patient's ability to convey accurate information about their medical problem. And patients with high attachment anxiety "may be difficult to reassure and may be perceived to require an excessive amount of contact and attention."

I don't recall my dad, even when facing cancer, ever catastrophizing. I went with him to many doctor appointments and don't recall him interacting with doctors in any way that could be construed as difficult.

Indeed, the night before his cancer surgery, the surgeon visited my dad in his hospital room. My sister and I were there too. The doctor explained the procedure and then invited my dad to sign the consent form. His signature looked as it always had: strong and with no trace of an elderly person's tremor.

The surgeon then asked if Dad had any questions.

An avoidant patient might have been stoically silent or questioned the need for care at all. A patient with anxious attachment might have burdened the doctor with expressions of neediness and fear. Instead, our secure dad used those last available moments to give the forty-something doctor a sort of pep talk, in effect recruiting him as a member of his optimistic, can-do team.

"Now, look," said Dad, handing the consent form back to the surgeon, "I want your best job tomorrow. Understand? I want your best work."

"Of course," the doctor said.

"No 'good enough' job," said Dad. "I want your best. A-plus."

Dad, lying in the bed in his hospital gown, clapped his hands for emphasis. "Of course," said the doctor again, smiling.

"You can do that for me? A-plus? I don't want any A-minus or B work!"

"You'll get my best," the doctor—evidently charmed—assured him.

The next morning, when they came to take my father to the OR, I leaned over and kissed his cheek. He'd been in the hospital several days by then and had not shaved. I felt the stubble of his beard and reveled in the remembered pleasure of that tactile closeness when he carried me piggyback up to bed, as a boy, and I would lean my cheek against his. I didn't know if I'd ever see him again. I hoped the surgeon would do an A-plus job.

Receiving Care and Role Reversals

"Mr. Lovenheim, welcome back!" called the doorman, holding the apartment building's front door open wide so my sister could push our father, in his wheelchair, inside.

In the six weeks since his surgery—three in the hospital and three in rehab—he'd recovered well, but we didn't know how long he might live. The doctors were prescribing no follow-up treatment for the cancer, he still had heart disease, and tests before the surgery had revealed an aortic aneurysm that, as his cardiologist put it, could "pop" at any time. "He could die fairly quickly," the doctor warned, "and it's actually not a bad way to go."

"So how does it feel to be home, Dad?" I asked, as we wheeled him into the apartment.

"Feels like heaven," he said. "You have no idea."

I asked, "You ever wonder if you'd get back here?"

"No," he said, coughing, "it never entered my mind. My only question was when."

He coughed some more, and then yawned.

"I've been up since five thirty this morning," he said. "I took a shit-load of pills. They over-pill you there."

Dad normally took fifteen pills a day; it was hard to imagine how many more they'd given him in rehab.

By early evening he was ready to sleep. An aide we'd hired readied him for bed. I kissed him good night, felt again the roughness of his cheek, and was deeply grateful he'd made it home.

———

Dependency, whether on family members or aides, can be a challenge for the older adult. "In later life, after decades of successful autonomy, encroaching dependency can seem a cruel denouement," write psychologist Carol Magai and colleagues.

Older adults who are secure tend to be good at recognizing their need for care, accepting it when offered, and trusting in the goodwill and competence of their caregivers. But avoidant individuals may deny their distress, insist they can take care of themselves, and therefore be less likely to receive care at all. One of my dad's aides recalled caring for an elderly man who all his life was independent. "'I can do it myself!' he'd say. He'd get frustrated that he needed help. He'd get angry and yell at us: 'Leave me alone! I can do this myself!' The danger there," she said, "is that the aides take it personally and get upset." Anxious individuals, on the other hand, while accepting the need for help, may jeopardize their care by being too needy. They may be "too eager to receive care and their potential caregivers may be put off by their sheer neediness, emotional intensity, and persistence," causing the caregivers to distance themselves, which in turn can generate even more insecurity.

My dad, home from rehab and with in-home care most of each day, appeared neither to deny his distress nor to display "neediness," but to accept help graciously. In this, he once again seems to have been aided by his attachment security. But my father's situation also involved another attachment issue, because not only were the aides helping care for him, so were my siblings and I.

Even before Dad had returned from rehab, my brother and sister and I had assumed a more active role in his care. We visited daily, went with him to doctor appointments, helped with the food shopping and bill paying, and more. In short, we each became his caregivers, and in this we—and he—experienced the common reversal of roles where middle-aged adults become caregivers to their parents. Research suggests that how the adult child handles this responsibility and how the parent receives the care are influenced by both the child's and the parent's attachment styles. "The quality of the child-parent bond . . . may well affect the kind of care aged parents received from their children," note researchers.

Adult children with a secure attachment will generally accept the responsibility of caring for their aged parents and feel prepared to provide care, approaching the task with empathy and diligence. But what of the nearly 50 percent of adult children who came out of early child-hood with insecure attachment due, at least in part, to the same parent who now requires care?

Avoidant adult children may show less sensitivity to a parent's dis-tress, while anxious adult children may feel unsure of their ability to provide care, be focused on their own needs, and thus shy away from the responsibility. However, researchers note, if the anxious adult is experiencing stress in his or her own life (e.g., child-rearing, job diffi-culties, divorce) and still relying on the parent as an attachment figure for emotional support, he or she will have a powerful incentive to pre-serve the well-being of that parent and so "rise to the occasion" to pro-vide the needed care.

And on a hopeful note, where there remain unresolved conflicts in the relationship between a grown child and aged parent, the parent-child role reversal can of-fer a last opportunity to heal old wounds. And that's what hap-pened with my dad and me.

The parent-child role reversal can offer a last opportunity to heal old wounds.

I wrote earlier (see chapters 1 and 2) about the mixed relationship I had with my dad when I was little. I noted he was my primary attach-ment figure—caregiver and nurturer—but also that at times he could be harsh, even scary. That tension had created some rough spots in our re-lationship that had never quite gone away. But in those last months when I helped as his caregiver, we had lots of time together. Sometimes we talked; sometimes we read; sometimes we just sat quietly together. The rough spots were not magically erased, but we were able to drop our guards and simply be together. One night I dreamed I was sitting with my dad and said to him, "I'm really liking this time together." It was a direct emotional statement that we were not accustomed to saying to each other, and I wondered if I could actually say it to him. So the next day at his apartment, I sat across from him, looked him in the eye, and said, "Dad, I'm really liking this time together." And in a tone more gentle than he typically used, he looked at me and said, "I'm liking it too."

Death Anxiety

How people cope with the approach of death—sometimes called "death anxiety"—varies according to attachment style. Anxious people tend to experience heightened fear, viewing death as yet another instance of being abandoned or forgotten. Avoidant people, in contrast, tend to suppress concerns about death. At an unconscious level, however, they may fear death for the loss of perceived control.

People with secure attachments, on the other hand, seem to approach death as they do much of the rest of life, by accepting it and making the best of it. As researchers Mikulincer and Shaver write:

> Even when faced with their biological finitude, securely attached people maintain felt security. They pursue the primary attachment strategy (seeking proximity to others); they heighten their sense of social connectedness and symbolically transform the threat of death into an opportunity to contribute to others and to grow personally.

In short, in the face of inevitable death, secure people double down on relationships.

And that's what I saw my father do. In his last months, having lost so many people in his life, he built new relationships with the only new people he did have: his aides. He learned about their families, lent them books from his library and later discussed those books with them, advised one who was hoping to start her own business, and helped arrange a job for another's son.

Secure as I believe he was, though, Dad was not immune to one attachment strategy seen among older adults. As we age and lose attachment figures—parents, spouses, siblings, close friends—one common response is to internalize the deceased loved ones as "symbolic" attachment figures. "People of all ages, but especially older adults, can rely on symbolic figures to serve attachment functions," note researchers Shaver and Mikulincer. Married adults, for example, who lose a spouse often continue to experience the spouse's symbolic presence and to "consult mentally with the spouse about important life decisions." For those of faith, an alternative is to internalize an attachment relationship with God or another deity who may be seen as a perfect safe haven and secure base: always nearby, always watching over one. (For more on religion and attachment, see chapter 13.) In this way, internalized attachment figures often become an important part of older people's social support system. Indeed, many older adults may "have a relatively high ratio of symbolic and internalized to real (i.e., living, human) attachment figures."

In this, my father was no exception. By his nineties, he had lost his wife, both brothers, and scores of lifelong friends. "The ranks have thinned," he told me. "Most people I ever knew are dead."

"I think about my mother often," he said, and he'd often refer to my sister as Mother—which is what he'd call our mother in our presence.

But as far as general death anxiety, Dad seemed at peace.

He often sat quietly, and once I asked him what he thought about.

Mostly about the past, he said. "The future isn't there, so you live a lot in the past. Most of it I can't do much about. I can't change things; they're already past."

What parts of the past did he think about?

"All of it," he said. "I think of times I was a kid in school. Of my life in business. I think of my brothers, how we stuck together, how we took care of one another. I have no regrets. I don't have any enemies; I'm not mad at anybody. I'm at peace."

Was he grateful?

"Yes, that's a good way to put it," he said.

My father even knew how he wanted to die. After his death, an aide told me, "I asked your dad once, 'Don't you want someone here overnight in case you fall or don't feel well?' But he said no, he wanted to be alone and hoped he would die at night by himself. He went just as he wanted to go."

Part III

———

Attachment All Around Us

CHAPTER 10

Securing a Position: Attachment in the Workplace

Pleasant Pops sits on a corner in a gentrified neighborhood in northwest Washington, DC, and while from time to time you might see an older customer—a senator or Supreme Court justice, for example—the regulars are mostly young professionals. One sunny morning in March, half a dozen customers—some carrying both briefcases and yoga mats—stood at the counter waiting to order coffee.

The two young men working as baristas that morning had arrived at seven to unlock the store. They'd removed chairs stacked upside down on tables the night before. They opened five-pound bags of Colombian coffee. They welcomed suppliers delivering coffee lids, paper towels, milk and eggs, and mini baguettes. They powered up the Italian-made espresso machine, set a bowl of water on the sidewalk for customers' dogs, turned on the electronic credit card reader, and at seven-thirty sharp, with sunlight streaming in through eastern-facing windows, turned on music and flipped the wooden sign on the front door to OPEN.

How attachment theory operates in the workplace is straightforward: work is a relational activity. Depending on the job and the type of workplace, most people at work are constantly involved in relationships: with colleagues, with managers, with customers. And given that attachment style influences behavior in relationships, research shows that many aspects of work will be affected by individual differences in attachment style. Thus, how we relate to others at work, how satisfying we find work, how we deal with job stress, whether we stay at a job or quit—indeed, how we choose a career path in the first place—all reflect our personal attachment style. And it doesn't matter if an organization is big or small: the influences of attachment are the same.

As a place to observe how attachment theory applies to work, Pleasant Pops seemed ideal. It was a business where people worked in close proximity to each other, to managers, and to customers. Moreover, founders and owners Roger Horowitz and Brian Sykora had generously agreed to give me complete access to the premises, including to their employees and themselves.

But what I didn't know until I had spent a good deal of time there was that Pleasant Pops would almost perfectly illustrate a recent discovery about a secret to business success: that *insecure* employees—those with avoidant or anxious attachment—not only contribute unique skills to a work team, but working together with secure employees can, under the right conditions, actually produce superior results.

Career Choice

Behind the café's kitchen, in a tiny office—really just a few plastic chairs and a table pushed against a wall—sat owners Roger and Brian. Both appeared uncomfortable, and not only because Roger at six foot one and Brian at six foot five were too tall for the chairs; they just seemed to have too much energy to sit still. They both wore zip-up sweatshirts and sneakers, adding to their boyish looks.

They'd become friends while rowing crew at the University of North Carolina. After graduation, both ended up in DC, and one day Brian e-mailed Roger: "There are a couple of empty storefronts in my neighborhood. We could sell something."

Roger, having grown up in Westchester County, outside New York City, recalled seeing Mexican-owned *paleterías*—small cafés selling ice pops, tortillas, and snacks. "They were mostly run by grandmothers, not young white guys," Roger told me. "But there wasn't anyone doing it in DC."

Neither Roger nor Brian had culinary experience, but they conceived the idea of using fresh, local ingredients to appeal to a young, health-conscious market. They began by selling handmade ice pops from a pushcart at local farmer's markets—and named their fledgling enterprise Pleasant Pops after the Mount Pleasant neighborhood where the farm market was located. Later, they took the plunge and leased a store. "We used money I'd saved for graduate school," said Roger, "plus we raised some on Kickstarter, and finally Brian and I signed personally on a quarter-million-dollar loan."

All that had happened just a few years ago. By the time of my visit, Pleasant Pops had expanded its menu to include upscale coffees, salads, and sandwiches. They were grossing a million dollars a year, employed more than a dozen people, and recently had leased space for a second location just a block from the White House. And that March morning they were in the grip of Pop Madness, the store's clever takeoff on college basketball's March Madness, where customers vote for their favorite all-natural ice pop by placing used pop sticks in one of two boxes near the front counter. Strawberry ginger lemonade was the favorite to win.

Sitting in Pleasant Pops' makeshift office, I wondered what allows two young people like Roger and Brian to move to an unfamiliar city, perceive a market opportunity, and risk their time and money by committing to a career in a field in which they have no background. What factors allow for that willingness both to risk and to commit?

One of those factors, it turns out, is attachment style.

A secure attachment, noted John Bowlby, permits a child to explore. And for adults, work can be understood as a form of exploration (or "functionally parallel" to exploration, as one researcher has put it).

In talking with Brian, I was struck by how his words echoed the idea of one's career being an adult form of exploration: "I get bored easily but want to pursue my interests," he told me, "even if it's not clear what the long term is. We had no idea where Pleasant Pops was going to take us, but figured there was no harm in trying to see where it might go."

Researchers note a strong link between attachment security and career exploration and commitment. In a longitudinal study, men and women whose attachment style had been measured at age one were interviewed at age eighteen about their career planning. Researchers found a "clear and statistically significant" relationship between attachment security in infancy and later ability to effectively explore career opportunities. In another study, adolescents who were more secure made more realistic career choices that coincided with their abilities.

In contrast, indecisiveness and confusion about choosing a career or "premature commitment to a career without sufficient exploration" are all associated with insecure attachment.

So was it secure attachments that had allowed both Roger and Brian to make such a bold commitment to starting Pleasant Pops? At my invitation, they both took the online version of the Experiences in Close Relationships quiz (see the appendix) in private and shared with me only the final scoring. Both scored exceptionally low on the scales for avoidance and anxiety, placing them solidly within the secure range.

The Secure Manager

At 10:00 a.m. Pleasant Pops' general manager, Hannah Smith, joined Roger and Brian for their weekly meeting to review operations. Twenty-five-year-old Hannah sat with perfect posture in an office chair across from Roger and Brian.

They reviewed routine issues: one employee leaving, a kitchen worker out ill, construction delays at the new store, some customer complaints about a shortage of organic bottled milk.

Of the milk shortage, Hannah said the employee responsible had failed to order enough. "But I think he just miscalculated," she said. "I'll meet with him later today."

At that moment, an employee rushed in from the kitchen.

"Health inspector's here!" he shouted.

An hour later, Roger returned to the back office. They'd passed inspection, but the inspector found that a refrigerator out front wasn't cold enough. They'd have to hire a technician to come fix it.

It wasn't noon yet, but already Roger and Brian had been hit with multiple stressors: an employee giving notice, another calling in sick, a third failing to order enough product, construction at the new store delayed, a surprise health inspection—and now a key piece of equipment needed costly and immediate repair.

And yet neither Roger nor Brian had panicked or complained. They'd done the grunt work of moving boxes during the inspection and been respectful and cooperative with the inspector. In short, in front of their employees they'd shown themselves to be confident and skillful managers. In a phrase used by attachment researchers, they'd adopted the role of "stronger and wiser" leader, a management skill that typically reflects a secure attachment and can inspire in employees themselves a sense of "courage and dedication."

But what might it have looked like if Roger and Brian were not secure? Insecure managers, particularly anxious ones, researchers have noted, may belittle others when under stress, causing "anger, disorganization, dishonesty, and despair." Roger and Brian might have panicked at the surprise inspection. Instead of quickly and calmly taking care of things and answering the inspector's questions, they might have questioned the inspector's competence or motives or tried to shift blame to their own kitchen staff. Roger might have called the refrigerator manufacturer to complain about the breakdown, rather than quickly scheduling the repair. And earlier, when told an employee had failed to order enough milk, they might not have assumed it was "just a miscalculation" as Hannah, their general manager, had—she also scored secure on the attachment quiz—but instead labeled the employee a slacker and taken disciplinary measures. Haven't we all known bosses like that?

Instead, they did none of these things and calmly took care of the problems—exactly the kind of response to business stressors we'd expect to see in managers with secure attachment.

Employees and Attachment Style

In the month I spent observing at Pleasant Pops, I got to know many of the employees. Among them were three full-timers who'd been there for years. They'd each had a difficult time plotting a career path and had come to Pleasant Pops when the need for work—almost any work—was crucial to them both economically and emotionally. And yet they'd all become skilled at tasks vital to the business.

"I'm an anxious person," one told me. Now a barista, he'd come to Pleasant Pops after losing his security clearance at a defense contractor. "I'm mostly happy but very vulnerable," he said. "There are days when what I really want to do is to stay alone in my room and write bad poetry." Another had found her way to Pleasant Pops after a bad breakup. "I was devastated and came to DC to make a fresh start," she told me. She now handles promotions and public relations. Finally, there was the "senior statesman" of the group: a man of thirty-three who'd earned a law degree but discovered he had no interest in practicing law. Teaching hadn't worked out either. "I had to do something or I'd fall apart," he told me. A chance meeting with Roger resulted in his being hired at first to sell ice pops at farmer's markets and later to become a barista.

I didn't ask them to take the attachment quiz, but in light of the career issues they had struggled with, I got the sense that each of these three probably had tendencies, like myself, toward a more insecure attachment style. And this, I learned, posed both challenges and—more interestingly—opportunities for the business.

Securely attached employees, according to many studies, function better in the workplace than their insecurely attached coworkers. They have more positive attitudes, report higher job satisfaction, are less likely to have hostile outbursts, and are less prone to both psychosomatic and actual physical illness.

Insecurely attached workers, in contrast, tend to have lower levels of job engagement, higher rates of job dissatisfaction, and more work-related distress and burnout.

Those with anxious attachment, note Mikulincer and Shaver, may see work as an additional opportunity to be accepted socially but also as a potential source of disapproval and rejection. They are more likely to feel unappreciated and misunderstood and to report greater anxiety over rejection. As such, they can present a "social challenge" to a work team by being "clingy, needy, and fearful" and may "frequently seek the approval of other team members." In sum, anxious workers may be so preoccupied with attachment-related worries while at work that they have trouble meeting job requirements.

Workers with avoidant attachments, on the other hand, may use work "to evade social involvements." They report more job dissatisfaction, more concerns about work hours, and exhibit fewer helpful behaviors toward colleagues. Often they don't make efforts to connect with colleagues, or outright avoid them, thus causing conflict among the team.

Job retention is another issue affected by attachment style. It's important because companies with low turnover—particularly start-ups—outperform those with high turnover. Studies suggest that insecurely attached employees—both anxious and avoidant—are more likely than secure colleagues to quit when dissatisfied with their jobs. A 2013 study, for example, of 125 workers in various public organizations, found a direct relationship between attachment style and intention to voluntarily leave a job. Anxious employees may display "dysfunctional interaction patterns" with colleagues and then consider quitting, while avoidant employees may "keep themselves aloof" but then think about leaving as "frustrations and resentment" toward colleagues mount.

Could a business, when making hiring decisions, somehow screen for securely attached employees? The cost of administering the gold standard for measuring attachment style in adults, the Adult Attachment Interview, would be prohibitive for all but the biggest corporations. Alternatively, managers could give applicants the Experiences in Close Relationships quiz I had asked the Pleasant Pops managers to take online.

Insecurely attached employees bring their own unique strengths to a work team.

But as advantageous as it might seem for a business to hire only secure employees, new research suggests that even if a company could screen for secure attachment, it would be a mistake to do so. This is because insecurely attached employees bring their own unique strengths to a work team.

Sentinels and Rapid Responders

People high in attachment anxiety, explains Israeli researcher Tsachi Ein-Dor, are especially sensitive to threats and therefore can function as a kind of early warning system—what he calls "sentinel" behavior. In a clever study, Ein-Dor and colleagues exposed test subjects to what appeared to be a threatening situation (a room gradually filling with smoke because of a supposedly malfunctioning computer). Those who were the most anxiously attached were the first to detect the threat.

Moreover, in a companion study, Ein-Dor also found the anxious "sentinels" to be the most diligent about delivering a warning message. In this study, he led test subjects to believe they had accidently activated a computer virus that erased an experimenter's computer. On their way to alert the department's computer technicians about the incident, they were presented with four decision points where they could choose either to delay their warning or to continue directly to the technicians' office. Again, those rated highest on attachment anxiety proved less willing to be delayed on their way to deliver the message. In yet another study, Ein-Dor found that anxious individuals were the most successful poker players—because they were best at detecting deceit, such as when other players bluffed.

In sum, these studies demonstrate that anxious individuals can benefit a group and contribute to its success. They do this by being vigilant to problems and threats, and reliably warning the whole group.

At the same time, workers with avoidant attachments also have an important role to play. In the experiment with an apparent fire emanating from a shared computer, those with avoidant attachments were the first to find a safe way out of the room. Avoidant people, accustomed to taking care of themselves, may in times of danger act promptly and effectively to find the best escape route from a threatening situation. Ein-Dor calls this "rapid response" behavior. Put another way, "When quick and/or focused action is required, when time is a factor, or when fearless deeds are needed," avoidant individuals may be the quickest to act.

So both anxious employees (sentinels) and avoidant employees (rapid responders) potentially bring valuable traits to a group. But "potentially" is the key word. The studies also show it is only within the security of a cohesive group—one with trust, acceptance, and comfort among team members—that employees with attachment insecurity are able to express their unique skills.

Creating a cohesive group involves, in the words of one researcher, creating an "island of security" by responding to employees' needs for security and protection. For anxious employees, managers can make sure they know they are accepted and valued as part of the team. For avoidant employees, managers can assign them roles that allow for maximum time to work independently. For both groups, managers can be alert to conflicts and help resolve disputes quickly before tensions escalate.

And that, it appeared to me, is what Pleasant Pops' trio of securely attached managers—Roger, Brian, and Hannah—had done. In their start-up café, they had created a true "island of security" for their key employees. I saw it consistently: in the encouragement they gave staff in facing both work-related and personal challenges, in the sensitivity they showed toward the unsettled nature of their young employees' lives, in the way they dealt with employee errors by assuming good intentions and not humiliating anyone. I saw it at the late-evening staff meeting when everyone was expected to help clean the store: it was Roger who climbed the ladder to dust light fixtures and Brian who got on his knees to clean the toilet in the customer bathroom.

Brian may have expressed it best when he explained to me his approach to management: "Roger and I can take the financial risk and be creative," he said, "but then that opens opportunities for the staff to be creative too, and without the financial pressure. Our goal has been to bring on smart people and give them support so they can succeed. It's empowering when we can do that. *Not* doing that—having the attitude that only we are the decision makers—that's what holds a lot of small operations down."

But the real proof is in what the employees themselves told me over the weeks I interviewed them:

"The reason why I'm still here [after two years] at Pleasant Pops is its culture of community," a barista told me. "You spend forty hours a week with these people. If there are problems, you talk it out. I'm sensitive and I like to have trust. I've gone from 'It's just a job' to 'These people are my friends and I have personal relationships with them.'"

"I moved here by default after a breakup," another told me, "but I've built myself up. Pleasant Pops and the people here have been a part of that. From the first day I felt my ideas and opinions were listened to. Hannah, Brian, and Roger always are open to suggestions and to empowering us."

"These guys did something at a pretty young age," another barista said admiringly, speaking of Roger and Brian's founding of Pleasant Pops. "I'm honestly happy to be a part of it." He also noted how few disputes occurred at work. "This particular group tends to be very conflict averse," he said.

The Best Functioning Teams

The research showing that anxious and avoidant employees have unique skills to offer at work would be significant enough, but a groundbreaking study by Shiri Lavy and colleagues takes that information an important step further.

At an Israeli university, researchers assigned fifty-two student work teams to complete an academic project. Each team had from three to five members representing a variety of attachment styles. When the work was completed and the results assessed, the surprising finding was that the most successful teams were not the ones with the most secure members but rather those that had a mix of attachment types: some secure, some avoidant, and some anxious.

These findings, say the researchers, provide the first evidence of a "significant contribution" of diversity of attachment styles to work-team performance and a "new perspective on the strengths and contributions of individuals" with insecure attachments. "Although insecure attachment patterns may yield undesirable outcomes for individuals," they note, "having individuals with diverse attachment patterns in a group . . . may be beneficial at the group level," enriching the team and improving team functioning. For managers looking to maximize results, they advise, "it may prove beneficial to include individuals with diverse attachment orientations on each team."

As in the earlier study, these results require a cohesive, supportive environment where workers feel "safe, accepted, and trusted."

So a key to business success may be—far from screening for only secure employees—to create a cohesive work environment where these diverse attachment types can thrive and together produce superior results.

I believe this is what the management team at Pleasant Pops had done. In a sense, the business itself had become an attachment figure providing for its employees a safe haven and secure base. In the process, the shop had flourished—exactly the function of effective, secure management.

And none of them knew it then, but before the year was out Pleasant Pops would enjoy—perhaps due to its success—some special recognition. Stopping in for an ice pop on a weekend afternoon, and with very little notice, would be the president of the United States. The occasion was Small Business Saturday, when the president visited a couple of local businesses. President Obama and daughters Sasha and Malia came to Pleasant Pops—ironically, not to the new store near the White House but to the original one. Dressed in jeans and fall jackets, they stared above the counter at the handwritten menu. After some hesitation, Malia ordered cookies and cream, and Sasha chose cranberry apple. To Obama's question about what was popular, an employee mentioned strawberry ginger lemonade. "You can't go wrong with that one," he advised. The tab was nine dollars. The president paid in cash and slipped a couple of bills into the tip jar.

———

Later that evening, the barista on duty swept behind the counter, wiped down tables, and stacked chairs upside down. Roger wheeled a trash barrel out the front door and down half a block to a trash room shared by local businesses. The night was cool and clear. Across the street, a red neon sign advertised ACE Cash Express, an all-night check-cashing service, a vestige of this trendy neighborhood before it gentrified.

At 10:00 p.m. Roger shut off the music and the lights, and flipped the wooden sign on the front door to CLOSED. Wishing the employees good night, he headed home.

CHAPTER 11

*Before the Buzzer: Attachment
and Sports*

The game that Sunday evening would begin in less than a minute. Players on both teams were on the court, warming up, chucking the ball toward the basket from twenty or thirty feet away. It was an impressive group of young guys: all under thirty, all with professional, DC-type jobs. Tommy worked for Homeland Security, monitoring foreign cables for nuclear threats. Todd and Dave both worked for military contractors. Jamiere was deputy finance director of a statewide political party. Marshall managed congressional campaigns. Of seven team members, four held security clearances, which meant they had access to highly classified material.

All of which meant nothing on the basketball court. What mattered there was whether they could run, dribble, pass, and put the ball in the basket.

So far, they mostly couldn't.

Going into tonight's game, they had two wins and three losses, but one of the wins was because the other team hadn't shown up.

———

These players were nice enough to let me stand with them at courtside and interview them between games, to examine the influence of attachment style on how people play sports. As I began getting to know the guys and rooting for them, I found I would also have liked to advise them about how they could improve their game: sport psychologists and a few forward-thinking coaches were starting to use attachment

175

theory to help their teams in ways that could make the difference between a losing season and a winning one.

But I wasn't their coach—none of the teams had coaches—and I didn't want to give unsolicited advice. Plus, they were all better athletes than I'd ever been. My athletic career had gone no further than high school junior varsity basketball—and even then I mostly rode the bench.

Athletes and Their Attachment Styles

In sports, players strive to achieve. They must take risks. They must cope with the pressure and stress of competition. As such, sports can be seen as an adult form of exploration, and an athlete's performance therefore will be influenced by attachment style and his or her ability to emotionally regulate in the face of the challenges presented by competitive sports. Moreover, sport is a relational activity: athletes are in constant relationship with teammates and coaches. How athletes navigate those relationships will also be influenced by attachment style—that is, by the "mental models" of relationship they formed in early childhood. Early attachment experiences, notes University of Washington psychologist Kelly A. Forrest, may help explain why some athletes are better at both handling the stress of competition and achieving high performance.

This understanding of attachment's influence on sports performance, however, has only recently begun to move from academia to the playing field, and for some reason more in England than in other countries. Not surprisingly, younger coaches and sports psychologists are leading the way.

One is Elliott Newell, sport and exercise scientist with the Manchester-based English Institute of Sport. "I use attachment theory to broadly understand how the athlete perceives trust and security in relationships and environments," says Newell, thirty-one, who holds a master's degree in sport and exercise psychology. Working with forty athletes and six coaches from the development squad of the British

Canoeing team, Newell and colleagues determined athletes' attachment styles based on interviews and "observable behaviors." They then created development plans that accounted for each athlete's specific attachment needs.

Attachment-theory-based practice is growing in popularity in the UK, Newell says, including for Olympic sports (both summer and winter) and with a range of professional sports clubs, including rugby, football, and English cricket.

Keeping Fit

The referee blew the starting whistle.

Games were three-on-three: three players from each team on the court at a time. Our center, Josh, won the jump and tipped the ball to Todd, who drove in and scored.

From there, it was downhill.

Tommy shot from the top of the key but missed the basket altogether. Josh rebounded aggressively under the boards but missed most of his shots. Marshall brought the ball down but dribbled high, and an opposing player stole it. At three minutes, Tommy took himself out, and Dave went in. A skilled shooter, Dave hit a long three-pointer but later passed to Todd—who'd gone in for Marshall—while Todd was going the other way. An opposing player grabbed the ball and scored.

By the half, we were down 39–31.

It was clear that one problem was simply that some of our guys were out of shape. They got winded easily—and then dribbled poorly, made sloppy passes, and took themselves out to rest after just a few minutes of play.

"I thought I was going to die," one player said, speaking of the season's first game, when not enough players showed up to allow for frequent substitutions. Another player, speaking of a teammate, said, "I know him and I've never seen him do anything remotely athletic. He doesn't even work out."

All the guys had heavy work schedules, often with frequent travel, so they had their reasons for not keeping fit. But their lack of conditioning could also be related to attachment style.

"Good health begins early in life," one researcher has observed, but "poor health also begins early in life." This is because of the link between an individual's attachment style and the discipline needed to stay fit and healthy. Higher attachment security, studies suggest, predicts a range of positive health behaviors, including good eating habits, dental care, good hygiene, and exercise. Securely attached people are more likely to view themselves as worthy of care and thus to take personal responsibility for engaging in health-promoting behaviors.

And yet failure to keep fit may not be just a matter of motivation and self-worth. For those with an anxious attachment style, another factor may be the physical pain associated with rigorous exercise. Research has shown that anxious individuals have a lower tolerance of pain—they actually feel pain more acutely than those who are secure or avoidant. As a result, anxious adults may develop an aversion to exercise. On the other hand, people with avoidant attachment can get deeply into impersonal activities like working out as a way of avoiding relationships, so it's possible that some ultrafit athletes we see in the gym are avoidant.

Either way, team members' attachment styles may be an indicator of both exercise habits and degree of fitness.

Risk-Taking

During the first half of that night's game, what I saw wasn't just a few out-of-shape players, but also a couple of guys who were noticeably timid on the court. For example, one had told me how eager he'd been to join the team, but in the game he was overly cautious in handling the ball. At least twice his hesitation before passing or shooting led to the other team getting the ball. (In those moments he reminded me of my young, hesitant self on the JV team.) Describing this player, a teammate told me, "He's skittish. He's afraid to shoot, afraid of embarrassing himself."

Risk-taking is another behavior related to attachment. Secure individuals, explains British researcher Sam Carr, tend to feel free to aggressively pursue their goals unhindered by fear of failure, because they are confident in their attachment figure's support regardless of whether they succeed or fail. Anxious individuals, on the other hand, may lack faith in their attachment figure's support if they fail and may "self-protectively avoid" failure by shying away from taking too much risk.

Athletes with insecure attachment, cautions Dr. Carr, thus "may be at a psychological disadvantage."

Which player's secure attachment was helping him drive boldly toward the basket, make the daring pass, or take the risky shot? And whose insecure attachment and fear of failure was holding him back?

Team Cohesion

The second half of that night's game was a long twenty minutes. Todd and Dave both sank impressive shots from the outside, and Marshall was effective on defense. But too often we passed the ball away or missed what should have been easy shots. Meanwhile, the opposing team sank shot after shot.

With two minutes left, we were getting trounced, 59–36. I remembered that when I played JV basketball, this was the moment when my coach would put me and the other third-stringers in—when all hope was lost and we couldn't do any damage. At least we'd get a little playing time.

With a minute left, any pretense of planning or cohesion was gone; the guys were just taking set shots from near half court.

Final, sad score: 64–38.

As the guys picked up their gear and headed outside into a snowy night, one remarked, "We just gotta work out the kinks." To which another answered, "We got plenty of kinks."

And so they did. If I were sharing insights from attachment theory with the players—if I'd been the coach—I'd start by inviting them all to take the Experiences in Close Relationships quiz (see the appendix) to assess their attachment styles. I'd keep the results private, between them and me, but that information would help me plan how to work with each player, including gaining their trust and addressing whatever relational issues they might have either with me or with teammates.

I'd work with my anxiously attached players to see which part of their workouts caused the most discomfort, and prescribe other exercises, perhaps of longer duration but that cause less pain. As far as hesitancy on the court, I'd work with my anxious players to help them understand how their attachment style may be the cause of the hesitancy. Then I'd reassure them—clearly and often—that I value them regardless of whether the risks they take on the court work out or not.

———

Sports history is filled with examples both of modest teams overcoming huge odds as well as talented teams failing. The 2004 US Olympic men's basketball team is often cited as an example. Composed of many talented players—sportswriters dubbed them "the Dream Team"—in the first round of competition, they were beaten by Puerto Rico. The upset was widely attributed to an absence of "group chemistry."

Research now shows that the players' attachment styles may be a factor that affects group chemistry or cohesion. Studies suggest, for example, that attachment avoidance might cause a person to distance himself from a group and contribute less to group morale. On the other hand, attachment anxiety might lead one to seek security from a group but also to doubt one's worth as a group member. Sports teams, therefore, as close-knit groups of people who spend months together under stressful and changing conditions, are especially vulnerable to the effects of individual members' attachment styles.

In terms of cohesion, my team was challenged from the start. It was formed by two different groups of friends and work colleagues: Tommy and three of the guys knew each other from work; Todd and two others had shared an apartment. Only one player, Dave, knew at least one person in both camps. "We're basically two separate teams," Dave told me. They'd had to learn on the fly how to work together. "Half of us met each other five minutes before the first game," Tommy said. Jamiere said, "Our biggest deficit is lack of chemistry."

Between games, Marshall, the team's organizer, had been trying to get everyone together for a happy hour, but so far that hadn't happened—they were all too busy, all at the beginning of professional careers with long hours and heavy responsibility. Carving out time for basketball games—let alone happy hours—was a challenge.

Not having a coach didn't help either. Eventually, the strongest player, Josh, would emerge as a sort of player-coach, but at this point—already past midseason—the team remained leaderless. This was too bad, I thought, because a good coach could help insecure players feel supported so they might more readily meld with the team, perhaps by matching secure players with insecure players as "team buddies" to help them get to know each other and create trust within the group. A coach could also be alert for avoidant players in need of support but who, as sport and exercise scientist Elliott Newell has written, "find it hard to ask for support." (A coach could also help check avoidant players' tendency to want to do it all themselves, to be the ball handler and star all the time.) Anxious players could be given extra reassurance about their value to the team. And with a bit more encouragement, they could all go out for happy hour too.

Coach as Attachment Figure

In a 2010 NCAA basketball game between Duke and West Virginia, West Virginia's Da'Sean Butler, about halfway through the second quarter, collided under the boards with a Duke player. Butler's left leg buckled, and he fell to the floor, writhing in pain, evidently from a knee injury. On the TV broadcast, the announcer declared, "Butler is in agony."

Soon, West Virginia head coach Bob Huggins walked onto the court. Huggins, nicknamed Huggy Bear, was one of only five Division I men's coaches with seven hundred or more career victories.

On the court, Huggins, a big man in a blue sweatshirt, knelt beside his injured player. He leaned over and with his face inches above Butler's—they were nearly nose to nose—cradled Butler's head in both his arms, stroked his cheek, looked him straight in the eye, and spoke consolingly.

"That's a very powerful moment with Coach Bob Huggins," commented the announcer.

Later, I discussed that "powerful moment" with one of the country's leading attachment researchers, Jude Cassidy at the University of Maryland. She, too, was impressed with how Coach Huggins got down on the floor with his player to comfort him.

"How does he know to do that?" she asked.

I said I didn't know.

"I suspect he knows," said Dr. Cassidy, "because his mother did it to him. So for this coach providing comfort to this athlete—in attachment terms, a safe haven—is probably the natural, automatic thing to do. The script he's learned: if there's distress, then comfort."

What explains the phenomenon of so-called winning coaches—those who win at one school or with one team and then go on to another school or team and win there too? To be sure, many factors contribute, such as a deep knowledge of the game, but could one reason be that some coaches—like Bob Huggins—become attachment figures for their athletes?

In a British study, more than three hundred young athletes were asked to complete the Experiences in Close Relationships quiz modified to reflect the player-coach relationship. Results suggest, researchers Louise Davis and Sophia Jowett found, that some athletes indeed may relate to their coach in a way that fulfills the basic attachment functions: "to explore and discover important aspects of the sporting environment" (secure base); to turn to a coach "during times of stress" (safe haven); and to "seek a level of closeness with the coach" (proximity maintenance).

Or consider the finding of Norwegian researchers who interviewed elite athletes—collectively, they had won seventeen Olympic medals—about their relationships with coaches. "A high-quality coach-athlete relationship," they concluded, "appears to be similar to the fulfillment of the attachment figure properties."

For me, when I look for coaches with whom I might have had an attachment relationship, I think of only one: my ninth-grade JV basketball coach—the one who would put me in when I couldn't do much damage.

In fact, my relationship with the coach predated the JV team. His name had come up when I took the Adult Attachment Interview and had been asked about "people outside the family" with whom I had a significant relationship.

His name was Clayton "Bud" O'Dell, and when I learned he would be coaching JV basketball, I wanted to be on the team—even though I wasn't much of a player. Earlier, as my sixth-grade teacher, he'd had a tremendous influence. I sensed he understood me and saw my potential, and that made me want to do my best in class. Later, in tryouts for his basketball team, I also wanted to do my best. I heard, for example, we'd need to dribble left-handed. This I couldn't do, but an older kid told me if you taped your right hand it would force you to practice dribbling with the left. So after school I'd come home, wrap my right hand in masking tape, and for hours, on the driveway, dribble with my left. I never became good at it, but I did make the team.

That was more than fifty years ago.

Now, long retired from both teaching and coaching, Bud O'Dell, eighty-six, and his wife, Jessie, lived near Charlotte, North Carolina.

I wanted to visit my old coach because there was something I was curious about. Clearly, he'd been an attachment figure for me, and I'd responded by doing everything I could to excel as his student and play on his team. But how had he done it? How had he managed to become my attachment figure?

At the door, he looked frail. He'd had cancer and undergone chemotherapy and three surgeries. His hair had thinned, turned gray and white, and was combed forward. In both ears he wore discreet hearing aids. And he seemed shorter. He told me he was recently measured at five foot eleven. "When I played basketball, I was six foot two—somewhere I lost three inches!"

We shook hands warmly, his grip still firm.

Bud and his wife showed me in to the living room of their modest apartment. He sat in an easy chair. The day was hot, yet he wore two shirts, one over the other. "I'm usually cold because I take the blood thinner," he said.

"So do you remember me on the JV team?" I asked. "I wasn't one of the more active players."

Bud paused before answering. I remembered those long pauses, how he spoke slowly and chose each word with care.

"My recollection is that you had a very deep interest in basketball," he said. "And you had some skills."

"That's a kind way to put it," I said, both of us laughing.

He surprised me by saying he regretted not giving me more playing time and cited the school's emphasis on having winning teams. "But I'm confident that my teaching of basketball to all of you on the team was evenhanded," he added.

"I wanted each of you to learn the same skills: how to dribble, how to pass, how to shoot, how to make a layup with the right hand, how to make a layup with the left hand—"

I interrupted. "Is it true you wanted everyone to know how to dribble left-handed?"

"I did," he said. He paused. "But, to be honest, I tried myself for twenty years to dribble left-handed and was never good at it, so I was sympathetic to anyone who had trouble with it."

Oh. Maybe in trying to make the team I needn't have been so concerned about learning to dribble lefty.

Then I asked Bud about his approach to coaching and the kind of relationship he tried to foster between coach and player.

"Well, I wanted to know each player personally, to understand who they are and what they can do, how they think, what interests them, what their strengths are—"

Bud was describing exactly what I'd felt fifty years earlier—his genuine interest in understanding me as a person.

"And I wanted to understand, for each of you, if you could accept challenges, how you reacted to challenges, and if you didn't react well, what I could do to help you, because there are so many challenges every day both in a classroom and on the court. The basic point was to understand what each kid needs and to figure out how I can help the kid get it. That was the basis of my coaching, and my teaching too."

My old coach hadn't used the language of attachment, but his method was clear: a true knowledge of the player, an attuned concern for the player, and giving the player the tools needed to achieve. These were, in essence, the keys to fostering an attachment relationship between coach and player. That approach was likely one of the factors that made him such a winning coach and teacher.

Home Court Advantage?

Since the disastrous game I'd watched several weeks before, the guys on the after-work team had made progress. With more time together, they'd learned each other's strengths: who was good on offense and who on defense, who could shoot from the outside and who could drive down the middle, etc. They never did meet for happy hour. ("Guys kept bailing," one told me. "Everyone's busy with work.") But through hard work on the court, the two halves of the team had begun to mesh.

Tonight would be the final game of the season, and the team had a lot riding on it. Their win-loss record was 4–4. If they ended the season with a losing record, they'd be matched in the first playoff game against one of the top teams and likely be quickly eliminated, but with a win tonight they'd be matched against a lesser team and have a shot at winning the finals.

Tonight's opposing team, however, looked tough. We'd all glanced at them as they warmed up, noting how big they were—bigger than anyone on our team. "They have two guys over six feet five," Dave said in awe.

As the team huddled to set the final strategy, the ref came onto center court to prepare for the tip-off. It was seven o'clock on a Sunday evening, in the middle of winter; aside from the players, the ref, the timekeeper, and me, the community center gym was empty; there were no spectators. One of the guys had commented on this. It felt "weird," he told me, to play their games in a silent, empty gym "where all you hear is the squeak of sneakers on the wood floor."

Weird it was, and from an attachment perspective, not helpful.

In a study, fifty children from ages three to twelve were told to run twice around a baseball diamond as fast as they could, once with their parents watching, and once with their parents staring at their phones instead. The results? When parents watched their children, four out of five kids ran an average of three seconds faster and with fewer trips and falls, but when parents stared at their phones—in essence, ignoring their child—the kids ran slower and stumbled more. And it made no difference if the attentive parents cheered or just watched quietly— the key was that they were present and paying attention. "When parents act as a secure base," concluded researcher Brandi Stupica, "children are more competent athletes."

That study involved young athletes and their parents, but researchers believe the effect is likely to be the same for adult athletes with loved ones. Separation from attachment figures, notes researcher Sam Carr, may provoke a "psychological state that is not conducive to optimal performance."

Could it be that what we think of as "home court advantage" is, at least in part, about having loved ones physically present and paying attention?

Unfortunately, coaches and team managers often get this backward, banning players from having contact with spouses, loved ones, and other family members, believing they're a distraction. In the 2010 World Cup, for example, England's coach reportedly banned players from contact with wives and girlfriends during team preparations and for the tournament itself. In attachment terms, that policy is counterproductive. A coach knowledgeable about attachment theory would encourage spouses, loved ones, and other attachment figures to attend the game, and then be sure they put away phones, electronic readers, and other devices that might distract them and instead pay attention to the game.

As it happened, on the night of our final regular-season game, one player's loved one did finally show up: Todd's girlfriend, Maggie. She and I sat together on the sideline as we waited for the ref's starting whistle.

Injury

On the opening jump, Josh tipped to Tommy, who passed to Dave, who shot from the corner of the free-throw line and scored. But then, just as quickly, the opposing team scored. By the half, we'd gotten the best of a close battle and were up 21–19. That meant the whole season would come down to the next twenty minutes. I wasn't playing and felt anxious; I could hardly imagine how the guys were handling the stress.

In the second half, with six minutes remaining, we'd increased the lead to 30–26.

But then the guys began passing the ball away and missing shots, while the behemoths on the other team got hot. With two minutes left, we'd fallen behind, 34–35. Todd went in for Tommy and then— perhaps inspired by his girlfriend's attentive presence—had a burst of energy. Under the boards, he wrestled a rebound away from a much larger player. Half a minute later he rebounded cleanly, drove straight through the center, sank a layup—and was pushed to the floor.

Todd lay still. His girlfriend leaped up, trying to get a better look, to see if he was okay.

The ref stopped play, and the guys went over to Todd and stood around him, waiting to see if he could stand.

Securely attached players will be better able to shake off injuries and get back in the game.

In general, securely attached players will be better able to shake off injuries and get back in the game than anxious players, who may stay focused on their injuries, or avoidants, who may deny the symptoms and thus worsen the injury. This is because they tend to be more confident that if help is needed, competent caregivers will be available and reliable. Secure players also tend to be more optimistic that an injury will heal. Insecure athletes, in contrast, will likely have more anxiety in response to pain because they don't trust that it's not serious or that people will be able to competently care for them. They are also prone to catastrophizing (e.g., "This is terrible and will never get better"), and as we've noted, they can actually experience physical pain more acutely.

A coach who becomes an attachment figure to players can comfort them in the event of injury—as Bob Huggins did. He can even go further and calibrate his reaction based on the player's attachment style. If the injured player had a secure attachment, he might reinforce the player's resilience and encourage him to get back in the game. If the player had an avoidant attachment style, he might keep the other players at a distance and talk with the injured player one-on-one, reinforcing a sense of self-reliance and higher tolerance for pain. If the player were anxiously attached, the coach could ask the team physician to reassure the player directly that the injury was not serious and then encourage teammates to come around and reassure the injured player that they care about his pain and support him.

Fortunately, that evening Todd was not hurt. He shook it off and got up.

Choking

With less than a minute to go, the guys were down by one point. The towering players on the other team froze the ball—passing it back and forth among themselves to keep us from having a chance to score. With thirty seconds left, Marshall deliberately knocked into an opposing player, fouling out of the game. The opposing player sank his foul shot, leaving us two points down with only seconds to go.

Dave, at five foot eight our shortest player but perhaps strongest shooter, went in for Marshall.

Now we had our best team in: Josh, Todd, and Dave.

If we could manage to keep control of the ball for these last few seconds, one of our guys could take a final shot just before the buzzer.

It was a clutch moment and crucial that he not choke.

Why are some athletes more prone to choking under pressure? It may be, notes researcher Kelly Forrest, that under increased stress, athletes with different attachment styles tend to experience different degrees of "concentration disruption."

Secure players under stress are generally able to focus on the task at hand, even when the pressure's on. But anxious players under stress tend to focus internally, on themselves; and avoidant players tend to focus on the external environment and on their own interests rather than the team's. In both cases, they are distracted and not able to "operate automatically" in accordance with their athletic training. These tendencies, suggests Forrest, may be responsible for whether an athlete chokes.

In my team's immediate situation, a coach familiar with attachment theory might call a time-out and set up the final play so that a securely attached player would be fed the ball for the final shot. That may not sound fair, because every player brings skills to the team, but to increase the odds of winning a secure player should, from an attachment perspective, take the clutch shot.

And that's exactly what the team did.

Dave took the final shot.

Dave was the team connector—the only player who knew both sets of friends and work colleagues before the team started. He valued and didn't take for granted those relationships. "You have to learn to trust your teammates," he told me. "And build those friendships. That's what's important, more than the winning." Dave also had a healthy perspective on what's important in life. He and his wife, Rebecca, had met as first-year college students and had now been married two years. "No game out there is as serious as my personal life and the relationship I have," he said. "This league is fun, but it's just an activity; I've already won the biggest game."

Was Dave securely attached? I can't say for sure; I hadn't assessed him or any of the other players using the Experiences in Close Relationships quiz. But from my observation and interviews, my hunch is yes.

Todd brought the ball down and passed to Dave—who was standing just above the half court line. We were two points down, and this would be the last shot of the game and of the regular season.

In Dave's later retelling: "I pass to Josh, thinking he wants to take the last shot, but then my defender comes off me, and Josh passes it right back to me. I'm a few feet back from the three-point line. I know I have to take the shot. It's a win-or-lose shot—not a tying shot—it's win or lose. I have no thoughts or feelings. It's just mechanical."

His attention undistracted, Dave took the shot.

As the clock hit zero and the buzzer sounded, the ball sailed through the net.

————

Later the guys walked out of the community center as a group.

Todd said, "Those guys were giants, but they didn't play smart."

Marshall said, "We played like a team tonight. I think we all learned how to play as a team."

Still in sneakers and shorts, they entered the darkened streets, excitedly reviewing the game and planning strategy for the playoffs.

CHAPTER 12

Following the Leaders: Attachment and Politics

When I visited Michael Dukakis to interview him, the difference between winning and not winning the presidency became starkly clear. On the ninth floor of Northeastern University's Department of Political Science, the door to Dukakis's modest office stood open; it wasn't even a corner office. Inside, the man nearly 42 million people voted for sat at his desk in shirtsleeves.

Other than his hair having turned mostly white, Dukakis looked, at eighty-two, just like the man I'd been thrilled to see enter the Democratic National Convention to Neil Diamond's "Coming to America" (the song a reminder of his Greek-immigrant heritage). He'd entered, not from backstage, as was traditional, but from the convention floor, walking among the cheering delegates.

In the campaign, however, Dukakis had failed to respond quickly enough to attacks by Republican nominee George H. W. Bush. And in a nationally televised debate, he'd answered a provocative question about his wife—"If Kitty were raped and murdered, would you still oppose the death penalty for her attacker?"—by repeating, with little emotion, his standard position against capital punishment. Commentators saw it as a gaffe that helped cost him the election.

But was it a gaffe, or was it a sign of something rooted in his personality and attachment style? In arranging the meeting that day, my goal was to ask Dukakis the questions from the Adult Attachment Interview. It would be the first time, as far as I knew, that the assessment would be given to a national political leader. And it would set me on the trail of a possible discovery about the attachment style of many politicians—one that has important implications for the well-being of the country.

How Attachment Affects Leadership

Attachment researchers occasionally speculate about the attachment styles of American presidents. It's a bit of a parlor game, though, because the only reliable way to assess the attachment style of an adult—whether king or commoner—is by use of either the Experiences in Close Relationships quiz or the Adult Attachment Interview. But since no president's attachment style has actually been measured by either tool—at least to my knowledge—we're left to speculate based on what is known of the president's personal history, public statements, and behavior.

And yet we do speculate. We speculate because the more researchers learn about the influence of attachment on adult behavior, the more we understand that a leader's attachment style can significantly influence both the substance and style of his or her leadership. Moreover, it can influence the well-being of citizens too. This is because once in office, a leader often fulfills the functions of an attachment figure: protecting citizens from foreign enemies (in attachment terms, a safe haven); maintaining domestic and economic order so we can pursue our lives (secure base); and keeping near to reassure us by their symbolic presence on TV, social media, etc. (proximity maintenance). And if we suddenly lose the leader—by illness or assassination, for example—then, as with other attachment relationships, we often experience the loss personally.

Once in office, a leader often fulfills the functions of an attachment figure.

A leader who is securely attached can use this attachment relationship to confidently and skillfully assume the role of what researchers call a "stronger and wiser" caregiver. In this capacity, he or she can build our sense of self-worth and competence, encourage our autonomy and creativity, and support our desire to take on new challenges. The secure leader, note researchers Phillip Shaver and Mario Mikulincer, thus has the potential to become "transformational"— that is, he or she can create conditions that infuse a sense of "courage, hope, and dedication" in citizens. But only *secure* leaders, with their positive sense of self and others, generally are able to do this. "Secure people are well equipped to occupy the role of security-enhancing leader, whereas insecure people are likely to have difficulty meeting followers' needs for a safe haven and secure base." Professor of psychology Tiffany Keller-Hansbrough concurs: "Transformational leaders tend to have secure internal working models of attachment."

Among modern American presidents, one who appears to have had a secure attachment and who displayed qualities of transformative leadership was Franklin Roosevelt. During the Great Depression and World War II, with his "fireside chats" and warning to the nation not to succumb to "fear itself," Roosevelt was a strong and protective leader who helped Americans feel secure and discover their hidden strengths during very troubled and insecure times. On news of his death, millions wept (as they did nearly two decades later at the news of the assassination of John F. Kennedy). More recently, and on the Republican side, Ronald Reagan may be considered transformative. With his optimistic message of "It's morning again in America" and his effective communication style, he popularized a pragmatic conservatism (the Reagan revolution) while reviving faith in patriotism and the presidency.

———

But what of leaders whose attachment styles are insecure? They can still be effective managers, researchers suggest, but probably not transformative. Their insecure attachment may motivate them to gain power but then, given the right circumstances, may also trip them up.

Leaders with avoidant attachment, for example, may view leadership as an opportunity to reinforce their view of themselves as "tough and independent," note Shaver and Mikulincer. Yet their "lack of comfort with closeness and interdependence" may block them from understanding their followers' needs and concerns. An example among modern presidents may be Richard Nixon. His social awkwardness as well as general distrust of others—even supporters and his own staff—may be evidence of avoidance. And after resigning the presidency, as he was about to be helicoptered away from the White House, Nixon declared in a farewell speech, "My mother was a saint." In fact, notes his biographer Evan Thomas, as a boy Nixon was often frightened of his mother. When a person can acknowledge that a parent was not perfect and at times may even have mistreated him but accepts the parent's imperfections and loves them anyway, that is evidence of a secure attachment. In contrast, the avoidant person often declares his parent perfect ("a saint") and insists he loves them completely—all without acknowledging obvious mistreatment. Idealization of parents despite disconfirming evidence, researchers say, is evidence of attachment avoidance.

Leaders with anxious attachment, on the other hand, may seek office "as a means of satisfying unmet needs for attention, closeness, and acceptance rather than as a means of meeting followers' needs and promoting their healthy development," note Shaver and Mikulincer. Once in office, they may exhibit a "self-preoccupied focus" on unsatisfied attachment needs that can "draw mental resources away" from fulfilling their sworn duties. An example may be found in Bill Clinton. Researchers note—and again this is conjecture—Clinton's evident need for attention and desire to please supporters, as well as his "inability to ignore a worshipful intern's thong underwear," which ultimately led to his impeachment.

Nixon and Clinton were both highly intelligent and talented politicians. If they had been aware of their attachment styles, it might have affected their behavior in office. All political leaders, in fact, might benefit from this knowledge. If Nixon, for example, had understood that some of the threat he felt from political opponents and the distrust of his staff may have stemmed from his own attachment avoidance, perhaps he could have resisted authorizing illegal behavior and not had to resign. And if Clinton had understood that his need for closeness to a young intern was tied, in part, to an anxious attachment, perhaps he could have better resisted the temptation.

How Attachment Affects Voters

As citizens, our attachment style influences our political leanings and whom we vote for. For example, there appears to be a correlation between secure attachment and beliefs that are centrist, either center-left or center-right. A secure attachment is marked by "self-confidence, empathy, and trust," note researchers Christopher Weber and Christopher Federico, and can lead to a general belief

> *There appears to be a correlation between secure attachment and beliefs that are centrist.*

that the world is a "safe, harmonious place" populated by people of goodwill. The secure voter, therefore, will tend to be tolerant of ambiguity and disinclined to embrace a rigid dogmatism. According to attachment expert Mario Mikulincer, a secure attachment produces "more moderate, more flexible, and more realistic political views."

Insecure attachment, on the other hand, can influence a voter toward a more extremist ideology, whether of the left or the right. "Insecurity is made worse by uncertainty," explains Union College psychology professor Joshua Hart, "so insecure people should also be drawn to . . . extremist ideologies of all stripes that provide a sense of having a strong and unerring view of the world." Sometimes, of course, there really *is* a reason to be insecure, such as a failing economy or threat of terrorism, but we're talking here about a generalized tendency toward extremist ideologies.

Voters who are avoidant, who often distrust others and prize self-reliance, may be attracted to right-wing conservatism, note researchers Weber and Federico, both in terms of economics (the world is an "uncaring, competitive jungle") and military policy ("we can only depend on our own strength"). Anxious voters, seeking security in a world that feels threatening, may embrace a far-left liberal orthodoxy that advocates redistribution of wealth and political power, and aggressively demands "inclusion" and protection in the form of a caregiving government that takes care of everyone's welfare. But this is not a hard-and-fast rule either. The avoidant voter could embrace the left-wing orthodoxy, and the anxious voter the right-wing conservatism—either way, they will be attracted to the perceived safety of dogmatism.

Anxiously attached voters, in particular, may project their unmet attachment needs onto leaders. And therein lies another concern: studies show that anxious voters may so crave attaching to a strong, caregiving leader that they may be unable to distinguish between a transformative leader—one who protects, encourages, and empowers them—and a leader without such qualities.

In one study, psychology professor Tiffany Hansbrough showed subjects video clips of two political speeches: one by Michael Dukakis accepting the Democratic presidential nomination and the other by Jesse Jackson, a candidate at the same convention. Both speeches had been previously evaluated for transformational qualities (for example, "appealing to followers' emotions and values and emphasizing a collective identity"). Jackson's speech was found to have these qualities, but Dukakis's speech, while "pragmatic," was found to lack them.

The results? Anxious subjects viewed the Dukakis speech as transformational, even though by objective measures it was not. The danger here, cautions Hansbrough, is that anxiously attached voters may so crave a strong and protective leader that they see transformational leadership where it is absent, confusing leaders who are genuinely transformative with those who are merely charismatic. This should be concerning, as it suggests that voters who are already far out on the extreme left or right may be prone to mistaking an unremarkable or even dangerous politician for a transformational leader and thus blindly follow someone who could turn out to be a demagogue.

The Governor's Attachment Interview

"Peter? Come in."

The former three-term governor of Massachusetts—once voted best governor by the nation's other governors—stood and came toward the door to greet me. He now walked, I noticed, with a slight stoop. I admired Mike Dukakis, had voted for him, and was grateful that he'd agreed to make the time to meet with me.

"So nice to meet you, Governor. Thanks for inviting me."

"I'm just finishing an e-mail," he said, seating himself behind the desk and swiveling around to a desktop computer behind him. "Never mind," he said, swiveling back to face me. "I'll finish that later."

The phone rang and he swiveled back to answer it.

"Hello. Yeah, what? Come on. He can't make what? Okay, all right. Yep."

I remembered that deep voice and clipped, rapid-fire speech.

When I quietly offered to step out, he motioned for me to stay.

It was an ordinary office—what I'd imagine for any full professor at the university—but from what I remembered of Dukakis, I knew he likely didn't mind the simple trappings. He and his wife, Kitty, had lived in the same modest house in Brookline for more than fifty years. As governor, he'd commuted to work by streetcar and without a security detail. "It wasn't an act," he told me. "I've been taking the streetcar since I was five. And what would I be doing driving around in a Cadillac with twenty state troopers for protection?" On the window ledge stood photos of Kitty and some of their seven grandchildren.

He continued on the phone: "She's . . . she's getting RSVPs, John. Okay, okay. We'll take care of it. We'll take care of it. Yep, okay. Okay, yep, we'll do it."

Finished with the call, he swiveled back toward me.

"So fire away. Fire away," he said.

I briefly explained my interest in attachment theory and said that for part of our conversation I'd be asking him questions from the Adult Attachment Interview for a book I was writing.

He said that would be fine.

The goal of the AAI, I'd learned earlier, is not to uncover the factual history of the person being interviewed. Instead, it's to activate the attachment system by asking the person to describe early relationships with primary caregivers—especially during periods of separation, illness, and loss—and see if the person can create a believable, internally consistent narrative of those childhood experiences. The questions are meant to "surprise the unconscious" and to reveal the state of mind of the person while discussing these attachment relationships.

People can become certified to administer the AAI by taking a training course offered by, among others, the very people who developed it. I had not taken that course and therefore was not certified to give the AAI. But as a journalist and author I had many decades of experience interviewing people. As recounted earlier (see chapter 2), I took the AAI myself with Mauricio Cortina, who was certified to give it. In writing about the experience, I had studied the AAI's structure carefully. All of which is to say that, although I was not officially trained or certified to give the AAI, by the time I arrived at Governor Dukakis's office, I was well familiar with its purposes, structure, and content.

Even so, as I sat across the desk from Dukakis, I was nervous at the prospect of asking so prominent a person such revealing questions. Both to assure him I was not out to trip him up and to provide a check against any errors I might make, I offered to review his responses before publication.

"It's all on the record. Not to worry," he said. "I'm not an off-the-record guy. It's too complicated."

So I checked that the tape recorder I'd put on the desk, with his permission, was running, and began.

"Okay," I said. "So why don't we just start by orienting me to your family: where you lived, who was in the family. Did you move around a lot? What did your parents do?"

"My parents were both immigrants," he began. His father worked in the mills, in restaurants, and went to night school. "That guy didn't speak a word of English when he got here," he said. "He didn't have a nickel in his pocket and twelve years later he was graduating from Harvard Medical School. How he did it, I have no idea."

I asked about his early relationship with his parents. "Just going back as far as you can remember, how would you describe that?"

"Well, I was a very happy kid," he began. "I loved school. Up to my eyeballs in sports, I mean, every season. For whatever reason, I seemed to do well in school. And I remember at one point, Peter, when I was about twelve or thirteen, kind of saying, 'I wish life could kind of stand still,' because, you know, I was just having a ball."

That was not quite responsive to the question, I thought, which had asked about his relationship with his parents. But the official guidelines for administering the AAI say not to correct the person's responses, just to move on.

Anyway, those first two questions are mostly just warm-ups. The next one—known as the "five adjectives"—is central.

"Thinking about your mom," I said, "could you give me five adjectives that would describe your relationship with her when you were little?"

"It was certainly loving," he began. "And disciplined. My parents set pretty high standards for us. We were expected to do well in school. And the Dukakis kids were always expected to work, you know. Nobody came around and cut the grass. We cut the grass; we shoveled the snow."

After a pause, he offered as a third adjective, "supportive."

Another lengthy pause.

"It's not always easy to come up with these," I prompted, as suggested by the guidelines.

"I don't know if there's a word for this," he said. "I mean . . . certainly attempted . . . to give us a pretty broad range of experience. You know, I mean . . . and ethnic. I don't want to overdo this, but we grew up in a Greek household where at least as long as my *yia-yia* [grandmother] was around we spoke Greek. And yet it was different from most Greek households because my parents obviously achieved a level of education, which was very unusual for Greek families at the time. So, you know, I went to Sunday school from the time I was five to the time I was thirteen . . . but I wouldn't call it a religious atmosphere as such."

"So as far as adjectives," I said, pulling him back to the question, "we have 'loving,' 'disciplining,' and 'supportive.'"

"'Educating,'" he offered.

He was not able to come up with a fifth adjective, and so we went on to the second part of the question: providing specific instances or episodes that support the chosen adjectives.

"So the first adjective you used to describe your relationship with your mom was 'loving.' Can you give me a specific memory or an instance that illustrates that for you?"

Twenty seconds went by. "I have to think about that," he said.

"You can take more time," I said.

"I can't remember an event or two or three. I mean it's just—"

"Some memory or image that stays in your mind showing how your mom was loving?" I prompted.

Ten more seconds.

"I have to think about that. It was much more, kind of the environment in which I grew up. I don't remember a particular, you know, kind of continuing thing, but—"

"Okay," I continued, "the second adjective you mentioned was 'disciplining.' Do you remember a specific instance when your mom was disciplining?"

The phone rang and he swiveled around to take the call.

"Hello. Hi. Yeah. He was on the working group. I told him so. Don't worry about that. Yeah. Okay. Okay. How about the labor guys, are they coming? I want them all there if we can get them. Okay. Okay. All right, thanks."

He swiveled back.

"I forgot the thread here," he said.

We were talking about his relationship with his mother, I reminded him, and looking for a specific memory to illustrate how it was "disciplining."

"Well, she'd whack us occasionally," he said, referring to himself and Stelian, his only sibling, four years his senior. "And we were two brothers who loved each other, but we were always fighting. Nothing new about that. In fact, one day she got so mad at us she wouldn't let us go to school with our belts on because every once in a while we'd take them off and start [fighting with them]—which was a little embarrassing, trying to keep your pants up, you know."

When I later asked Dukakis for five adjectives to describe his relationship with his father, he said they'd be the same as those for his mother, only "less intense." That's because while his mother was mostly a homemaker, his father worked seven days a week in his medical practice, so he had less time with him.

"So when you think about your dad as being 'loving,'" I asked, "is there a particular memory that comes to mind that illustrates that?"

"Not really," he said. "Just a kind of ongoing, very warm, supportive relationship."

He had little to offer in support of the other adjectives as well.

We moved on.

"Do you remember the first time you were separated from your parents?"

He did. At age eleven, he went to overnight camp in New Hampshire.

"I was horribly homesick and embarrassed about it," he began, "because I really wanted to go. There's lots of sports up there, and I was learning how to swim, but man was I homesick. It was the weirdest kind of feeling. I couldn't . . . I couldn't even comprehend what happened to me. I was crying a lot in private. It was the damnedest thing I ever—you know. And maddening, as you could imagine from a personal standpoint, because I couldn't understand why this was happening to me."

"Were your parents ever threatening in any way," I asked, moving to another question, "for discipline or even jokingly?"

In response, he told a story about his father. On Sunday afternoons his father took a break from his medical practice to come home for dinner and a nap. But one Sunday, when Michael was nine or ten, he and Stelian were playing football in the living room and woke their father. "Man, I mean, he was furious," Dukakis recalled. "He came downstairs, grabbed a poker from the fireplace. I managed to jump into the bathroom and lock myself in before he"—and here Dukakis laughed—"swatted me," he said.

One of the challenging things about asking someone the AAI questions is that the interviewer is not supposed to comment on the answers. I found this tough when I took the test and retold sometimes painful stories from my own childhood only to have Dr. Cortina listen in silence. And I found it tough now to hear such stories from Dukakis and not offer a sympathetic word.

"So looking back," I said, moving on, "how do you feel your childhood experiences affected your adult personality?"

"I have no idea," he said. "I can't really tell you, except that I was a very happy kid who loved what I was doing and really didn't spend a lot of time thinking about it."

How about other adults important to him growing up? Earlier, he'd mentioned his paternal grandmother, Olympia (after whom his cousin, the actress Olympia Dukakis, is named). She was the grandmother who lived with the family and whom he called *yia-yia*.

"We had a great relationship," he said. "When we'd have Sunday dinner, I'd go to the living room and she'd grab my arm, and I'd bring her into the dining room and seat her. I was about six."

She died the next year.

What did he remember of that?

"She was laid out in a casket in our living room," he said, and people visited.

And how did he experience that?

"I don't remember," he began. "I mean, obviously I was sad, but I don't remember anything other than a certain amount of sadness. You know, my *yia-yia* had died. How does a seven-year-old kid deal with death? I mean, it happens. You're sad. I think you kind of accept it and move on."

While Stelian, Dukakis's older brother, was in college, he developed a "severe psychological disorder" and was hospitalized. "It was the first time we'd ever had anything quite like that" in the family, said Dukakis. When Dukakis was thirty-nine, Stelian died after being hit by a car.

"I've always been instinctively an optimist, Peter," he said. "I don't care what the problem is. There's a solution out there someplace. But it was confusing. My older brother seemed to be fine, was doing well in school, doing well athletically, and all of a sudden—bingo. We know a lot more now about the biological basis for mental illness, and it was one of those classic cases. And we've seen this over and over again, except it was my brother."

Toward the end of our interview, Dukakis spoke of how Kitty, his wife of fifty-two years, struggled with depression and some memory loss. By press accounts I'd seen, Dukakis was devoted to her and to her care. "She's feeling great. Thanks to electroconvulsive therapy," he said. "Honest to God, Peter, I mean, she would not be alive today without it. Kitty and I are still out helping people every day, and I introduce her as the best-looking Medicare recipient in America. She is. But, you know, we've had a hell of a ride. I mean it's just been an extraordinary life."

———

Later, I sent a transcript of the interview to psychotherapist Dr. Shoshana Ringel, who has coded hundreds of them, including mine. A few weeks later, she sent me the coded Dukakis transcript, including margin notes in which she commented on specific answers:

On the five-adjectives questions: "Has difficulty finding memories or experiences that reflect the adjectives, especially regarding love." Also, "Emphasis on academic achievement, not emotional support."

On being disciplined by his mother: "Endorses mother's disciplining even when harsh and shaming."

On homesickness at summer camp: "Admits to missing parents but is unable to reflect on it, understand it or accept it, even so many years later."

On threats and punishment from his father: "Does admit to some adverse experiences and father's temper, but makes fun of the event and minimizes it."

On his grandmother's death in the family home: "Generic description of experience, remote and impersonal."

And on his brother Stelian's mental illness: "Discusses the process of brother's illness but not how it affected him . . . uses logic but minimizes feelings."

In sum: "Qualities throughout include abstract responses that are remote from memories and feelings, self is described as strong, independent, and if vulnerable, subject minimizes it. . . . There is little expression of feelings and of needing or depending, actually there is an active dismissal of those feelings. There is minimizing and downplaying of negative experiences, emphasis on achievements, academic success, and athletics rather than emotional intimacy."

Her assessment: "Attachment classification: Avoidant."

So one of the national political figures I most admired—and whom I'd enthusiastically voted for—had an insecure avoidant attachment?

Initially, it made me wonder if the AAI itself was valid. Could the fact that I'd done the interview rather than a psychotherapist have skewed the results? A fair question, noted Dr. Ringel, but it appeared Dukakis had sincerely tried to answer the questions and, anyway, many AAIs are not conducted by psychotherapists but by researchers.

Could the AAI be culturally biased? Dukakis was in his eighties, raised in a time when families—perhaps especially immigrant families— did not talk much about emotions and instead emphasized hard work and achievement. Did the AAI penalize him for not being more emotionally open? As a society, we used to admire the strong, silent John Wayne type. Dr. Ringel replied that there could be a cultural bias, but also noted that she had coded interviews with other people of similar age and background and found them "much more open and emotional."

In light of Dr. Ringel's assessment, I had to consider Dukakis's political career through a new lens. If the coding was correct, perhaps it was his avoidant attachment that helped give him the drive and self-reliance to become a successful governor. But the avoidant attachment might also have been what led him as a presidential nominee to give an acceptance speech so lacking in uplift that it became a model for "nontransformative" rhetoric. And it might also have been what led him in a televised debate to respond to a question about his wife's hypothetical rape with an emotionless statement of policy. In short, his debate answer may not have been a gaffe at all but an honest, if unfortunate, reflection of his attachment style.

Are Most Politicians Avoidant?

I asked the AAI questions to several other politicians—current and former members of Congress—and was surprised to find that in each instance the responses, like Dukakis's, were most consistent with avoidant attachment.

Dr. Ringel, in a personal note to me after scoring the AAI of one of those former members of Congress, posed the question: Might an avoidant style be a "professional hazard" among politicians?

It was an intriguing question, and yet I did find one exception: the young mayor of my hometown, Rochester, New York. Lovely Warren had been mayor for three years when I visited her office in city hall to ask her the questions from the AAI.

In response, she recalled important events from childhood: stories of love (a warm household where her mom would "hug and kiss us and tell us that she loves us," and her dad would encourage her to do her best and was the one she went to when upset); stories of loss (at thirteen, life "just started to unravel" when she found out her dad was using drugs and her parents separated; "My childhood for me was over that day," she recalled); stories of trauma ("And I ran out after [my dad] and he got in the car and drove away and [I screamed], 'Dad, are you really going to choose drugs over me?' And he left."); and stories of resilience (after high school she earned bachelor's and law degrees, became president of the city council, and at thirty-five was elected mayor).

Dr. Ringel reviewed the transcript of my interview and scored the mayor secure. Her comments included:

> Has evidence for her adjectives . . . shows self as vulnerable . . . recognizes impact of attachment experience on her though it was painful . . . poignant description of rejection . . . is reflective and insightful and seems to have her own personal identity as separate from parents.

My mayor was, it seemed to me, a prime example of how an early secure attachment can provide resilience, helping one cope with even the most hurtful events and losses later in life. If my theory that most politicians are avoidant is correct, then Mayor Warren is an exception to the rule: a leader with secure attachment. Whether in the future she can use that base of attachment security to become a truly transformational leader is too soon to tell. But the promise is there.

———

A handful of random interviews, of course, is insufficient to draw broad conclusions, but—my hometown mayor notwithstanding— might avoidant attachment, which describes about 25 percent of the general population, indeed be overrepresented among politicians? If so, why? And with what consequences?

I could see how aspects of avoidance could be an advantage to someone pursuing public office. Avoidants tend to be self-reliant—a necessary trait among those seeking elective office. They also tend to do well spending long stretches of time away from home and family—a necessity for those campaigning for and then holding statewide or national office. In this regard, I was reminded of the Israeli study showing that among professional tennis players on the singles circuit, an avoidant attachment predicted higher rankings. Professional tennis, the study noted, is a competitive arena where one operates alone and that requires frequent travel and thus time away from home and significant others—both factors that reward self-reliance. Even more so, perhaps, in politics.

Moreover, avoidants also tend to be reluctant to trust others—a trait that could confer an additional advantage in a field seemingly rife with double-dealing and betrayal. "That probably makes a lot of sense," agrees Tim Petri, a former member of Congress. Until his recent retirement, Petri served thirty-six years in the House, representing his district in eastern Wisconsin. It was during his years in Congress, during the early 1980s, that the FBI conducted a sting operation known as Abscam. In it, federal agents videotaped politicians accepting bribes from a fraudulent Arabian company in return for political favors. Six representatives and one senator were convicted. "Politicians have to have a pretty good nose for detecting people's motives and sensing something isn't right," says Petri, "so those who have a healthy reluctance to trust and who are cautious about getting too close, they're the ones who at the crucial moment are likely to say 'this doesn't sound right' or 'get lost,' and keep themselves out of trouble."

The 2016 presidential contest appeared to continue this pattern.

Democrat Hillary Clinton's tendency to protect herself and perhaps not to be too trusting of others—her use of a private e-mail server when serving as secretary of state might be an example—would be consistent with the self-reliance and general distrust characteristic of attachment avoidance. Her campaign speeches, while filled with policy details, were by most accounts not uplifting—similar in that regard to those of Michael Dukakis. And Clinton's apparent difficulty in revealing what many voters could perceive as an authentic personality would also be consistent with the avoidantly attached person's disinclination to self-disclose.

Republican Donald Trump also showed traits consistent with attachment avoidance: strong self-reliance, not acknowledging self-doubts, referencing sexual relations as bragging points rather than intimacy, and idealization of parents despite disconfirming evidence. An evident need to be in the spotlight, if it were aimed primarily at receiving approval, might be evidence of attachment anxiety, but in Trump's case it appears to be more about adulation, which would be consistent with avoidance. In sum, the weight of the evidence—particularly his apparent extreme self-reliance—would place our forty-fifth president among the long line of politicians whose dominant attachment style is avoidant.

If this hypothesis is right—if many or even most politicians are, in fact, avoidant in their attachment style—what might the implications be? To be sure, it doesn't mean that we don't have effective political leadership. Mike Dukakis was a successful public servant, re-elected three times, voted best governor by his peers, an effective advocate for sound policies at both the state and national level, still active today in public affairs, and respected by citizens and political leaders alike.

But effective is not the same as transformative. That rarer type of leadership seems to be reserved for the politician who comes to office with a secure attachment, who can be the "stronger and wiser" caregiver, especially in times of crisis, providing emotional support, uplifting the populace, and empowering followers to reach their full potential both as individuals and as a nation. Such leaders, to repeat the assessment of researchers Phillip Shaver and Mario Mikulincer, can inspire in citizens of all attachment styles a sense of "courage, hope, and dedication."

The biggest implication of having avoidantly attached political leaders might just be that for long stretches of time we must endure a lack of secure leadership and muddle through with no sense of a "stronger and wiser" leader at the helm. Instead of a public mood of confidence, harmony, and well-being, we might experience a general sense of insecurity. That absence, in turn, might prompt unease and unleash infighting, with regular eruptions of conflict among competing groups. In short, a situation like many nations have experienced throughout most of history.

———

To be sure, we are left merely to speculate about politicians' attachment styles. Clues may be found in what is known of their personal history, in their public statements, and in their behavior in and out of office. Do memoirs or accounts by other family members reveal details about early childhood? Who was the primary caregiver and what was the relationship like? Were there major disruptions in the relationship? In the politician's adult life, does he or she generally assume good intentions on the part of others until proven wrong—often a mark of attachment security? Have relationships with friends, colleagues, and office staff generally been trusting and stable? Does the primary relationship with spouse or significant other seem healthy and stable? Is the politician's message to the public uplifting and empowering rather than self-serving or divisive?

None of these factors by themselves indicate secure attachment—plenty of politicians, for example, maintain the facade of a stable marriage only to be revealed as philanderers—but taken together they may give some indication of relationship patterns that can point to either a secure or insecure attachment style.

We can get along without transformative leaders, but it's better when we have them. In peaceful times, they can help us find creative solutions to complex societal problems—a form of exploration—and in times of war or financial crisis, when we do need that "stronger and wiser" man or woman to be our secure base and safe haven, they can reliably guide us. For that reason, let's keep an eye out for securely attached candidates who at least have the potential to be transformative leaders.

CHAPTER 13

Thou Art with Me:
Attachment and Religion

The basilica, nearly empty, sat silent. The Christmas Eve children's service, which had included a Nativity pageant, had ended, but Midnight Mass would not begin for another hour.

I took a seat at the end of a pew about two-thirds of the way back from the altar. In that church, it was a long way back. The basilica on the campus of Catholic University in northeast Washington, DC, is the largest Roman Catholic church in the United States and one of the ten largest in the world. Its dome is nearly as big as the dome of the US Capitol. In size and with its Byzantine-Romanesque design, it is meant to rival the great cathedrals of Europe. Yet it is not the cathedral of Washington. That is St. Matthew's, located downtown. Instead, the basilica was built as a shrine to the Virgin Mary. Presidents and popes visit, as do more than a million people every year, many of them on sacred pilgrimages.

Yet I was curious: in attachment terms, what is belief in God and attendance at a religious service about? Does attachment style influence whether we believe in God, how we relate to God, and what particular religion we embrace?

I'd never been to Midnight Mass. As a Jew, Christmas to me meant Chinese food and a movie. But these were questions I'd come to the great Basilica of the National Shrine of the Immaculate Conception to explore, while immersed in the spiritual richness of Midnight Mass.

God as Attachment Figure

For many people of faith—particularly those who follow the monotheistic religions—a core idea is belief in a personal God with whom one can have a personal, interactive relationship. In a Gallup survey, for example, most Americans said their religious faith is defined by "a relationship with God."

For many Christians, this relationship is directly with God. For others, it is with Jesus or Mary. The God of Judaism is also a personal God with whom one can relate—or argue or question—as figures have done from Abraham and Moses down the ages to Tevye, the milkman of *Fiddler on the Roof.*

Similarly, researchers examining the divine attributes of Allah—for example, al-Mu'min (the Preserver and Bestower of security) and al-Mujib (the Responsive)—as well as stories and verses from the Qur'an, have found evidence of Allah having "key attributes" of an attachment figure. "Allah fulfills critical attachment functions of proximity, safe haven, and secure base," conclude University of Tehran professor Bagher Ghobari Bonab and others.

Even in religions outside the Judeo-Christian-Islamic tradition, including those Westerners may think of as not based on the idea of a god—Hinduism and Buddhism, for example—followers may focus on, as professor of psychology Lee A. Kirkpatrick notes, "personal gods imported from ancient folk religions."

Yet it was with some skepticism that I read in the attachment literature about how the relationship with God can be a true attachment relationship for people of faith—not a metaphor but an actual attachment. That seemed a stretch. When I was younger, mostly when my kids were little, I believed in God but since then had been unable to sustain it. I went to religious services and said the words of the liturgy, but I didn't have quite the degree of faith that would allow me to see an invisible, noncorporeal God as an attachment figure.

And yet the argument has been made that for people of faith a relationship with God can, indeed, fulfill the five psychological criteria of a true attachment relationship. Kirkpatrick, who has done much of the work in this field, makes the case as follows:

Secure Base: An attachment figure who is "simultaneously omnipresent, omniscient, and omnipotent," and who watches over us, writes Kirkpatrick, would provide "the most secure of secure bases." Scripture frequently describes God as a source of security: a "shield," a "rock," and a "fortress." One of the most well-known Psalms makes the point explicitly: "Yea, though I walk through the valley of the shadow of death, I will fear no evil: for thou art with me; thy rod and thy staff they comfort me." Thus God functions psychologically as a secure base, providing the believer, as Kirkpatrick notes, "with strength, self-assurance, and a sense of peace to tackle the problems and challenges of everyday life."

Safe Haven: Frightening events, illness and injury, and threat of separation—situations that John Bowlby believed activate the attachment system—are the same situations in which people are most likely to turn to God as a haven of safety. The old saying that "there are no atheists in foxholes" aptly captures the truth that in dire situations we often seek comfort from God, even if we never have before. Whether soldiers under fire, patients facing serious illness, or those bereaved, people of faith as well as newly minted believers seek in God a source of strength for getting through tough times.

Proximity Seeking: When frightened, children may need a caregiver physically present, but for adults the value of an attachment figure depends not so much on physical as on psychological proximity. Therefore, though not present physically, God can still function psychologically and spiritually as an attachment figure. In contrast to loved ones, who die or may leave, an omnipresent God can always be by our side. Religious objects such as paintings, crosses, garments, or a synagogue's eternal light also remind us of God's presence. And there are places we can go to feel nearer to God: houses of worship and sites of miracles and mountaintops. Prayer, too, keeps a sense of closeness. In prayer we perceive ourselves to be in relationship with an immediate, personal God.

Separation and Loss: The fourth and fifth criteria of attachment (as discussed in chapter 1) are that the threat of separation from the attachment figure causes anxiety (often accompanied by protest) and that the loss of the attachment figure causes grief. Talking about the loss of God can be difficult because, as professor of psychology Pehr Granqvist and Lee Kirkpatrick wryly note, God "does not die, sail off to fight wars, or file for divorce." Even so, we understand what it means to be separated from God: if we suffer a tragedy and come to feel that God has abandoned us, that loss of secure base and safe haven can trigger anxiety, anger, and grief. In Jewish tradition, to be cut off from God (*karet*) is the worst punishment. In Islam, Bagher Ghobari Bonab and colleagues note, "perceived abandonment by Allah" creates among followers "an acute form" of separation anxiety. "Just as the child unable to obtain proximity to its attachment figures cries out in distress, so too, believers lament when faced with separation from Allah, their ultimate attachment figure." In Christian belief, separation from God is "the essence of hell." Christ himself cried out on the cross: "My God, my God, why hast thou forsaken me?" (Matthew 27:46).

Mother of Sorrows

On either side of the basilica's upper church—where Mass would be held—were small chapels each dedicated to Mary. The powerful appeal of Mary, notes Kirkpatrick, "is to be found . . . in the marvelous possibility that God loves us the way a mother loves her baby" and is an important reason "why modern Catholics remain Catholic," even if they dissent from church doctrine. Even for non-Catholics, Mary is "a universal symbol of maternal love, as well as suffering and sacrifice," writes journalist Maureen Orth, who also notes that when asked what Mary means to him, Pope Francis answered simply, "She is my *mama*."

Jews also have this concept. One of the names for God, Av HaRachaman, means Father of Compassion, and the root of the Hebrew word for compassion means "womb."

In the basilica, each of the Mary chapels sits in its own alcove. They are gifts from Catholic groups around the world: Our Lady of China chapel; Mary, Help of Christians chapel; Our Lady of Guadalupe chapel, and others.

To the right of where I was seated was a chapel called Mother of Sorrows. Inside was a pietà: a life-size, marble sculpture of Mary holding the dead body of Jesus. I left my seat to have a closer look.

The sculpture resembled the famous *Pietà* by Michelangelo, but this was not a copy of Michelangelo's masterpiece; it was an original work by American artist Ernest Morenon. In the sculpture, made from beige Italian marble, Jesus is cradled by his mother, his head hanging back and one arm limp at his side. Mary stares into the middle distance with a look suggesting resignation but also peace. Below are the words: "Mother of Sorrows, Pray for Us."

The sculpture moved me but not so much as a religious expression. Instead, when I looked at it I thought of my only sister, Jane. Seven years older than me, Jane had nurtured and played with me throughout my childhood, always in a supportive, mothering way. As adults, we lived in the same town and remained close. After my father's death, the task of replacing him as a primary attachment figure was made easy by my having few choices: with no current romantic partner, there was no one else to turn to other than Jane: someone who had been an attachment figure for me—a substitute mother, really—all my life.

But I was still mourning my father when I lost my sister. She and her husband had been flying south, to a vacation in Florida, when their private plane lost pressurization, causing them within minutes to lose consciousness. After four hours flying on autopilot, the plane crashed off the coast of Jamaica, killing them both.

That night, Christmas Eve, would have been Jane's birthday. Had the accident not happened, I'd be calling her to wish her happy birthday. Instead, gazing at the pietà, I imagined myself holding my sister's lifeless body, her brown hair hanging limp and wet from the ocean where she fell.

In front of the sculpture was a kneeler, and at that moment part of me wanted to kneel. My sister's sudden death was still an open wound, and in my sadness I sensed it would be comforting to be nearer the ground. As a Jew, though, kneeling would be alien and inappropriate, and I couldn't do it.

Against one wall of the chapel, however, was a shelf with rows of large candles. A sign said, "Votives $4." I wasn't sure what a votive was, but I very much wanted to light a candle for my sister. Doing things like that kept me feeling close to her. I have her photos and some of her belongings, including her cell phone salvaged from the Caribbean, the edges still stained with rust. Sometimes I'll talk to her—most often silently. Though she's gone, I feel our attachment continues.

Kneeling was alien, but lighting a candle was familiar: in a Jewish tradition that actually comes from the Catholics, each year on the anniversary, or *yahrzeit*, of a parent or other close relative's death—for Jane that was September 5—we light a candle that burns for twenty-four hours.

I put a five-dollar bill in the offering box and lit a votive candle.

On my way out of the chapel, I stopped to read a plaque: the Mother of Sorrows chapel, coincidentally, had been dedicated years earlier on September 5. September 5—I could hardly believe it—the same date as my sister's death.

I would feel the pull of that chapel throughout the rest of my evening at the basilica, and it would turn out to be the key to my understanding of religion and attachment.

Secure and Insecure Relationships with God

A piercing blast from the basilica's two organs—with a combined 9,365 pipes—roused me from thoughts of my sister. They were playing "Hark! The Herald Angels Sing," a carol I was familiar with from the final scenes of *It's a Wonderful Life* and *A Charlie Brown Christmas*, but I didn't recall ever hearing it live.

In anticipation of the start of the Mass, the basilica had filled to capacity: thirty-seven hundred people. Many, I presumed, had a true attachment relationship with God. Yet all came with their own attachment style. How did that affect the relationship?

People approach their relationship with God, researchers say, pretty much as they approach all other relationships. That is, the "mental model" of relationships we form in early childhood colors whatever relationship we later have with God. "Beliefs about what God or gods are like, and one's ability to have a personal relationship with God, appear to be consistent with one's experience in human relationships with attachment figures," notes Kirkpatrick.

If our attachment style is secure and we tend to view attachment figures as loving and trustworthy, then we are likely to have an image of God as a loving protector, and to view God as available, reliable, and responsive. As such, feeling secure with God can give believers extraordinary strength and a sense of meaning to get through difficult times.

Those with an anxious attachment style, however, who tend to view attachment figures as unreliable and unpredictable, may tend to view God in similar terms; for some, Kirkpatrick says, the relationship with God may be "deeply emotional, all-consuming, and 'clingy.'" People whose attachment style is avoidant, in contrast, may tend toward agnosticism or atheism, or view God as stern or punishing.

These are generalizations, of course, and while valid over large populations, they may not apply to any one individual. Even so, as I looked out over the thousands of worshippers at the basilica I presumed that most who had chosen to come to Midnight Mass that evening were securely or anxiously attached and fewer were avoidant.

Choosing a Religion

But why had the thousands of people surrounding me decided to come to *tis* religious service—Midnight Mass at a Roman Catholic church—istead of some other? Some may have been raised Catholic and have chosen to remain so; others may have converted. Does attachment style influence such choices?

Research suggests there are two broad paths by which attachment influences how we choose a religion (or no religion).

First, studies show that if your parents raised you to have a secure attachment *and* you observed your parents being religiously observant, then you are likely to follow your parents' religion. But note this model has *two* parts: raising a child to have secure attachment *and* the parents' religious observance. For religious parents who wish for their children to embrace their own religion, Granqvist and Kirkpatrick caution, religious preaching and teaching are not enough; in fact, they believe, "it may fall on entirely deaf ears unless combined with placing a high priority on sensitive caregiving that meets the childrens need for protection and security." In other words, if you're Catholic and want your kids to share your faith when they grow up, you'll not only need to raise them to see you living as a sincere and devout Catholic, but you'll also need to raise them to have a secure attachment

What if a child is raised in a religious family but *without* a secure attachment? In that case, asserts Kirkpatrick, the adult child, reacting to a problematic childhood relationship with his or her parents, may shun the parents' religious tradition and perhaps religion altogether. These adult children may, Kirkpatrick adds, become "the apostates . . . or the militant atheists."

That said, some individuals with insecure attachment who turn away from their childhood religion might later find their way back to religion through conversion to a different faith. It may come in response to distress or a loss, such as after a romantic breakup or the death of a loved one. In essence, studies show that individuals with an anxious attachment style often find religion an effective way to regulate distress.

Studies show that individuals with an anxious attachment style often find religion an effective way to regulate distress.

Often the conversion will be dramatic: the sudden discovery of God or Jesus, for example, as a substitute attachment figure.

When people with *secure* attachments convert, the process looks much different from the sudden, dramatic conversions of the insecure. These conversions tend to occur, for example, not *after* a romantic breakup, but rather after the establishment of a new intimate relationship, and they tend to be gradual rather than sudden.

Sudden converts may discover in God "a kind of attachment relationship one never had with one's parents," note Granqvist and Kirkpatrick. "Converts suddenly come to see God or Jesus . . . as someone who loves them, cares about them, faithfully watches over them . . . in direct contradiction to a lifetime's worth of personal experience with attachment figures to the contrary." For someone with an insecure attachment, "this idea must be emotionally very powerful," comparable perhaps to "falling in love for the first time."

Many studies on sudden religious conversion were conducted largely with Christian samples, but one study of non-Orthodox Jews who became Orthodox also found a high level of attachment insecurity among those who underwent this transformation. Another study found that insecurely attached Christian women (especially those with anxious attachment) were more likely to report being "born again" and speaking in tongues than securely attached Christian women.

A Foxhole of Grief

From my vantage point at the end of the pew, I could see in the Mother of Sorrows chapel an elderly, white-haired man lighting a votive candle. It was close to the candle I'd lit for my sister. He put money in the box and then sat on a bench, bowed his head, and folded his hands in prayer. While he prayed, a young woman entered the chapel and knelt before the pietà. I envied them both their faith and apparent serenity.

I felt powerfully drawn to the Mother of Sorrows chapel. When I looked at the pietà, not only did I associate the lifeless body of Jesus with Jane after her accident, but I knew the chapel itself had been dedicated on the very calendar day of her death. And Christmas Eve was her birthday. The truth was, with my sister's death following so closely on my father's death, I'd fallen into a deep hole of grief—a foxhole, to reference the adage about atheists—and I didn't know how to get out.

I wondered what it would feel like to sit in the chapel and pray for my sister. I wouldn't have to kneel; I could just sit on the bench in front of the votive candles as I'd watched the white-haired man do.

My pew was just twenty feet from the chapel. I was tempted and yearned to be comforted. But what would it mean to pray? In attachment terms, it would mean allowing God to be my safe haven. But that would mean accepting God as an attachment figure, and I couldn't quite see that relationship with an invisible being. So I resisted. Anyway, even if I could pray, I wasn't sure that as a Jew doing so in a chapel dedicated to Mary in a basilica on Christmas Eve were the best circumstances. Still, if I was going to pray for Jane, I felt it would have to be in the chapel, in that place I now associated with her, where at that moment a candle that I had lit for her still burned.

Suddenly, the lights in the basilica shut off—all of them. I couldn't see the pietà. People around me didn't appear surprised, but I'd been lost in thought and hadn't paid attention. Everyone was holding a lighted candle—I remembered they'd passed them around, but I hadn't taken one. Only slender white candles held by thirty-seven hundred worshippers—minus one—now lit the basilica. Oh my—it was beautiful.

After the proclamation for Christmas was read aloud, we stood to sing "Silent Night." Until that point, I hadn't participated in the service; it felt too much like celebrating Christmas. But with the lights off and the candles lit all around me, I could not resist joining in and did so on the second verse, "Shepherds quake at the sight."

It was so welcoming, so enticing—the image and very idea of Mary so comforting in my grief, and everyone singing together, holding candles in the dark, the sound of the choir lifting over the deep notes of the organ. I felt swept up and held, comforted to be part of something bigger than myself and bigger than my own loss.

For a moment, I did wonder: was I experiencing a sudden conversion? I fit the model: anxious attachment, grief over the loss of an attachment figure, and the reactivation of my attachment system on this, my sister's birthday.

Fortunately for me (and probably also for the Roman Catholic Church), just then a procession of priests came by carrying a statue of Jesus on the cross. The bubble burst. That really was too foreign to my Jewish sensibility. The magic of the moment was lost.

Archbishop Carlo Maria Viganò, the apostolic nuncio to the United States, in white robe and red skullcap, delivered the homily.

"My dear brothers and sisters," he began in a pleasant Italian accent, "both here in this national shrine, and around the world"—the Mass was being broadcast internationally—"on behalf of the holy father Pope Francis, greetings and blessings to you on this Christmas night."

He continued, "Tonight we meet the face of God's mercy in the face of a Child. . . . We must not be afraid to approach God and to pour out our hearts before him—and allow him to embrace us, to feel the warmth of his love, and to wipe the tears from our eyes."

That's when it struck me: of course I can have a true attachment relationship with God even though God cannot be seen. My sister, after all, had been unseen by me for more than a year now, yet I still had a relationship with her that met the attachment criteria. I'm not sure I believe in life after death, but I do believe in love after death. I continue to keep her close (proximity) with photos and other objects, and by talking to her. And our love continues to strengthen me (secure base) and comfort me in times of stress (safe haven). My love for Jane and hers for me survives her death, as does our attachment relationship.

By eleven fifteen the lights were back on. The service ended after Communion, concluding with "Joy to the World."

I hadn't made plans for how to get home but ran into a young couple heading in the same direction, and we agreed to share a cab.

"Excuse me just one minute," I asked them. "Don't leave—I'll be right back."

In the Mother of Sorrows chapel, a half-dozen people were viewing the pietà, some taking pictures with their cell phones.

I looked up at Mary holding her lifeless son, and then bent my head.

"Happy birthday, Jane," I said to myself. "I miss you."

"And, God," I prayed, "please let Jane be at peace under the sea."

Then I found my ride and headed home.

––––––––––––––

There are no atheists in foxholes, but that Christmas Eve I had found myself unexpectedly in a deep foxhole of grief. Fortunately—and thanks in part to a heartrending sculpture, thirty-seven hundred candles, and the piercing blasts of two organs—I was able to find some comfort in that foxhole by accepting a new attachment relationship. I left the basilica feeling reassured by the notion that as we age and inevitably lose so many "real-life" attachment figures, there is some consolation in having an invisible, internalized one that will never leave. Despite being in a foreign religious environment, I had found a sense of connection and faith for which I had longed.

Religious affiliation has been declining in the United States, as it has in most Western countries. Among millennials (those born between 1980 and 1994), nearly 35 percent say they are atheist, agnostic, or that religion is "not a big deal." I respect everyone's choice about belief in God, but I do wonder what that 35 percent of millennials might do in years to come when their parents are gone, and they are not in a relationship, and their sister's plane falls into the sea. It's comforting to know that at least they'll always have an option.

Epilogue

When I began exploring attachment theory, I didn't anticipate the number of attachment-related events that would occur in my life during the nearly six years that I worked on this book. These included the death of my father—my primary attachment figure—followed soon after by the sudden death of my sister. Amid these losses, however, I also had the joy of attending both of my daughters' weddings and of becoming a grandfather. And I was fortunate to enjoy a relationship with a woman with—of all things!—secure attachment.

That I began this journey to understand attachment as a result of a difficult romantic relationship was unfortunate, but, looking back, I'm okay with that because the subject has turned out to be so enlightening. I had no idea, when I started, how broad the whole field of attachment research had become, nor how important.

Attachment is important because it helps us understand ourselves. It explains why we often feel and act as we do, especially in response to uncertainty or fear or loss. It's important, too, because it helps us understand others. It shows us how to create and maintain close bonds, and how best to respond to others' uncertainties, fears, and losses. Attachment is important because it can help us choose our partners and treat them in ways that respect their own attachment needs. It's important because it helps us be forgiving—of our parents, of our partners, and of ourselves—because now we know that everyone at times is struggling to meet their own attachment needs. And attachment is important because it guides us in how to be sensitive and responsive to our children. As such, it may be one of our best new tools to help forge a better life for all, because when a critical mass of humanity comes to understand attachment and works to endow a new generation with the gift of attachment security, we just might find we've built ourselves a better world.

In this book I've tried to explain attachment theory and show how our attachment system affects us in many ways throughout life. We've covered a lot of territory, and so it might be helpful to finish by recapping with what, on reflection, seem like some of the most practical and useful points.

Ten Lessons of Attachment

1. Know Your Attachment Style

Just as it can help to be aware of other aspects of your personality—introvert versus extrovert, for example—it can help to know your own attachment style. Take the quiz in the appendix (as discussed in chapter 2), or find someone qualified to give you the Adult Attachment Interview. Then use the information in this book to better understand how your attachment style influences your thoughts, feelings, and behavior. Knowing this can help you better regulate your emotions and actions, and anticipate how you're likely to react in certain situations, particularly those that are stressful or threatening.

2. Live with, or Work Around, Your Attachment Style

If you were fortunate enough to have come out of early childhood with a secure attachment, be grateful for the sense of self-worth, comfort with intimacy, resiliency, and stable relationships that tend to come with attachment security.

But if you're among those with insecure attachment, there's no need to despair; this is not a lifetime sentence to relationship hell. Once you learn your attachment style and understand how it affects you, you can begin to anticipate those effects and avoid situations that trigger them, if possible, and if not (such as with breakups, illness, or death of loved ones), learn to recognize and possibly temper your normal reactions.

And keep in mind that insecure attachment styles sometimes have their own advantages. Anxious people, sensitive to threats, can act as "sentinels," warning others of danger; avoidant people, inclined toward self-reliance and independent action, can act as "first responders," quickly finding solutions to threatening situations.

3. You Can Work to Change Your Attachment Style

Though most people spend their whole lives with the same attachment style, some are able to change. People with insecure attachments can, as discussed in chapter 2, become "earned secure." The change can come from a long-term relationship with a supportive adult, such as a teacher, mentor, or coach; from therapy or deep reflection; from the experience of very mindful parenting; or from a long-term relationship with a secure spouse or romantic partner.

4. Try to Give Your Children the Gift of Attachment Security

As discussed in chapter 6, we needn't embrace all the practices of attachment parenting, but neither can we ignore the reality of our babies' attachment needs—the stakes are just too high. If we're going to raise emotionally healthy people, a consistent attachment figure must be present at least for the first eighteen months to two years of life. This is not a gender-specific role; it could be mother, father, grandparent, nanny, among other possibilities. But someone has to do it.

It's not about "hovering" or being with our babies all the time; it's about being sensitive and attuned when we are with them—and ensuring that others to whom we entrust their care are similarly attuned. Attachment parenting's core practices—breast-feeding, babywearing, and cosleeping—can help keep babies close enough so we learn to correctly read their cues and respond.

As Glen Cooper, a clinician who works with children and families, has observed, "Children don't come with an instruction manual—they *are* the instruction manual, and behavior is how they communicate their needs."

5. Remember That Others Are Affected by Their Attachment Styles Too

Just as our behavior reflects our own attachment style, so does everyone else's behavior. As discussed earlier, being aware of this can help explain behaviors of friends, work colleagues, and sports teammates.

People who are avoidant are going to be less comfortable disclosing emotionally to their friends, getting chummy at the office, or passing the ball to others on the basketball court. Those who are anxious, on the other hand, may consistently overdisclose to friends, be hypersensitive if excluded from work meetings, or overreact to minor injuries on the ball field.

Give the avoidant person more space and the anxious person more reassurance.

But if we bear in mind that at least some of these behaviors are simply others' attachment systems speaking, we can sometimes help them with their attachment needs or at least just cut them some slack. As a rule of thumb: give the avoidant person more space and the anxious person more reassurance.

6. *Make a Good Match with the Help of Attachment Knowledge*

There's no magic formula for finding a romantic partner, but since romantic love is an adult form of attachment, it makes sense when looking to consider people's attachment styles.

As discussed in chapter 5, even on a first date you can try to assess a person's attachment style. In general, securely attached people are easy company: upbeat, fairly relaxed, and pleasant to converse with. They won't withhold personal information but neither will they over-disclose to the point of sounding needy or too eager. Avoidantly attached people, in contrast, wouldn't talk about feelings or personal matters much but would focus on things like their jobs or favorite sports teams—nothing personal or deep. Anxiously attached people, on the other hand, can be funny and engaging, but part of that comes not from a genuine interest in the other person, but from fear of rejection and a desire for the other person to like them and offer them security. They also tend to disclose too much too soon, thus coming across as needy or overeager.

Anyone, regardless of attachment style, can make a good partner, but some combinations of attachment styles work better than others. The pairing of an avoidant person with an anxious person (the anxious-avoidant trap) is the most problematic. It can work if each person is aware of and willing to accommodate the other's attachment needs, but without such effort it can lead to an unstable, on-again, off-again relationship. Overall, the best combinations occur when at least one partner is secure. "If you can find someone secure," psychology professor Harry Reis says, "you're five steps ahead."

7. *Save a Relationship with the Help of Attachment Knowledge*

It's when partners don't meet each other's attachment needs—when they fail to be each other's safe havens and secure bases—that relationships become threatened. Fights, notes Canadian psychotherapist Sue

Johnson in chapter 7, are really protests over emotional disconnection. That's why Johnson developed Emotionally Focused Therapy (EFT), a counseling method based on attachment theory.

In EFT, explains Johnson, the counselor helps draw a couple back into an emotionally appropriate bond and reestablish a sense of safe connection. Thousands of counselors, both nationally and internationally, are now trained in EFT. Studies show an exceptionally high rate of success. Many counselors also use the same principles in work with individual clients.

To locate an EFT-trained counselor near you, see the website of the International Centre for Excellence in Emotionally Focused Therapy: iceeft.com.

———

Beyond the way attachment theory affects individuals, it also has important political and moral implications for society as a whole. For example, professors Kenneth Corvo and Ellen deLara note, "Attachment theory raises the question of how well a society creates 'persons.'" They ask, Is our society organized to support healthy bonding between children and caregivers?

With these larger societal issues in mind, here are my final three attachment lessons:

8. Increase Support for Parental Education, Paid Parental Leave, and Day Care

John Bowlby, the British psychotherapist who developed attachment theory, in one of his later essays lamented society's values when it comes to raising emotionally healthy children. He wrote:

> Man and woman power devoted to the production of material goods counts as a plus in all our economic indices. Man

and woman power devoted to the production of happy, healthy, and self-reliant children in their own homes does not count at all. We have created a topsy-turvy world.

A good start to righting this "topsy-turvy" state would include better education about parenting. Future parents learn about immunizations, toy safety, and proper use of car seats, but where do they learn about attunement and sensitive responsiveness to their baby? These topics—and attachment theory in general—should be part of regular parenting education, and it wouldn't be a bad idea to start early, perhaps even with mandated parenting classes in high school and as part of regular prenatal care.

And once baby arrives, there are few things more important than consistent parental care, especially during the first eighteen months to two years—a crucial period for the formation of attachment bonds. But in the United States, almost alone among developed countries, few parents are eligible for paid leave from work. Currently, the federal Family and Medical Leave Act mandates twelve weeks of *non-paid* leave but only for full-time employees at companies with fifty employees or more. Fortunately, some states mandate more generous provisions and some private companies—particularly those in high tech—now offer significant paid time off. Examples include Amazon (twenty weeks), Google (five months), and Cisco (five months). The Bill and Melinda Gates Foundation offers a full year. We should support fiscally responsible measures—local, state, and federal—that encourage paid parental leave.

Day care, too, needs increased public support. Child-development experts, while often wary of day care in the first year, seem confident that day care for toddlers and older children can be, when combined with sensitive parenting, a fine option for working parents, and even beneficial in promoting development. This assumes, however, that day care workers are of high quality (able to correctly interpret a child's signals), that the staff-to-child ratio is high (one to three for infants and one to four for children under three), that children are assigned a particular caregiver, and that staff turnover is low.

But much day care available in the United States falls far short of these standards, particularly for poor children. In one study, fewer than half of US child-care centers met minimum standards of the American Public Health Association and the American Academy of Pediatrics, with most rating poor or mediocre in quality. We should welcome any legislation or corporate policies that improve the availability, affordability, and quality of day care.

9. Help At-Risk Kids with Disorganized Attachment

Disorganized attachment results when an infant comes to fear the same caregiver on whom he or she relies for protection and support. In the general population, only about 5 percent of children have disorganized attachment, but among at-risk kids—those living in poverty and who have been neglected or maltreated—the frequency has been measured at 80 percent or greater.

As discussed in chapter 3, kids with disorganized attachment and the dissociative disorders they spawn often lack the social skills and behavioral self-control to succeed in school, from Head Start and pre-K right up through high school. They show higher levels of oppositional behavior, hostility, and aggression. In adolescence and early adulthood, this attachment type may also be a risk factor for delinquency and violent criminality.

As psychiatrist Thomas Lewis and colleagues have observed:

> Children who get minimal care can grow up to menace a negligent society. . . . These avenging phoenixes arise from the neural wreckage of what once could have been a healthy human being.

And yet researchers have developed interventions that in careful studies have been shown to turn disorganized attachments into secure ones. These include Child-Parent Psychotherapy, where therapists meet weekly for a year with mothers and infants in the mother's home. In one study, as noted in chapter 3, the number of kids with disorganized attachment fell by more than half. Good results also have been shown with another program, Circle of Security, in which groups of parents meet with workshop leaders to learn about attachment theory and parenting skills.

Disorganized attachment among at-risk kids comes at enormous costs, not only to these children and their families, but also to the larger community. Intervention programs are expensive but the cost is tiny when compared to the costs to society of dealing with school dropouts, delinquency, and violent criminality. We need to urge elected officials—local, state, and national—to generously fund these programs.

10. Recognize That We Are All Creatures Who Need to Attach

Most adults do not understand their attachment needs; indeed, even to acknowledge them runs counter to our society's notion of adulthood: that the height of maturity is to be independent and self-sufficient and that dependency is a weakness. Yet John Bowlby saw "effective dependency" (we might also call it mutual dependency) and the ability to turn to others for emotional support not as a weakness but as both a sign and a source of strength.

If we could recognize and accept the very human need for connection and support, I believe we could build a healthier and, ultimately, happier society. This will take a gradual change in attitude, but toward that end we can take a few practical steps. For example, those who plan and administer our communities can place less emphasis on people living self-sufficiently and more on neighborliness. The design movement called New Urbanism is a promising start: it promotes walkable neighborhoods, homes closer to the street—often with front porches— a common green, or other public spaces. Also promising are innovative work and living spaces. Consider, for example, WeWork, which provides shared work spaces for young entrepreneurs, and new apartments for young people often designed with shared kitchens and social programming. Similar designs for seniors would be most welcome. "Toy libraries" and "tool libraries"—recent innovations in some communities—encourage people to pool resources and connect.

But the major attitudinal shift will come only when we recognize that we all need attachment. If as a society we were able to make this attitudinal shift, and stop denying our own biology and the thing we crave most—connection—then through interdependence we could become our strongest selves.

———

It's a hard thing to watch your own child in pain, but at the same time I was grateful to my daughter, Valerie, for allowing me into her hospital room to witness—along with her husband, her sister, and her mother—the birth of her first baby. It was in Val's college psychology textbook that I had, years earlier, first read about attachment theory, and now, six years later, I was with her in a hospital room and about to see the real-life expression of the beginning of the attachment process.

As Val labored, I was both humbled and exhilarated: humbled because I was, of course, helpless to ease my daughter's pain; exhilarated because to witness the birth of one's first grandchild—what a marvel!

And then suddenly there came a little baby girl, a helpless new human being. I watched as she began searching with her eyes, moving her arms, and crying—all to find and attach to a caregiver for protection. That the new human being was my own granddaughter, and the caregiver my daughter, was a joy and a wonder, and gave new meaning to all I'd been learning about attachment.

Moments later, the baby was placed, skin to skin, on her mother's breast, and I watched as Val held her protectively, looked into her eyes, and gently positioned her to nurse. At that moment, I recalled something I'd once heard an attachment researcher suggest: if you want to *feel* how a baby sees its mother, listen to Joe Cocker singing "You Are So Beautiful" as if it were sung to the mother by her child.

Just over a year later, as I was finishing the edits on this book, my older daughter, Sarah, and her husband had their first child. After a long labor—this time the grandfathers were not in the delivery room—they were blessed with a healthy son. And as I witnessed mother and son, I marveled at what seemed to me the beginning of yet another attuned and loving attachment bond.

Added to the blessing were the names my daughters and their husbands chose for these beautiful children: Maya Jane, after my sister, Jane; and Andrew, after my dad. In these two new lives, the two attachment figures I'd lost during the course of writing this book were memorialized.

I have the chance to see these little ones often, and for that I am grateful. As I watch them grow, and see their parents working hard and thoughtfully to meet their attachment needs, I pray they—and all babies everywhere—will be blessed with attachment security and with it the confidence, resilience, and easy ability to love that will be their lifelong reward.

Acknowledgments

The list of those I need to recognize for making this book possible is long, and it begins with John Bowlby, who developed attachment theory. It's an honor to have had the opportunity to try to convey the basics of Bowlby's brilliant work; I wish I could have met him in person to thank him.

In my hometown of Rochester, New York, people are generally friendly and helpful, but Professor Harry Reis of the University of Rochester went beyond anything I reasonably could have expected. Harry welcomed me into his classroom, spent many late afternoons patiently answering my questions, read and commented on all three hundred–plus pages of the final draft, and then contributed the foreword. For all his help and support, I am so grateful.

I'm grateful, too, to many of today's top national and international attachment researchers for their time and patience in helping me understand their field of study. These include Jude Cassidy of the University of Maryland, my earliest and most valuable guide to understanding childhood attachment; Phillip R. Shaver of the University of California, Davis; and Mario Mikulincer of the Interdisciplinary Center Herzliya (ICH) in Israel.

I also thank clinical psychiatrist Mauricio Cortina of Silver Spring, Maryland, for administering my Adult Attachment Interview and for many hours of helpful conversation; Gurit Birnbaum, also at the ICH, for her insights into attachment and sexuality; Jim Coan of the University of Virginia for a stimulating day in Charlottesville (although if I never see a red X again, that'll be fine); Susan Paris of Portland, Maine, for sharing her expertise in coding the strange situation;

therapist Reena Bernards of Silver Spring, Maryland, for sharing her knowledge of couples counseling using Emotionally Focused Therapy (EFT); Sue Johnson of Ottawa, developer of EFT, for many helpful suggestions; Shoshana Ringel for her skill in scoring the Adult Attachment Interview and for her thoughtful responses to many questions; Julie Potter for her accurate and prompt transcriptions; and Musie Tadesse and all the genial and supportive staff at my home office at the Post Massachusetts Avenue in Washington, DC.

Other researchers to whom I owe thanks include Josh Hart at Union College; Cindy Hazan at Cornell University; Paula Pietromonaco at UMass Amherst; Amir Levine at Columbia University; Paul Howes of Fairport, New York; Sam Carr at the University of Bath, England, for his groundbreaking work on sports and attachment; and Elliott Newell with the English Institute of Sport in Manchester, England.

In Rochester, at Mt. Hope Family Center—an important research center and valuable public clinic—I thank executive director Sheree Toth, clinical director Jody Manly, research director Fred Rogosch, and many staff therapists. Also in Rochester, I thank those associated with the Monroe County Pediatrics and Visitation Center for allowing me to observe at that excellent facility, especially Ellen McCauley, Moira Szilagyi, and Deborah Rosen. Thank you also to Dr. Robin Adair at the University of Rochester Medical Center and to family counselor David Schwab.

Many people gave of their time and entrusted me with their stories. In Rochester they include Alexa Weeks, therapist, doula, and coach; Matias Pivas; Xuechen Bao; Scott Miner, DVM; and Padme Livingston; in the DC area: Chris Wilson, Rachael Petersen, Jennifer Fink, and a great couple, Tiffany and Edgar; at Pleasant Pops café: Roger Horowitz, Brian Sykora, Hannah Smith, Ben Thelen, Aaron Steely, and Emily Platt; at the DCJCC: health and fitness director Andre Dixon, as well as Marshall Cohen and all the guys on the basketball team.

For their help on the subject of attachment and politics, I thank Marty Linsky, Alan Posner, Adi Shmueli, Norm Ornstein, and especially Governor Michael Dukakis for allowing me an intimate interview.

Thanks, too, to former representative Tim Petri, former representative Mickey Edwards, Rep. Louise Slaughter, and Mayor Lovely Warren.

For his help on the subject of attachment and religion, I thank Monsignor Stephen J. Rossetti of the Catholic University of America in Washington, DC.

Thank you, too, to the Elizabeth Writers Center for providing a workspace so supportive of sustained writing—and with skilled editorial assistance close at hand. And for sustaining me in a different, and delicious, way—especially through first drafts—I'm thankful for Turkish figs, roasted pumpkin seeds in the shell, So Delicious Mini Mocha Almond Fudge Bars, Whole Foods Cape Cod Trail Mix, and Klondike Bars.

On some of the earliest chapter drafts, Patricia McClary and Gail Hosking provided helpful comments. Editor Sarah Flynn skillfully helped shape those early drafts into book form.

Shira Klapper came into this project in the bottom of the ninth but pitched an excellent final inning checking and correcting source notes, copyediting, and generally improving everything I'd written.

I remain ever grateful to two wonderful teachers: Clayton "Bud" O'Dell and Elizabeth Hart. While researching this book, Bud and his wife, Jessie, warmly welcomed me into their home in North Carolina, and with Jessie and her family I mourn Bud's recent passing.

Readers who value clear thought and clean writing will join me in thanking a loyal band of good and patient friends who commented on every chapter through multiple drafts. That anything I write even gets published is pretty much due to their help:

Byron Rubin, who was there from the beginning of my fascination with attachment theory and whose steadfast friendship and constant encouragement are more than anyone could ask;

Nancy Heneson, whose editing skills and wit are a marvel; reading whole chapters over the phone and dissecting them together was a pleasure;

Elisa Siegel, whom I'm so grateful to have met, thank you for our "security checkpoint," and thank you for every single edit, especially the ones where you just wrote it the way it should be and let me take the credit; and

Rabbi David A. Katz, my lifelong friend, whose intelligence, keen editorial eye, humanity, and good humor make me sound a lot smarter and more pleasant on the page than I often am.

I'm also blessed with excellent homegrown readers and editors. For their practical advice, insight, steady encouragement, and valuable suggestions throughout, I thank Sarah Lovenheim Goldfarb, Valerie Lovenheim Adaki, Ben Lovenheim, Oren Adaki, Zachary Goldfarb, and Marie Lovenheim. I'm so grateful to be attached to you all.

To my wonderful agent, Geri Thoma of Writers House: once again you stayed firmly in my corner when things looked uncertain and once again, thanks to you, it all worked out.

To Marian Lizzi, my editor, thank you for embracing this project, for the fun of working together again, and for the way you make whatever I write come out so much better.

And, finally, to my grandchildren at the time of this writing, Maya, Andrew, and Talia, as well as those to come: though I can be with you for only a small part of your journey, I hope what I've written here may help guide and smooth your way.

Glossary

Adult Attachment Interview (AAI): A structured, hour-long interview designed to assess an adult's attachment style.

Ainsworth, Mary (1913–99): Canadian-born developmental psychologist and research assistant to John Bowlby, Ainsworth developed the "strange situation," a laboratory procedure used to assess attachment style in young children.

Anxious attachment style: An insecure attachment pattern that develops when a child becomes unsure of whether the parent or other primary caregiver will meet the child's needs. This is often the result of caregivers responding to the child's needs either inappropriately or inconsistently, or both. Individuals with anxious attachment often crave high levels of intimacy, approval, and responsiveness from relationship partners but have difficulty trusting them and constantly seek reassurance.

Attachment: The deep and enduring emotional bond that connects one person to another as an attachment figure.

Attachment figure: A person who provides for another the essential elements of an attachment relationship: a *secure base* from which to explore, and a *safe haven* to return to when fearful or hurt. An attachment figure is also a person one strives to keep in *close proximity*. Threats of separation from an attachment figure typically cause distress, often accompanied by protest. Loss of an attachment figure typically causes grief.

Attachment style: The core emotion or personality structure that an individual forms in early childhood as a result of interaction with caregivers, and which in turn creates a set of beliefs and expectations about relationships and serves as a prototype for later intimate relationships.

Attachment system: An inborn behavioral system developed through evolution in human beings and most other mammals designed to protect infants from danger by assuring their proximity to competent, reliable caregivers who can support and protect them.

Attachment theory: A psychological model that explains the emergence of the emotional bond between an infant and primary caregiver, and the way this bond affects the child's behavioral and emotional development. John Bowlby, who developed attachment theory, argued that attachment evolved as a way to keep infants—immature and vulnerable—close to their parents, thus protecting them from danger and giving them a survival advantage.

Avoidant attachment style: An insecure attachment type in which a child has lost hope that a parent or other primary caregiver will meet his or her needs. This is often the result of caregivers consistently failing to provide sensitive and reliable care. Individuals with this attachment pattern find it difficult to trust others and desire a high level of independence, viewing themselves as self-sufficient and not needing close relationships.

Bowlby, John (1907–90): A British psychotherapist and developer of attachment theory who devoted his life to the study of the mother-child bond. His major work was the trilogy known as *Attachment and Loss*: *Attachment*, published in 1969; *Separation*, in 1973, and *Loss*, in 1980.

Disorganized attachment: An insecure attachment style that most often results when an infant comes to fear the same caregiver on whom he or she relies for protection and support. This may result from negligent or abusive treatment or from a general lack of care as may be found when infants are orphaned and institutionalized. Individuals with this attachment pattern measure high in both avoidance and anxiousness. Seen in only about 5 percent of the general population, the frequency of this attachment style rises to as much as 80 percent among maltreated children.

Earned secure: This condition is achieved when a person who should have had attachment insecurity due to unreliable or unresponsive caregiving nevertheless achieves attachment security. This can result from a long-term relationship with a supportive adult such as a teacher, mentor, or coach; through therapy or deep reflection; or through a long-term relationship with a secure spouse or romantic partner.

Experiences in Close Relationships quiz: A thirty-six-item questionnaire designed to measure an adult's attachment style based on responses concerning past romantic relationships.

Internal working model: A set of beliefs and expectations born of a child's earliest experience with caregivers about the availability of attachment figures and their likelihood of providing support during times of stress.

Protest behavior: How infants respond—by crying, for example—when they perceive that the primary caregiver is not readily available. The adult version is seen, for example, when an individual is faced with a romantic breakup and cries, argues, or even threatens self-harm or violence in response to the impending loss of an attachment figure.

Proximity seeking: The efforts by infants to maintain physical contact with, or at least be physically close to, primary caregivers. Adults make a similar effort to keep in touch—or at least to know the whereabouts of—romantic partners and other attachment figures.

Safe haven: One of the defining criteria of an attachment relationship. For an infant, a parent or caregiver functions as a safe haven when the infant is confident he or she can turn to that person for safety and reassurance when stressed or faced with a threatening situation. For an adult, a person functions as a safe haven when he or she is a reliable source of protection and support in times of need.

Secure attachment: An attachment pattern in which a child has come to trust that the parent or other primary caregiver will meet the child's needs. This is often the result of caregivers responding to a child's needs appropriately and consistently. Individuals with secure attachment generally are resilient in the face of setbacks, have high (but not overinflated) self-esteem, are able to communicate well about their own needs, are comfortable with intimacy, and tend to trust others and to have stable, long-term relationships.

Secure base: One of the defining criteria of an attachment relationship. For an infant, a parent or caregiver functions as a secure base when the infant, in the security of that person's care, feels safe to explore and master the environment. For adults, a person functions as a secure base when, within the security of their relationship, the individual feels safe to take risks in pursuit of his or her goals.

Strange situation: A laboratory procedure designed by developmental psychologist Mary Ainsworth to assess attachment style in young children from about one to two years of age.

Appendix:
Attachment Quiz

Experiences in Close Relationships Questionnaire

This thirty-six-item questionnaire, developed by attachment researchers, is designed to help you assess your own attachment style.* The statements concern how you feel in emotionally intimate relationships. You are asked to respond to the questions in terms of how you *generally* experience relationships—not just in what is happening in a current relationship—by giving a number from 1 through 7 to indicate how much you agree or disagree with the statement, with 1 = strongly disagree and 7 = strongly agree.

Computing your score for the quiz can be complicated, so it's easiest to take the quiz online where your score will be automatically computed, illustrated on a graph, and analyzed.

Go to www.web-research-design.net/cgi-bin/crq/crq.pl and choose Survey B.

---

* Originally published in Kelly A. Brennan, Catherine L. Clark, and Phillip Shaver, "Self-Report Measurement of Adult Romantic Attachment: An Integrative Overview," in *Attachment Theory and Close Relationships,* eds. Jeffrey A. Simpson and Steven Rholes (New York: Guilford Press, 1997), 46–76. Later revised by R. Chris Fraley, Niels G. Waller, and Kelly A. Brennan, "An Item-Response Theory Analysis of Self-Report Measures of Adult Attachment," *Journal of Personality and Social Psychology* 78, no. 2 (2000): 350–65. The questionnaire in this book is adapted from the Fraley, Waller, and Brennan version.

1. It's not difficult for me to get close to my partner.
2. I often worry that my partner will not want to stay with me.
3. I often worry that my partner doesn't really love me.
4. It helps to turn to my romantic partner in times of need.
5. I often wish that my partner's feelings for me were as strong as my feelings for them.
6. I worry a lot about my relationships.
7. I talk things over with my partner.
8. When I show my feelings for romantic partners, I'm afraid they will not feel the same about me.
9. I rarely worry about my partner leaving me.
10. My partner only seems to notice me when I'm angry.
11. I feel comfortable depending on romantic partners.
12. I do not often worry about being abandoned.
13. My romantic partner makes me doubt myself.
14. I find that my partner(s) don't want to get as close as I would like.
15. I'm afraid that I will lose my partner's love.
16. My desire to be very close sometimes scares people away.
17. I worry that I won't measure up to other people.
18. I find it easy to depend on romantic partners.
19. I prefer not to show a partner how I feel deep down.
20. I feel comfortable sharing my private thoughts and feelings with my partner.
21. I worry that romantic partners won't care about me as much as I care about them.
22. I find it difficult to allow myself to depend on romantic partners.
23. I'm afraid that once a romantic partner gets to know me, he or she won't like who I really am.
24. I am very comfortable being close to romantic partners.
25. I don't feel comfortable opening up to romantic partners.
26. I prefer not to be too close to romantic partners.

27. I get uncomfortable when a romantic partner wants to be very close.
28. I find it relatively easy to get close to my partner.
29. I usually discuss my problems and concerns with my partner.
30. I tell my partner just about everything.
31. Sometimes romantic partners change their feelings about me for no apparent reason.
32. When my partner is out of sight, I worry that he or she might become interested in someone else.
33. I am nervous when partners get too close to me.
34. It's easy for me to be affectionate with my partner.
35. It makes me mad that I don't get the affection and support I need from my partner.
36. My partner really understands me and my needs.

Resources

Attachment Theory, Generally

Several US universities operate laboratories that conduct research on aspects of attachment theory. The labs train graduate students, publish research findings, and run experiments for which they often recruit volunteers. Some also provide training for therapists and those in related fields.

Davis, California
Adult Attachment Lab at the University of California, Davis
adultattachment.faculty.ucdavis.edu

College Park, Maryland
Maryland Child & Family Development Lab, University of Maryland
www.childandfamilylab.umd.edu/index.html

New York City
The Center for Attachment Research at the New School for Social Research
www.attachmentresearch.com

Stony Brook, New York
SUNY Stony Brook Attachment Lab
www.psychology.sunysb.edu/attachment

Charlottesville, Virginia
The Ainsworth Attachment Clinic (Independent*)
theattachmentclinic.org
*The independent Ainsworth Attachment Clinic in Charlottesville

provides evaluation and consultation services for children from birth through adolescence—including those in foster care or adoptive care—who have experienced significant challenges to attachment bonds with parents or other caregivers.

Further Reading

A Secure Base, by John Bowlby (Basic Books, 1988). A collection of some of Bowlby's later lectures, presenting his ideas on various attachment-related issues, including guidelines for child-rearing.

Becoming Attached, by Robert Karen (Oxford University Press, 1998). A comprehensive and readable account of the development and scope of attachment theory.

Attachment in Adulthood, second edition, by Mario Mikulincer and Phillip R. Shaver (Guilford Press, 2016). A compendium of current research on all aspects of attachment's influence on adult behavior. Written for psychologists and other practitioners.

Handbook of Attachment, third edition, edited by Jude Cassidy and Phillip R. Shaver (Guilford Press, 2016). This is the most comprehensive analysis of current findings on all major aspects of attachment research. The book is written for psychologists and other practitioners.

Child Development and Parenting

Attachment parenting promotes practices that are meant to produce healthy emotional bonds between parents and children. Caregivers need not endorse all of attachment parenting's precepts in order to find that some of its core practices—babywearing, breast-feeding, cosleeping—may help enable a sensitive and responsive approach to a baby's attachment needs. Helpful websites include the following:

Attachment Parenting International: www.attachmentparenting.org

Babywearing International: babywearinginternational.org

La Leche League International (provides education and support for breast-feeding): www.llli.org

Mother-Baby Behavioral Sleep Laboratory at University of Notre Dame (includes FAQ on cosleeping): cosleeping.nd.edu

Further Reading

The Attachment Parenting Book, by William Sears, MD, and Martha Sears, RN (Little, Brown and Company, 2001).

Being There: Why Prioritizing Motherhood in the First Three Years Matters, by Erica Komisar (TarcherPerigee, 2017). A veteran psychoanalyst gives stay-at-home and working parents practical advice on raising emotionally healthy, secure, and resilient children.

The Mother-Infant Interaction Picture Book: Origins of Attachment, by Beatrice Beebe, Phyllis Cohen, and Frank Lachmann (W. W. Norton & Company, 2016). Using video microanalysis—which captures moment-to-moment interactions—an internationally known researcher enables readers to see details of mother-infant communication and response that are too rapid to grasp with the naked eye and that can predict future attachment styles.

Couples Counseling and Individual Therapy

The International Centre for Excellence in Emotionally Focused Therapy, based in Ottawa, Canada, promotes Emotionally Focused Therapy (EFT), the form of couples counseling developed by Dr. Sue Johnson and based on principles of attachment theory. Many therapists trained in EFT also use the same principles in their work with individual

clients. To locate a therapist near you trained in EFT—or for information on training, tapes, and other support services—see iceeft.com.

Further Reading

Hold Me Tight, by Sue Johnson (Little, Brown and Company, 2008). The origin
    and workings of Emotionally Focused Therapy.
Love Sense: The Revolutionary New Science of Romantic Relationships,
    by Sue Johnson (Little, Brown and Company, 2013). Reflections on
    how and why we love, and discussion of current research.

Dating

The Experiences in Close Relationships questionnaire, composed of
thirty-six statements about how you feel in emotionally intimate relationships, is a quick way to assess your attachment style and, if a
significant other is willing, to assess that person's attachment style too.

Sample statements from the questionnaire appear in the appendix.
To take the quiz and have the results automatically computed, illustrated on a graph, and analyzed, see www.web-research-design.net/
cgi-bin/crq/crq.pl and choose Survey B.

Further Reading

*Attached: The New Science of Adult Attachment and How It Can Help You
    Find—and Keep—Love*, by Amir Levine and Rachel S. F. Heller (Jeremy P.
    Tarcher / Penguin, 2010). An excellent guide to how attachment knowledge
    can help with dating success.

International Organizations

These groups organize international conferences on attachment, report on new research, and promote understanding and use of attachment theory.

The Bowlby Centre
thebowlbycentre.org.uk

The International Association for the Study of Attachment
www.iasa-dmm.org

Society for Emotion and Attachment Studies (Hosts an annual international conference and publishes the journal *Attachment and Human Development*.)
www.seasinternational.org

Measuring Attachment

The Adult Attachment Interview is considered the best way to measure attachment style in adults. To locate a person accredited to administer the interview, use the website attachment-training.com or e-mail Naomi Gribneau Bahm, coordinator of the AAI Trainers Consortium, at ngbreliability@gmail.com.

Another option is to take the Experiences in Close Relationships quiz. It measures different factors from the AAI but also gives a general measure of attachment style. A sample of the questionnaire appears in the appendix. To take the quiz and have the results automatically computed, illustrated on a graph, and analyzed, see www.web-research-design.net/cgi-bin/crq/crq.pl and choose Survey B.

Measuring attachment in children under two years of age is done with the laboratory procedure called the "strange situation" (see chapter 3). You can see what the strange situation looks like from this (and many other) videos available on YouTube: www.youtube.com/watch ?v=QTsewNrHUHU.

Note: The strange situation is not designed to be a valid measure of an individual child's attachment style. This is because the procedure is designed for research with large numbers of children and is statistically valid with such groups. But the accuracy rate with any one child on any one day is not 100 percent. On any given day, for example, a child may be tired, the parent may be stressed, or the stranger may not relate well to that particular child. Therefore, if parents wish to determine their children's attachment styles, instead of using the strange situation they should find a child and family therapist skilled in attachment theory and familiar with assessing the attachment styles of children of various ages. Depending on the child's age and family situation, the therapist can use a combination of approaches—observation of the child, conversation with the parents, and diagnostic tools such as "story stems" (storytelling combined with doll play) to assess an individual child's attachment style.

Notes

Introduction

xviii **"leave the relationship":** Joyce Parker, PhD, "Using Attachment Theory Concepts in Couple Therapy," Independent Psychotherapy Network, Summer 2005, accessed on October 6, 2017, www.therapyinla.com/articles/article0905.html. Emphasis has been added. Dr. Parker appropriately uses the attachment terms "preoccupied" and "dismissive" but I use the roughly equivalent "anxious" and "avoidant" to simplify terminology for the general reader and make it uniform throughout the book.

xviii **a relationship killer:** The term "anxious-avoidant trap" was coined by authors Amir Levine and Rachel S. F. Heller in their book *Attached: The New Science of Adulthood Attachment and How it Can Help You Find—and Keep—Love* (New York: Jeremy P. Tarcher/Penguin, 2010).

xix **"from the cradle to the grave":** John Bowlby, *Attachment and Loss*, vol. 1 *Attachment* (New York: Basic Books, 1969), 208.

xix **what love *feels* like:** Thomas Lewis, Fari Amini, and Richard Lannon, *A General Theory of Love* (New York: Vintage, 2001), 160.

xx **first to find a way out to safety:** Tsachi Ein-Dor, Mario Mikulincer, and Phillip R. Shaver, "Effective Reaction to Danger: Attachment Insecurities Predict Behavioral Reactions to an Experimentally Induced Threat Above and Beyond General Personality Traits," *Social Psychological and Personality Science* 2, no. 5 (2011): 467–73.

xxiii **"21st-century psychology":** Jude Cassidy and Phillip R. Shaver, eds., preface to *Handbook of Attachment: Theory, Research, and Clinical Applications*, 2nd ed. (New York: Guilford Press, 2008), xi.

xxiii **"most successful theories in psychological science":** Lee A. Kirkpatrick, *Attachment, Evolution, and the Psychology of Religion* (New York: Guilford Press, 2005), 25.

xxiii **"the business of understanding people":** Sue Johnson, *Hold Me Tight: Seven Conversations for a Lifetime of Love* (New York: Little, Brown and Company, 2008), 16.

xxiii **Mount John Bowlby:** "Mount John Bowlby and Peak Mary Ainsworth," Department of Psychology, State University of New York, Stony Brook, accessed on June 29, 2017, www.psychology.sunysb.edu/attachment/mount_john_bowlby/mountains.htm.

xxiv **do not have a single other person to confide in:** Sean Alfano, "The Lonely States of America," *CBS News,* June 28, 2006, www.cbsnews.com/news /the-lonely-states-of-america/.

xxiv **"depriving people of what they crave most":** Lewis et al., *A General Theory of Love,* 225.

Chapter 1. When the Tiger Comes:
Origin of the Attachment System

6 **"physical contact and comfort":** Lee A. Kirkpatrick, *Attachment, Evolution, and the Psychology of Religion* (Guilford Press, 2005), 27. (For a video of Harry Harlow discussing the "wire mother" experiment, see www .youtube.com/watch?v=_O60TYAIgC4.)

6 **"part of a relationship":** Donald Winnicott, *The Child, the Family, and the Outside World,* 2nd ed. (Perseus Publishing, 1992), 88.

8 **"to whom the child would run first":** Kirkpatrick, *Attachment, Evolution, and the Psychology of Religion,* 37–8.

8 **"stores an impression of what love feels like":** Thomas Lewis, Fari Amini, and Richard Lannon, *A General Theory of Love* (New York: Vintage, 2001), 160.

11 **"and maybe (anxious)":** Kirkpatrick, *Attachment, Evolution, and the Psychology of Religion,* 38, citing Cindy Hazan and Phillip R. Shaver, "Attachment as an Organizational Framework for Research on Close Relationships," *Psychological Inquiry* 5, no. 1 (1994): 5.

11 **"a nanny and some nursemaids":** Suzan van Dijken, *John Bowlby: His Early Life: A Biographical Journey into the Roots of Attachment Theory* (London: Free Association Books, 1998), 19.

11 **"wouldn't send a dog to boarding school at that age":** Robert Karen, *Becoming Attached: First Relationships and How They Shape Our Capacity to Love* (New York: Oxford University Press, 1998), 30–1.

16 **"Attachment Patterns in Adulthood":** Harry Reis, lecture from Relationship Processes and Emotions, University of Rochester, New York, October 27, 2011. Slide modified by Harry Reis from one used in a talk by Phillip R. Shaver, and additionally modified by the author to use terms consistent with those used in this book.

17 **"your mother's arms and life in your lover's arms":** Theodore Waters, "Learning to Love: From Your Mother's Arms to Your Lover's Arms," *The Medium: The Voice of the University of Toronto* 30, no. 19 (February 9, 2004): 12.

18 **"more intimate than I feel comfortable being":** Based on research from Cindy Hazan and Phillip Shaver, "Romantic Love Conceptualized as an Attachment Process," *Journal of Personality and Social Psychology* 52, no. 3 (1987): 511–24.

19 **"scares people away":** Ibid.

20 **"experience deals the hand you can play":** Lewis et al., *A General Theory of Love.*
21 **between genes and attachment style:** Marinus van IJzendoorn, from remarks presented at the 7th International Attachment Conference, New York, New York, August 7, 2015.
21 **to protect the community:** Tsachi Ein-Dor, Mario Mikulincer, Guy Doron, and Phillip R. Shaver, "The Attachment Paradox: How Can So Many of Us (the Insecure Ones) Have No Adaptive Advantages?" *Perspectives on Psychological Science* 5, no. 2 (2010): 123–41, as cited in Sam Carr and Ioannis Costas Batlle, "Attachment Theory, Neoliberalism, and Social Conscience," *Journal of Theoretical and Philosophical Psychology* 35, no. 3 (2015): 160–76. See also Willem Eduard Frankenhuis, "Did Insecure Attachment Styles Evolve for the Benefit of the Group?" *Frontiers in Psychology* 1 (November 2010): 1–3, dx.doi.org/10.3389/fpsyg.2010.00172.
23 **substitutes for the caregiver:** Mario Mikulincer and Phillip R. Shaver, *Attachment in Adulthood: Structure, Dynamics, and Change*, 2nd ed. (New York: Guilford Press, 2016), 132, 142.

Chapter 2. Five Adjectives: Measuring Adult Attachment

26 **how he sees himself in relation to others:** Jude Cassidy, "Truth, Lies and Intimacy: An Attachment Perspective," *Attachment & Human Development* 3, no. 2 (September 2001): 121–55.
26 **"across countries and cultures":** Marian Bakermans-Kranenburg and Marinus van IJzendoorn, "The First 10,000 Adult Attachment Interviews: Distributions of Adult Attachment Representations in Clinical and Non-clinical Groups," *Attachment and Human Development* 11, no. 3 (May 2009): 223–63.
29 **"contradictions and inconsistencies":** Erik Hesse, "The Adult Attachment Interview," in *Handbook of Attachment: Theory, Research, and Clinical Applications*, 2nd ed., eds. Jude Cassidy and Phillip R. Shaver (New York: Guilford Press, 2008), 555.
32 **selection of each word:** Ibid., 557.

Chapter 3. When Mother Returns: Attachment Styles in Children

53 **"resisting contact angrily once it is achieved":** Nancy S. Weinfield et al., "The Nature of Individual Differences in Infant-Caregiver Attachment," in *Handbook of Attachment: Theory, Research, and Clinical Applications*, 2nd ed., eds. Jude Cassidy and Phillip R. Shaver (New York: Guilford Press, 2008), 81.
55 **orphanages or other institutionalized care:** Bert Powell, Glen Cooper, Kent Hoffman, and Bob Marvin, *The Circle of Security Intervention:*

Enhancing Attachment in Early Parent-Child Relationships (New York: Guilford Press, 2014), 79.

55 **themselves had secure attachments:** Mario Mikulincer and Phillip R. Shaver, *Attachment in Adulthood: Structure, Dynamics, and Change*, 2nd ed. (New York: Guilford Press, 2016), 135.

57 **"fearing their caregiver at the same time":** Powell et al., *Circle of Security Intervention*, 74–5.

58 **"And it's really sad":** Jude Cassidy, lecture at the Department of Psychology, University of Maryland, College Park, Maryland, April 24, 2013, and personal communication, December 1, 2013.

61 **"dissociative disorders":** Mary Dozier, K. Chase Stovall-McClough, and Kathleen E. Albus, "Attachment and Psychopathology in Adulthood," in *Handbook of Attachment*, 2nd ed., 736.

61 **in combination with childhood maltreatment:** L. Alan Sroufe et al., *The Development of the Person: The Minnesota Study of Risk and Adaptation from Birth to Adulthood* (New York: Guilford Press, 2005), 296–97.

61 **"including . . . speech and language development":** Anna T. Smyke and Angela S. Breidenstine, "Foster Care in Early Childhood," in *Handbook of Infant Mental Health*, 3rd ed., ed. Charles H. Zeanah Jr. (New York: Guilford Press, 2009), 504.

62 **girls were also at risk:** R. Pasco Fearon et al., "The Significance of Insecure Attachment and Disorganization in the Development of Children's Externalizing Behavior: A Meta-Analytic Study," *Child Development* 81, no. 2 (2010): 435–56.

62 **82 percent of psychiatric patients:** J. Reid Meloy, "Pathologies of Attachment, Violence, and Criminality," in *Handbook of Psychology, vol. 11 Forensic Psychology*, ed. Alan M. Goldstein (Hoboken, NJ: John Wiley & Sons, 2003), 519.

62 **delinquency and violent criminality:** Ibid.

62 **sensitively to her child's needs:** Erin P. Stronach, Sheree L. Toth, Fred A. Rogosch, and Dante Cicchetti, "Preventive Interventions and Sustained Attachment Security in Maltreated Children," *Development and Psychopathology* 25 (2013): 919–30.

62 **drop in disorganized attachment:** Dante Cicchetti, Fred A. Rogosch, and Sheree L. Toth, "Fostering Secure Attachment in Infants in Maltreating Families through Preventive Intervention," *Development and Psychopathology* 18 (2006): 623–49.

Chapter 4. In the Scanner: Attachment and the Brain

66 **"using measures of neural activity":** James A. Coan, "Toward a Neuroscience of Attachment," in *Handbook of Attachment: Theory,*

Research, and Clinical Applications, 2nd ed., eds. Jude Cassidy and Phillip R. Shaver (New York: Guilford Press, 2008), 254.

66 **"Why We Hold Hands"**: James Coan, "Why We Hold Hands," YouTube video of talk at TEDx Charlottesville, filmed on November 15, 2013, posted January 25, 2014, www.youtube.com/watch?v=1UMHUPPQ96c.

68 **mothers who were avoidant:** Lane Strathearn et al., "Adult Attachment Predicts Maternal Brain and Oxytocin Response to Infant Cues," *Neuropsychopharmacology* 34 (2009): 2655–66.

68 **threats to the self:** Pascal Vrtička et al., "Individual Attachment Style Modulates Human Amygdala and Striatum Activation During Social Appraisal," *PLOS ONE* 3, no. 8 (2008): e2868, accessed July, 7, 2017, doi:10.1371/journal.pone.0002868.

69 **"differences in anxious and avoidant attachment"**: C. Nathan DeWall et al., "Do Neural Responses to Rejection Depend on Attachment Style? An fMRI Study," *Social Cognitive and Affective Neuroscience* 7, no. 2 (2012): 184–92.

71 **"'You're not enough people!'"**: Kurt Vonnegut Jr., *Timequake* (New York: Berkley Publishing Group, 1998), 24.

72 **normal distribution of attachment styles:** Marinus van IJzendoorn, "Attachment in Context: Kibbutz Child-Rearing as a Historical Experiment," paper presented at the Biennial Meeting of the International Society for the Study of Behavioral Development, Amsterdam, the Netherlands, June 27–July 2, 1994, openaccess.leidenuniv.nl/bitstream/handle/1887/1477/168_144.pdf;jsessionid=882039C799E3AB7C332D6A24 AF68FDD6?sequence=1.

75 **"grief" over the loss of Minnie:** Suzan van Dijken, *John Bowlby: His Early Life: A Biographical Journey into the Roots of Attachment Theory* (London: Free Association Books, 1998), 26.

79 **either secure or avoidant attachment:** Mario Mikulincer and Phillip R. Shaver, *Attachment in Adulthood: Structure, Dynamics, and Change*, 2nd ed. (New York: Guilford Press, 2016), 250–51.

Chapter 5. A Date for Coffee: Attachment and Dating

84 **"It's that difficult"**: Genesis Rabbah 68.4; see also www.myjewishlearning.com/article/our-god-our-matchmaker.

84 **"grieving over someone"**: John Bowlby, *Attachment and Loss, vol. 3 Loss: Sadness and Depression* (New York: Basic Books, 1980), 40.

84 **"in couple relationships"**: Mario Mikulincer and Phillip R. Shaver, *Attachment in Adulthood: Structure, Dynamics, and Change*, 2nd ed. (New York: Guilford Press, 2016), 346.

85 **"their ultimate fate"**: Ibid., 286.

86 **"their partners' needs"**: Amir Levine and Rachel S. F. Heller, *Attached: The New Science of Adulthood Attachment and How It Can Help You Find—and Keep—Love* (New York: Jeremy P. Tarcher / Penguin, 2010), 135.

87 **style's relative share of the population:** Ibid., 95.

88 **to break up within the three-year study period:** Mikulincer and Shaver, *Attachment in Adulthood*, 336.

94 **"to be irresistibly desired":** Gurit Birnbaum, "Attachment and Sexual Mating: The Joint Operation of Separate Motivational Systems," in *Handbook of Attachment: Theory, Research, and Clinical Applications*, 3rd ed., ed. Jude Cassidy and Phillip R. Shaver (New York: Guilford Press, 2016), 464–83.

94 **"a lost sense of identity":** Mikulincer and Shaver, *Attachment in Adulthood*, 209.

95 **"poignant but incapacitating":** Thomas Lewis, Fari Amini, and Richard Lannon, *A General Theory of Love* (New York: Vintage, 2001), 158.

99 **"disapproval and rejection":** Mario Mikulincer and Phillip R. Shaver, *Attachment in Adulthood: Structure, Dynamics, and Change*, 1st ed. (New York: Guilford Press, 2010), 286.

99 **enjoy the experience:** Ibid.

100 **"explored or established":** Ibid., 287.

Chapter 6. Raising a Human Being: Attachment and Parenting

105 **cover story on "attachment parenting":** Kate Pickert, "The Man Who Remade Motherhood," *Time*, May 21, 2012, accessed July 9, 2016, time.com /606/the-man-who-remade-motherhood.

106 **"responding appropriately to those cues":** William Sears and Martha Sears, *The Attachment Parenting Book: A Commonsense Guide to Understanding and Nurturing Your Baby* (New York: Little, Brown and Company, 2001), 2.

106 **and responds appropriately:** Klaus Grossmann et al., "Maternal Sensitivity: Observational Studies Honoring Mary Ainsworth's 100th Year," *Attachment & Human Development* 15, nos. 5–6 (2013): 443–47.

108 **her child on her back:** Maria Blois, *Babywearing: The Benefits and Beauty of This Ancient Tradition* (Amarillo, TX: Praeclarus Press, 2016), 30–2.

111 **"behavior is how they communicate their needs":** Glen Cooper, during training for Circle of Security Parenting, Baltimore, Maryland, January 22, 2013.

111 **"will alleviate this distress":** Judi Mesman, Marinus van IJzendoorn, and Abraham Sagi-Schwartz, "Cross-Cultural Patterns of Attachment: Universal and Contextual Dimensions," in *Handbook of Attachment: Theory, Research, and Clinical Applications*, 3rd ed., eds. Jude Cassidy and Phillip R. Shaver (New York: Guilford Press, 2016), 853.

112 **"years later, a secure child":** Thomas Lewis, Fari Amini, and Richard Lannon, *A General Theory of Love* (New York: Vintage, 2001), 75.

112 **researchers call "family ecology":** Mario Mikulincer and Phillip R.
Shaver, *Attachment in Adulthood: Structure, Dynamics, and Change*, 2nd
ed. (New York: Guilford Press, 2016), 123.

114 **including sexual offenses and domestic violence:** Ibid., 396, 433–35.

115 **some even walked out of his early lectures:** Deborah Blum, *Love at Goon
Park: Harry Harlow and the Science of Affection* (Cambridge, MA: Perseus
Publishing, 2002), 234.

115 **than just day care alone:** NICHD Early Child Care Research Network,
"Child-Care and Family Predictors of Preschool Attachment and Stability
From Infancy," *Developmental Psychology* 37, no. 6 (2001): 847–62.

116 **particularly for poor children:** Robert Karen, *Becoming Attached: First
Relationships and How They Shape Our Capacity to Love* (New York:
Oxford University Press, 1998), 339.

116 **Breast-feeding is a "built-in" attachment tool:** Sears and Sears, *The
Attachment Parenting Book*, 53.

116 **if both mother and child desire:** American Academy of Pediatrics, policy
statement, "Breastfeeding and the Use of Human Milk," *Pediatrics* 115
(2005): 496–506.

118 **"learns to trust his parents and his ability to communicate":** Sears and
Sears, *The Attachment Parenting Book*, 6.

118 **"all the world's parents sleep with their children":** Thomas Lewis, Fari
Amini, and Richard Lannon, *A General Theory of Love* (New York: Vintage,
2001), 194.

119 **not perfectly so and not all the time:** Donald Winnicott, *The Child, the
Family, and the Outside World*, 2nd ed. (Perseus Publishing, 1992).

121 **"lessen a baby's need to cry":** Sears and Sears, *The Attachment Parenting
Book*, 4, 82.

121 **"the frequency and intensity" of an infant's crying:** Robert S. Marvin
and Preston A. Britner, "Normative Development: The Ontogeny of
Attachment," in *Handbook of Attachment*, 2nd ed., 276.

Chapter 7. Dancing Close:
Attachment, Marriage, and Couples Counseling

122 **"when most couples walk through my door":** David Schwab
(psychotherapist and EFT-trained family counselor), interview with author,
Rochester, New York, June 8, 2014.

123 **"rules for fighting effectively":** Sue Johnson, *Hold Me Tight: Seven
Conversations for a Lifetime of Love* (New York: Little, Brown and
Company, 2008), 84.

124 **the core issue: love:** Ibid., 6.

124 **"destroyed their marriage and themselves":** Ibid., 3.

124 **"the best survival mechanism there is":** Ibid., 47.

124 **"safe haven from the storms of life":** Ibid., 15.
124 **"neural duet":** Ibid., 253.
124 **"bodily processes and our emotional lives":** Coan quoted in ibid., 26.
125 **"deny this at our peril":** Ibid., 24.
125 **"Do I matter to you?":** Ibid., 30.
125 **"Nothing else will do":** Ibid., 254, 47.
125 **"innate part of being human":** Audrey Brassard and Susan M. Johnson, "Couple and Family Therapy: An Attachment Perspective," in *Handbook of Attachment: Theory, Research, and Clinical Applications*, 3rd ed., eds. Jude Cassidy and Phillip R. Shaver (New York: Guilford Press, 2016), 806.
126 **"responsive to each other":** Ibid., 7.
126 **"longings for caring and connection":** Ibid., 44.
126 **"respond with soothing care":** Ibid., 47–48.
127 **"presence of a romantic partner":** Susan M. Johnson et al., "Soothing the Threatened Brain: Leveraging Contact Comfort with Emotionally Focused Therapy," *PLOS ONE* 3, no. 8 (2013): e79314, accessed July 10, doi:10.1371/journal.pone.0079314.
127 **"comforts the neurons in our brain":** Sue Johnson, "Soothing the Threatened Brain," YouTube video, posted December 10, 2013, www.youtube.com/watch?v=2J6B00d-8lw.
130 **"low commitment to their primary relationship":** Gurit Birnbaum, "Attachment and Sexual Mating: The Joint Operation of Separate Motivational Systems," in *Handbook of Attachment*, 3rd ed., 464–83.
130 **"anger born of fear":** Mario Mikulincer and Phillip R. Shaver, *Attachment in Adulthood: Structure, Dynamics, and Change*, 2nd ed. (New York: Guilford Press, 2016), 338.
131 **"partner unavailability and lack of responsiveness":** Ibid., 337–40.

Chapter 8. Sassy and Classy: Attachment and Friendship

138 **from parents to same-sex peers:** Mario Mikulincer and Phillip R. Shaver, *Attachment in Adulthood: Structure, Dynamics, and Change*, 2nd ed. (New York: Guilford Press, 2016), 54.
138 **the WHOTO scale:** Mario Mikulincer et al., "Attachment, Caregiving, and Altruism: Boosting Attachment Security Increases Compassion and Helping," *Journal of Personality and Social Psychology* 89, no. 5 (2005): 817–39.
138 **"separated involuntarily from their friends":** Wyndol Furman, "Working Models of Friendship," *Journal of Social and Personal Relationships* 18, no. 5 (2001): 583–602.
140 **forecasting later qualities of friendship:** L. Alan Sroufe, "The Place of Attachment in Development," in *Handbook of Attachment*, 3rd ed., 1004.
140 **"more troubled relations":** Mikulincer and Shaver, *Attachment in Adulthood*, 297.

140 **greater satisfaction with their friendships:** Ofra Mayseless and Miri
Scharf, "Adolescents' Attachment Representations and Their Capacity for
Intimacy in Close Relationships," *Journal of Research on Adolescence* 17, no.
1 (2007): 26.

140 **thus pushing friends away:** Chong Man Chow and Cin Cin Tan,
"Attachment and Commitment in Dyadic Friendships: Mediating Roles of
Satisfaction, Quality of Alternatives, and Investment Size," *Journal of
Relationships Research* 4, e4 (2013): 1–11.

140 **less satisfied with their friendships:** Ibid.

142 **online versus offline friendships:** Vanessa M. Buote, Eileen Wood, and
Michael Pratt, "Exploring Similarities and Differences Between Online and
Offline Friendships: The Role of Attachment Style," *Computers in Human
Behavior* 25 (2009): 560–67.

144 **"reach for or rely on their partners":** Yuthika U. Girme, et al., "'All or
Nothing': Attachment Avoidance and the Curvilinear Effects of Partner
Support," *Journal of Personality and Social Psychology* 108, no. 3 (2015):
450–75.

144 **"insatiable desire for closeness and care":** Ibid., 452.

144 **"fail to appreciate or be calmed by the support":** Ibid., 471.

145 **rupture will be only temporary:** Harry Reis, personal communication
with author, March 2, 2017.

Chapter 9. Getting Old: Attachment and Aging

148 **"less of a drop in well-being":** Juliann Hobdy et al., "The Role of
Attachment Style in Coping with Job Loss and the Empty Nest in
Adulthood," *International Journal of Aging and Human Development* 65,
no. 4 (2007): 335–71, cited in Carol Magai, Maria Teresa Frías, and Phillip
R. Shaver, "Attachment in Middle and Later Life," in *Handbook of
Attachment: Theory, Research, and Clinical Applications*, 3rd ed., eds. Jude
Cassidy and Phillip R. Shaver (New York: Guilford Press, 2016), 538.

149 **less frequent but emotionally richer:** Laura L. Carstensen, Derek M.
Isaacowitz, Susan T. Charles, "Taking Time Seriously: A Theory of
Socioemotional Selectivity," *American Psychologist* 54, no. 3 (1999):
165–81.

150 **relied more on sleeping medication:** R. Niko Verdecias et al., "Attachment
Styles and Sleep Measures in a Community-Based Sample of Older Adults,"
Sleep Medicine 10, no. 6 (2009): 664–67. See also Cheryl L. Carmichael and
Harry T. Reis, "Attachment, Sleep Quality, and Depressed Affect," *Health
Psychology* 24, no. 5 (2005): 526–31.

151 **smoking, drinking, and drug abuse:** Mario Mikulincer and Phillip R.
Shaver, *Attachment in Adulthood: Structure, Dynamics, and Change*, 2nd
ed. (New York: Guilford Press, 2016), 248, 251.

151 **failed to take the necessary steps to do so:** Ibid., 248.

151 **lived longer than those who did not:** Lynne C. Giles et al., "Effect of Social Networks on 10 Year Survival in Very Old Australians: The Australian Longitudinal Study of Aging," *Journal of Epidemiology and Community Health* 59 (2005): 574–79, cited in Magai, Frías, and Shaver, "Attachment in Middle and Later Life," in *Handbook of Attachment*, 3rd ed., 536.

151 **challenge the ability to maintain a supportive social network:** Phillip R. Shaver and Mario Mikulincer, "Attachment in the Later Years: A Commentary," *Attachment & Human Development* 6, no. 4 (2004): 451–64.

153 **"excessive amount of contact and attention":** Robert G. Maunder et al., "Physicians' Difficulty with Emergency Department Patients Is Related to Patients' Attachment Style," *Social Science & Medicine* 63, no. 2 (2006): 552–62.

155 **"a cruel denouement":** Magai, Frías, and Shaver, "Attachment in Middle and Later Life," in *Handbook of Attachment*, 3rd ed., 545.

156 **generate even more insecurity:** Ibid.

156 **"care aged parents received from their children":** Ibid., 543.

157 **shy away from the responsibility:** Ibid., 545–48.

157 **heal old wounds:** Shaver and Mikulincer, "Attachment in the Later Years," 461.

158 **loss of perceived control:** Mikulincer and Shaver, *Attachment in Adulthood*, 2nd ed., 215.

158 **"an opportunity to contribute to others and to grow personally":** Ibid., 216.

158 **"rely on symbolic figures to serve attachment functions":** Shaver and Mikulincer, "Attachment in the Later Years," 452.

159 **"(i.e., living, human) attachment figures":** Ibid., 453.

Chapter 10. Securing a Position: Attachment in the Workplace

163 **affected by individual differences in attachment style:** Mario Mikulincer and Phillip R. Shaver, *Attachment in Adulthood: Structure, Dynamics, and Change*, 2nd ed. (New York: Guilford Press, 2016), 244.

166 **effectively explore career opportunities:** Glenn I. Roisman, Mudita A. Bahadur, Harriet Oster, "Infant Attachment Security as a Discriminant Predictor of Career Development in Late Adolescence," *Journal of Adolescent Research* 15, no. 5 (2000): 531–45.

166 **career choices that coincided with their abilities:** Mikulincer and Shaver, *Attachment in Adulthood*, 2nd ed., 241.

166 **"premature commitment to a career without sufficient exploration":** Ibid., 240, 241.

167 **"courage and dedication":** Ibid., 481.

167 **"anger, disorganization, dishonesty, and despair":** Ibid.

169 **work-related distress and burnout:** Ibid., 244.

169 **potential source of disapproval and rejection:** Ibid.

169 **"approval of other team members":** Shiri Lavy, Tariv Bareli, and Tsachi Ein-Dor, "The Effects of Attachment Heterogeneity and Team Cohesion on Team Functioning," *Small Group Research* 46, no. 1 (2015): 35.

169 **"to evade social involvements":** Mikulincer and Shaver, *Attachment in Adulthood*, 2nd ed., 245.

169 **behaviors toward colleagues:** Hadassah Littman-Ovadia, Lior Oren, and Shiri Lavy, "Attachment and Autonomy in the Workplace: New Insights," *Journal of Career Assessment* 21, no. 4 (2013): 502–18. See also Patrice Wendling, "Attachment Styles Predict Workplace Behavior," *Clinical Psychiatry News* 38, no. 6 (June 2010): 10.

169 **conflict among the team:** Lavy et al., "The Effects of Attachment Heterogeneity," 35.

169 **as "frustrations and resentment" toward colleagues mount:** Aharon Tziner et al., "Attachment to Work, Job Satisfaction and Work Centrality," *Leadership & Organization Development Journal* 35, no. 6 (2014): 560, 561.

170 **first to detect the threat:** Tsachi Ein-Dor, Mario Mikulincer, and Phillip R. Shaver, "Effective Reaction to Danger: Attachment Insecurities Predict Behavioral Reactions to an Experimentally Induced Threat Above and Beyond General Personality Traits," *Social Psychological and Personality Science* 2, no. 5 (2011): 467–73.

170 **most diligent about delivering a warning message:** Tsachi Ein-Dor and Orgad Tal, "Scared Saviors: Evidence That People High in Attachment Anxiety Are More Effective in Alerting Others to Threat," *European Journal of Social Psychology* 42, no. 6 (2012): 667–71.

171 **when other players bluffed:** Tsachi Ein-Dor and Adi Perry, "Full House of Fears: Evidence That People High in Attachment Anxiety Are More Accurate in Detecting Deceit," *Journal of Personality* 82, no. 2 (2014): 83–92.

171 **may be the quickest to act:** Lavy et al., "The Effects of Attachment Heterogeneity," 31–32.

171 **able to express their unique skills:** Ibid., 35.

171 **before tensions escalate:** Littman-Ovadia et al., "Attachment and Autonomy in the Workplace," 514.

173 **"safe, accepted, and trusted":** Lavy et al., "The Effects of Attachment Heterogeneity," 27–49.

174 **president of the United States:** "Obamas Celebrate Small Business Saturday with Shopping Trip," YouTube video, filmed November 2015, posted November 28, 2015, www.youtube.com/watch?v=Pj17MXg7XKw.

Chapter 11. Before the Buzzer: Attachment and Sports

176 **achieving high performance:** Kelly A. Forrest, "Attachment and Attention in Sport," in *Journal of Clinical Sport Psychology* 2, no. 3 (2008): 243.

176 **"trust and security in relationships and environments":** Elliott Newell, e-mail message to the author, October 25, 2016.

178 **"poor health also begins early in life":** Sam Carr, *Attachment in Sport, Exercise and Wellness* (London: Routledge, 2012), 107, quoting Rena L. Repetti, Shelley E. Taylor, and Teresa E. Seeman, "Risky Families: Family Social Environments and the Mental and Physical Health of Offspring," *Psychological Bulletin* 128, no. 2 (2002): 330–66.

178 **engaging in health-promoting behaviors:** Carr, *Attachment in Sport*, 112, and Elaine Scharfe and Deborah Eldredge, "Associations Between Attachment Representations and Health Behaviors in Late Adolescence," *Journal of Health Psychology* 6, no. 3 (2001): 295–307.

178 **feel pain more acutely than those who are secure or avoidant:** Pamela Meredith, Jenny Strong, and Judith A. Feeney, "Adult Attachment, Anxiety, and Pain Self-Efficacy as Predictors of Pain Intensity and Disability," *Pain* 123, nos. 1–2 (2006): 146–54. See also Zoe Chrisman-Miller, "Exercise Habits, Adult Attachment Styles, and HPA-Axis Hypersensitivity" (undergraduate thesis, Oregon State University Honors College, Corvallis, 2015), ir.library.oregonstate.edu/xmlui/handle/1957/57896.

179 **"may be at a psychological disadvantage":** Carr, *Attachment in Sport*, 46–48.

180 **talented teams failing:** Ibid., 60.

180 **group chemistry or cohesion:** Ibid., 60–64.

181 **"find it hard to ask for support":** Elliott Newell, "Using Attachment Theory to Better Understand Your Athletes," *Believe Platform*, 2015, believeperform.com/performance/using-attachment-theory-to-better -understand-your-athletes/.

182 **"Butler is in agony":** "Da'Sean Butler Knee Injury vs. Duke. Bob Huggins," YouTube video, recorded on April 3, 2010, posted on February 12, 2012, www.youtube.com/watch?v=VtRJXLyS0_U.

182 **or more career victories:** "Bob Huggins," *Wikipedia*, accessed July 12, 2016, en.wikipedia.org/wiki/Bob_Huggins.

183 **"closeness with the coach" (proximity maintenance):** Louise Davis and Sophia Jowett, "Investigating the Interpersonal Dynamics Between Coaches and Athletes Based on Fundamental Principles of Attachment," *Journal of Clinical Sport Psychology* 4, no. 2 (2010): 126.

183 **"attachment figure properties":** A. F. Frøyen and A. M. Pensgaard, "Relationship Quality in Elite Sport: The Perspective of Athletes and Coaches," *Norwegian School of Sport Sciences, Olympiatoppen*, accessed July 12, 2017, www.olympiatoppen.no/om_olympiatoppen/aktuelt /media43113.media

186 **ran slower and stumbled more:** Brandi Stupica, "Rounding the Bases with a Secure Base," *Attachment & Human Development* 18, no. 4 (2016): 373–90.

186 **"children are more competent athletes":** Brandi Stupica, personal communications with author, August 8, 2015, and June 12, 2015.

186 **"not conducive to optimal performance":** Carr, *Attachment in Sport*, 83.

187 **for the tournament itself:** Ibid., 82.

188 **deny the symptoms and thus worsen the injury:** Ibid., 86.

189 **"concentration disruption":** Forrest, "Attachment and Attention in Sport," 249–50.

Chapter 12. Following the Leaders: Attachment and Politics

193 **"followers' needs for a safe haven and secure base":** Mario Mikulincer and Phillip R. Shaver, *Attachment in Adulthood: Structure, Dynamics, and Change*, 2nd ed. (New York: Guilford Press, 2016), 480–82.

193 **"secure internal working models of attachment":** Tiffany Keller-Hansbrough, "The Construction of a Transformational Leader: Follower Attachment and Leadership Perceptions," *Journal of Applied Social Psychology* 42, no. 6 (2012): 1537.

193 **was Franklin Roosevelt:** Mikulincer and Shaver, *Attachment in Adulthood*, 2nd ed., 481.

194 **understanding their followers' needs and concerns:** Ibid., 482.

194 **often frightened of his mother:** Evan Thomas, *Being Nixon: A Man Divided* (New York: Random House, 2015), 9.

194 **evidence of attachment avoidance:** Mario Mikulincer, personal communication with author, October 3, 2015. See also, in regard to calling one's mother "a saint," Jude Cassidy, "Truth, Lies and Intimacy: An Attachment Perspective," *Attachment & Human Development* 3, no. 2 (2001): 141.

194 **"away" from fulfilling their sworn duties:** Mikulincer and Shaver, *Attachment in Adulthood*, 2nd ed., 482.

194 **"intern's thong underwear":** Ibid., 442.

195 **people of goodwill:** Christopher Weber and Christopher M. Federico, "Interpersonal Attachment and Patterns of Ideological Belief," *Political Psychology* 28, no. 4 (2007): 389–416, at 392.

195 **"more realistic political views":** Mario Mikulincer, personal communication with author, September 9, 2015.

195 **"strong and unerring view of the world":** Joshua Hart, personal communication with author, September 8, 2015.

196 **("we can only depend on our own strength"):** Weber and Federico, "Interpersonal Attachment and Patterns of Ideological Belief," 394.

196 **could turn out to be a demagogue:** Keller-Hansbrough, "The Construction of a Transformational Leader," 1533–49.

198 **"surprise the unconscious":** Erik Hesse, "The Adult Attachment Interview: Protocol, Method of Analysis, and Selected Empirical Studies: 1985–2015," in *Handbook of Attachment: Theory, Research, and Clinical*

Applications, 3rd ed., eds. Jude Cassidy and Phillip R. Shaver (New York: Guilford Press, 2016), 555.

204 **"Attachment classification: Avoidant":** Dr. Ringel appropriately uses the term "dismissive," rather than "avoidant." I use the roughly equivalent "avoidant" to simplify terminology for the general reader and make it uniform throughout the book. The substitution is mine and not Dr. Ringel's.

207 **avoidant attachment predicted higher rankings:** Tsachi Ein-Dor et al., "Standoffish Perhaps, but Successful as Well," *Journal of Personality* 80, no. 3 (2012): 749–68.

208 **more about adulation:** See, for example, Frank Bruni, "Donald Trump's Demand for Love," *The New York Times*, November 22, 2016.

209 **"courage, hope, and dedication":** Mikulincer and Shaver, *Attachment in Adulthood*, 2nd ed., 480–82.

Chapter 13. Thou Art with Me: Attachment and Religion

212 **personal, interactive relationship:** Pehr Granqvist and Lee A. Kirkpatrick, "Attachment and Religious Representations and Behavior," in *Handbook of Attachment: Theory, Research, and Clinical Applications*, 3rd ed., eds. Jude Cassidy and Phillip R. Shaver (New York: Guilford Press, 2016), 918.

212 **"a relationship with God":** Ibid.

212 **"proximity, safe haven, and secure base":** Bagher Ghobari Bonab, Maureen Miner, and Marie-Therese Proctor, "Attachment to God in Islamic Spirituality," *Journal of Muslim Mental Health* 7, no. 2 (2013): 77, 99.

212 **"personal gods imported from ancient folk religions":** Lee A. Kirkpatrick, *Attachment, Evolution, and the Psychology of Religion* (New York: Guilford Press, 2005), 98.

213 **makes the case as follows:** Ibid., 55–74.

213 **"challenges of everyday life":** Ibid., 66.

214 **"or file for divorce":** Granqvist and Kirkpatrick, "Attachment and Religious Representations and Behavior," in *Handbook of Attachment*, 3rd ed., 921.

214 **"Allah, their ultimate attachment figure":** Bonab et al., "Attachment to God in Islamic Spirituality," 77, 99.

214 **"why modern Catholics remain Catholic":** Kirkpatrick, *Attachment, Evolution, and the Psychology of Religion*, 92, citing Andrew Greeley, *The Catholic Myth: The Behavior and Beliefs of American Catholics* (New York: Touchstone, 1990), 252.

214 **"She is my *mama*":** Maureen Orth, "How the Virgin Mary Became the World's Most Powerful Woman," *National Geographic*, December 2015, 36.

214 **Jews also have this concept:** For this understanding of the Hebrew name, I am indebted to Rabbi David A. Katz, personal communication with author, January 2, 2017.

217 **"consistent with one's experience in human relationships with attachment figures":** Kirkpatrick, *Attachment, Evolution, and the Psychology of Religion*, 125–26.

217 **view God as available, reliable, and responsive:** Granqvist and Kirkpatrick, "Attachment and Religious Representations and Behavior," in *Handbook of Attachment*, 3rd ed., 928.

218 **choose a religion (or no religion):** Ibid., 923–30.

218 **"need for protection and security":** Ibid., 929.

218 **"the apostates . . . or the militant atheists":** Kirkpatrick, *Attachment, Evolution, and the Psychology of Religion*, 137, 134.

219 **as a substitute attachment figure:** Ibid., 131. Note that the same discovery can also lead one to embrace a cult. In studies, members of religious cults have acknowledged troubled relationships with parents, unhappy childhoods, and traumatic events experienced during childhood.

219 **gradual rather than sudden:** Granqvist and Kirkpatrick, "Attachment and Religious Representations and Behavior," in *Handbook of Attachment*, 3rd ed., 929.

219 **"never had with one's parents":** Ibid., 924.

219 **"to the contrary":** Kirkpatrick, *Attachment, Evolution, and the Psychology of Religion*, 135.

219 **"falling in love for the first time":** Ibid., 135.

219 **underwent this transformation:** Granqvist and Kirkpatrick, "Attachment and Religious Representations and Behavior," in *Handbook of Attachment*, 3rd ed., 925.

219 **than securely attached Christian women:** Ibid.

222 **"not a big deal":** "America's Changing Religious Landscape," Pew Research Center, May 21, 2015, www.pewforum.org/2015/05/12/americas-changing-religious-landscape.

Epilogue

226 **"behavior is how they communicate their needs":** Glen Cooper, during training for Circle of Security Parenting, Baltimore, Maryland, January 22, 2013.

228 **"how well a society creates 'persons'":** Ken Corvo and Ellen deLara, "Bowlby's Ghost: The Political and Moral Reverberations of Attachment Theory," *Attachment: New Directions in Psychotherapy and Relational Psychoanalysis* 4, no. 1 (2010): 63.

229 **"a topsy-turvy world":** John Bowlby, *A Secure Base* (New York: Basic Books, 1988), 2.

229 **fifty employees or more:** "Family and Medical Leave Act of 1993," *Wikipedia*, accessed July 13, 2017, en.wikipedia.org/wiki/Family_and_Medical_Leave_Act_of_1993.

229 **and Cisco (five months):** Julia Quinn-Szcesuil, "20 Companies with Great Maternity Leave," Care@Work, October 6, 2014, workplace.care.com /20-companies-with-great-maternity-leave.

229 **Gates Foundation offers a full year:** "19 Companies and Industries with Radically Awesome Parental Leave Policies," *Entrepreneur*, accessed on July 14, 2017, www.entrepreneur.com/slideshow/249467#3.

230 **most rating poor or mediocre in quality:** Corvo and deLara, "Bowlby's Ghost," 65–6, citing Peggy Patten and Omar Benton Ricks, "Child Care Quality: An Overview for Parents," *ERIC Digest* (December 2000), eric .ed.gov/?id=ED447969.

230 **80 percent or greater:** Dante Cicchetti, Fred A. Rogosch, and Sheree L. Toth, "Fostering Secure Attachment in Infants in Maltreating Families Through Preventive Interventions," *Development and Psychopathology* 18, no. 3 (2006): 623–49.

230 **"could have been a healthy human being":** Thomas Lewis, Fari Amini, and Richard Lannon, *A General Theory of Love* (New York: Vintage, 2001), 218.

231 **not as a weakness but as both a sign and a source of strength:** Sue Johnson, *Hold Me Tight: Seven Conversations for a Lifetime of Love* (New York: Little, Brown and Company, 2008), 21.

232 **shared kitchens and social programming:** Shilpi Malinowski, "D.C. Developer Bets Big on Apartments with Shared Eating Spaces," *The Washington Post*, April 28, 2015, www.washingtonpost.com/news /where-we-live/wp/2015/04/28/d-c-developer-bets-big-on-apartments -with-shared-eating-spaces/?utm_term=.ef1894db8e11, and Kim Velsey, "Sharing an Apartment with Strangers," *The New York Times*, May 5, 2017, www.nytimes.com/2017/05/05/realestate/rent-long-island-city-room-share .html.

233 **as if it were sung to the mother by her child:** Bert Powell, during training for Circle of Security Parenting, Bethesda, Maryland, September 8, 2015. "You Are So Beautiful" was written by Billy Preston and Bruce Fisher.

Index

About the Author

Peter Lovenheim is an author and journalist whose articles and essays have appeared in *The New York Times*, *New York Magazine*, *Los Angeles Times*, *Parade*, and *The Washington Post*.

His previous works include *In the Neighborhood: The Search for Community on an American Street, One Sleepover at a Time*, a Barnes & Noble Discover Award winner and recipient of the inaugural Zócalo Public Square Book Prize, and *Portrait of a Burger as a Young Calf*, a firsthand attempt to understand the food chain.

Lovenheim holds a degree in journalism from Boston University and in law from Cornell Law School. He teaches narrative nonfiction writing at the Writer's Center in Bethesda, Maryland, and splits his time between his hometown of Rochester, New York, and Washington, DC. See www.peterlovenheim.com.